LINCOLN'S
UNSUNG HEROES

Hampshire Co south Dist

VOLUNTEER ENLISTMENT.

STATE OF   TOWN OF

Mass   *South Hadley*

I, *George Cole*   born in *Ireland*

in the State of   aged *twenty seven* years,

and by occupation a *Clerk*   Do HEREBY ACKNOWLEDGE to have

volunteered this *twenty third* day of *June*   186 *4*

to serve as a **Soldier** in the Army of the United States of America, for the period of *THREE YEARS*, unless sooner discharged by proper authority: Do also agree to accept such bounty, pay, rations, and clothing, as are, or may be, established by law for volunteers. And I, *George Cole*   do solemnly swear, that I will bear true faith and allegiance to the **United States of America**, and that I will serve them honestly and faithfully against all their enemies or opposers whomsoever; and that I will observe and obey the orders of the President of the United States, and the orders of the officers appointed over me, according to the Rules and Articles of War.

Sworn and subscribed to, at *Boston*

this *23rd* day of *June*, 186 *4*

Before *W. F. Traword M.S.*   *George Cole*

     I CERTIFY, ON HONOR, That I have carefully examined the above-named Volunteer, agreeably to the General Regulations of the Army, and that, in my opinion, he is free from all bodily defects and mental infirmity, which would in any way disqualify him from performing the duties of a soldier.

J. F. Harlow.
Mass.
EXAMINING SURGEON.

     I CERTIFY, ON HONOR, That I have minutely inspected the Volunteer, *George Cole* previously to his enlistment, and that he was entirely sober when enlisted; that, to the best of my judgment and belief, he is of lawful age; and that, in accepting him as duly qualified to perform the duties of an able-bodied soldier, I have strictly observed the Regulations which govern the recruiting service. This soldier has *Blue* eyes, *Black* hair, *Dark* complexion, is *five* feet *nine* inches high.

                  Regiment of   *Mass*   Volunteers,

                               RECRUITING OFFICER.

(A. G. O No. 74 & 75.)

Mustered into the service of the United States, in Company ____ Regiment of ____ Volunteers, on the 23" day of June, 1864 at Boston Mass

The volunteer enlistment form of George Cole.
The form, which was filled out for every new soldier, includes
a physical description and declarations of the soldier's
qualifications for enlistment. (National Archives)

Lincoln's Unsung Heroes

PHILIP KATCHER

ARMS AND
ARMOUR

To the memory of the men whose lives are described here within as well as a member of Colonel Lee's regiment, Private Charles Katcher, who died a prisoner of war in Salisbury, North Carolina, August 1864.

Arms and Armour Press
An Imprint of the Cassell Group
Wellington House, 125 Strand, London WC2R 0BB

Distributed in the USA by Sterling Publishing Co. Inc.,
387 Park Avenue South, New York, NY 10016-8810.

British Library Cataloguing-in-Publication Data:
a catalogue record for this book is available from
the British Library

ISBN 1-85409-350-9

Designed and edited by DAG Publications Ltd.
Designed by David Gibbons; edited by John Gilbert;
Printed and Bound in Great Britain
by Creative Print and Design Wales, Ebbw Vale.

Contents

Introduction

The story of the Civil War is a story, in the end, of the people who lived through it. It is one thing to speak of great charges, of regiments and ships moving this way and that, of victories won and battles lost. But in the final analysis these activities were all performed by men – most of them white, young and unlearned in the ways of the world.

In all, some two million men served in the armed forces of the United States during the Civil War. Today, when so many armed forces personnel are employed as support, rather than combat, troops in positions ranging from commissary officer to radar operator, it is customary to think that virtually everyone in the Civil War had a direct fighting role. True, most of them were combat soldiers first and foremost. But the Union armed forces were amazingly sophisticated and there were all kinds of positions that an individual could and was required to fill. It was not unusual for an individual who had signed up as an infantryman to spend most of his time as a clerk in a provost office in some outpost or as a general's orderly. The notion that everyone who joined a volunteer unit at the beginning of the war spent his entire enlistment period in that same unit, in a combat role, perhaps working up to commissioned rank, is not wholly accurate. There were plenty of opportunities to move about in jobs and places in the army of the Civil War.

In thinking of the men in the Union army and navy it may be useful to consider a modern corporation in the United States. There are various different levels of workers. Managing directors, vice presidents and chief executive officers are 'top management'. These relate to the generals and admirals of the armed forces. Below them are 'middle management', such as department managers, who are equivalent to field grade officers, colonels and majors in the army and to commanders and captains in the navy. The lower management level, heads of sections and departments, are akin to company-grade officers – captains and lieutenants in the army, lieutenants, masters and ensigns in the navy. Below them are the workers, enlisted men and seamen. Each level is occupied by men with different amounts of experience, training and abilities.

In the old regular army, before the Civil War, where things were done correctly in a military fashion, most officers were educated in the United States Military Academy, which offered a Bachelor of Science degree after four years of education. Indeed, just prior to the war, the length of a term of study at the Academy was upped to five years. The core of the top army command was made up of these Academy graduates, or at least attendees. The lives and motivations of such men are well covered in a variety of biographies. Yet the Academy also turned out men such as William Raymond Lee, Jnr.

For its part, a Naval Academy produced a number of senior navy officers, although since this institution was much younger than West Point, the majority of the most senior naval management came up through the older system of shipping aboard a man of war as a midshipman, and learning, as it were, on the job. William Penn McCann was a man whose professional career started both as a sea-going midshipman and an Academy cadet.

These were professional military men, and any study of Civil War soldiers has to include such individuals, who generally represent the top and middle management levels.

Yet the men who officered the volunteer Civil War army unit or ship – middle and lower management – were rarely professionals. They were usually elected or granted a state commission for raising a certain number of troops at the beginning of the war, which meant that a number of less than outstanding officers were enrolled. Later boards weeded out many of these men while other boards passed judgement on those applying for commissions; it became harder to obtain a commission, although some misfits always found a way to slip through the cracks in the system. These were men like J. Henry Sleeper, George Adams, Charles Rohan and Franklin Case.

The Navy and Revenue Marine Cutter Service, too, was hard pressed to get enough officers for all its vessels and commissioned all manner of men directly from civilian life as volunteer acting officers. Jerry Benson, John Thomas and William Muse were examples of such men.

Finally, the average enlisted man rarely had much if any previous military experience. Nor was he especially driven to advance in ranks or make the army a career. His country was threatened, or he was looking for a little adventure away from a humdrum life at home, or he simply could not find work elsewhere, and he was here merely to do a job and then go home. Statistically, the average Union soldier was an infantryman from a farm or rural area, five feet nine inches tall, weighing 160 pounds, eighteen years of age, with brown hair and blue or light grey eyes. He had at least a grammar school education.

With typical variations, he was a David Barnett, Winsor Smith, Grant MacAllister and Eli Nichols.

War in the mid-nineteenth century had become ever more complicated. The Industrial Revolution, which had begun some fifty years earlier, had brought technological wonders, while science advanced on all fronts. Sailors no longer depended on the winds to propel their ships; they used great steam engines. Therefore, the armed forces of the Civil War had to call upon a number of specialists in technical fields – men such as David Cole, Marshall Price, Lyman Sweeney and Charles Trotter.

To sum up, then, this book takes a look at a selection of men who fought in the armed forces of the United States in that war. However, these are not just individual stories. They reflect the wide variety of experiences undergone by Civil War military personnel. There are good soldiers who fought well and paid the price; men who joined up and spent the war in relative safety – through no fault or desire of their own, as they simply did what they were told to do; and men whose records leave much to be desired. They include cavalrymen, infantrymen, engineers, sailors and artillerymen. Some are enlisted men, non-commissioned officers and commissioned officers; others jumped from the ranks to a commission. Some survived without injury; others paid the ultimate price. There are those who mainly served away from front lines. And there is one man who was described by a superior officer as a 'cad and a swindler'.

These individual stories aim to explore the backgrounds of the men who served in the war, to explain the precise nature of the jobs they performed, to describe their daily lives and to place their activities in the overall context of the Union armed forces. Finally, it is worth noting how these men were affected by the war. Two of the eighteen died during the course of the conflict, and another two, as a result of wounds, disease, life as a prisoner-of-war or physical stress, were left with health problems from which they never recovered. One man's war-time marriage failed, in an age where divorce was rare. The war was the major event in most of these men's lives, and it was an event that seldom left them the better for having participated in it.

Acknowledgements

Many people have helped to put this book together. Harry Roach, publisher of Military Images Magazine, has helped to raise overall understanding of and interest in individual portraits and the stories behind them. Thanks are due to Tod Butler, Bob Scanlon and the rest of the staff of the National Archives for digging up individual service and pension records. Henry Deeks found a number of the images on which this book is based and did a great deal of research on the individuals shown in them before passing them on to me. Nancy Eckerman of the University of Indiana's Medical School turned up a copy of the rare period history of the 8th Indiana Infantry. Charles Greifenstein of the College of Physicians of Philadelphia dug up valuable information on Dr Marshall F. Price. Sue Kerekgyarto gave me the image of Captain and Mrs Case of the 2nd Ohio along with much information on them and the regiment. Michael J. Winey, US Army Military History Institute, Carlisle Barracks, supplied information on A. Macalister Grant's battery. Roderick Dymott of Arms and Armour had faith in the entire project. Thanks are due to them all.

1

George W. Adams
Captain, 8th Indiana Volunteer Infantry Regiment

The shells that burst over Fort Sumter in the Charleston, South Carolina, harbour on 12 April 1861 might just as well have burst over every city and town in the north. Within days flags and all manner of red, white, and blue bunting appeared as if by magic on houses, offices and public buildings. People gathered in small and large groups, asking what they could do to avenge this insult to the flag and save the country which they had been taught to believe held out the last opportunity for all people to live in freedom.

On 15 April, the day after the fort formally surrendered, President Abraham Lincoln gave them their answer. He sent a telegram to every governor asking for a certain number of troops to put down this rebellion. From Governor Oliver Morton of Indiana, he requested six infantry regiments, led by a brigadier general, and including 225 officers and 4,458 enlisted men, to be mustered in at Indianapolis, the state capital. 'On behalf of the State of Indiana I tender to you for the defense of the nation and to uphold the authority of the Government 10,000 men,' Morton immediately telegraphed back.[1]

Although Lincoln's telegraph had asked the governors to draw their men from the various state militias, by and large that was not a viable option. Most states had ignored their militia, and Indiana was one of them. Although a law had been passed in 1852 to organise a general militia from all able-bodied Hoosiers, there were actually very few militia companies in existence by 1861. Another state act was passed in 1855 to recognise officially volunteer companies, formed by individuals to meet and drill from time to time. By April 1861 there were perhaps about a hundred such companies that had been chartered by the state, but these, too, were neither uniformly equipped nor trained organisations.

Therefore, on 16 April Morton issued a proclamation to all 'loyal and patriotic men' of Indiana 'to organise themselves into military companies' and report to the state's Adjutant General in Indianapolis.[2] 'On the morning of April 17, a call, signed by the leading citizens was issued for a public meeting at the court house in the evening of the same day,' recalled a citizen of Vanderburg County, Indiana, of a scene that was being played out all over the state.

'Warren's Crescent City Band paraded the streets playing inspiring airs. It being ascertained that hundreds desirous of participating were in the streets unable to get into the house, an adjournment was had to the street about the Washington House, from the balcony of which the band continued to discourse enlivening music.'[3] Following the music came patriotic speeches, a general pledge to support the Union, and the raising of an infantry company which quickly departed for Indianapolis.

One such company was raised this way in Wayne County, Indiana. It was the practice in democratic America for officers of such companies to be elected. Sometimes it was the individual who raised the company initially who was elected captain; sometimes it was another local civic leader, perhaps someone active in the local volunteer militia company or with previous experience in such military exploits as the Mexican War. In this particular case a man named M. M. Lacy was elected captain, while twenty-five-year-old George W. Adams was elected his first lieutenant, the second-in-command. Then the company bade farewell to family and neighbours and headed off to the great adventure in Indianapolis.

Elections were often fiercely contested. Indeed, some candidates were reported as spending as much as $400 in the contest, for such items as barrels of whiskey rather than as outright bribes, in their campaigns. Losers sometimes took their complaints to as high as the governor and were occasionally successful in having the elections overturned by state government officials.

These state officials formed the incoming companies into regular infantry regiments. Ten companies, each containing a captain, a first lieutenant, a second lieutenant, a first sergeant, four sergeants, eight corporals, two musicians, a wagoner and sixty-four privates, made up a regiment. When enough companies had been organised, the governor appointed three field grade officers, a colonel, a lieutenant colonel and a major, to the regiment and had it mustered into service. The colonel would then select a couple of lieutenants to become adjutant and quartermaster. As well, he would pick a sergeant major, a regimental quartermaster sergeant, a regimental commissary sergeant, a principal musician and a hospital steward. Each regiment was also authorised a twenty-four-piece band, but this was not common to all regiments.

The majority of states took the first regiment to be organised and formally mustered into Federal service and numbered it the 1st. Not so Indiana. Proud of its five regiments of volunteers that saw service in the Mexican War, the state authorities decided to muster in its first regiment of 1861 as the '6th Indiana Volunteer Infantry Regiment'. As it happened, Lacy's company became Company D of the third regiment mustered into Federal service, the 8th Indiana, commanded by Judge William P. Benton. In line of battle, Lacy's company would be posted third from the right, it being ordered that the companies should be lined up, from the right: first, sixth, fourth, ninth, third, eighth, fifth, tenth, seventh and second, according to the captains' ranks.

While during the years before the Civil War states received shipments of infantry weapons on a regular basis, these were largely issued to various volunteer companies and were not available for these new regiments. A survey of Indiana's armoury turned up only 54 Mississippi rifles, 80 'muskets with accoutrements', 13 M1847 musketoons, 75 'holster pistols,' 26 Sharps rifles, and 20 Colt 0.36 calibre revolvers.[4] This would not even arm one regiment. Indiana was not alone in this respect. Governors from all the northern states bombarded the War Department with pleas for arms. On 19 April Morton telegraphed the Secretary of War, 'Twenty-four hundred men in camp and less than half of them armed. Why has there been so much delay in sending arms? We have received none, and cannot learn that they have ever been shipped. No officer here yet to muster troops into service. Not a pound of powder or a single ball sent to us, or any sort of equipment. Allow me to ask what is the cause of all this?'[5]

The cause was a tremendous rush of requests on a War Department that simply did not have enough weapons itself. In a relatively short time, however, the Allegheny Arsenal supplied Morton's men with some 3,500 smooth-bore, 0.69 calibre, M1842 muskets, sufficient for most volunteers in the state's first regiments.

Uniforms were another problem, with the Federal government hard-pressed to clothe all its new volunteers. Indiana officials filled the gap, arranging for local tailors to make uniforms for its first volunteer regiments. The men of the 8th received waist-length, single-breasted light blue jackets and plain light blue trousers. Whereas uniforms of the period were generally made of wool, in this case jeans cloth, a mixture of wool and cotton, was used for the uniforms of the 8th. They also received plain black broad-brimmed hats.

George and his fellow new officers, however, had to supply their own uniforms. Regulations called for dark blue trousers with a line of sky blue piping down each leg; and a single-breasted, almost knee-length dark blue coat with rank indicated in dress by gold-fringed epaulettes and by gold-edged boxes, or shoulder straps, of sky blue with the rank badge worn inside the box. In George's case, the rank badge was a single gold bar at each end of the strap. For dress, a black broad-brimmed hat, pinned up on the left side, with three ostrich feathers, a black and gold cord and acorns, and a gold-embroidered bugle surrounding the silver number 8 in its centre, would be worn. The same cap badge would also appear on the fatigue cap of dark blue with brass side buttons and leather peak and chin-strap. On duty, he would wrap a crimson sash, knotted at the left side, under his sword belt.

Photographs of George and other officers of the 8th indicate that they improved the uniform by adding gold lace around the crown of the cap, up the sides and front and back, and forming a trefoil on its top. One line of gold lace represented each grade; as a first lieutenant, George's cap would have two lines of gold lace. When he became captain, an additional line would be added.

The regimental tailors also added a gold Austrian knot on each sleeve: one line of gold lace for a lieutenant, two for a captain and three for a field-grade officer. These knots were adopted from the French service, where they made up the rank indicators, and were regulation in the Confederate Army and Marines as well. Usually such additions to the uniforms rarely lasted past the first several months of service, but in the case of the 8th, they appear on photographs taken as late as 1864.

As an officer, too, George would have to supply his own weapons. Most line officers carried a revolver by choice. Regulations, however, only called for an M1850 foot officer's sword. In some families, heirloom swords were given to the new officer, but in most cases they had to dig up some money to buy their arms. One newly elected Ohio lieutenant wrote home just after receiving his commission: 'What I want to say, John, is that I need some money to get my rig. I do not intend to get anything expensive, but would like to look like the rest of the officers... Now if you can send me, amongst you, about seventy-five dollars, $75, I think I could get along.'[6]

In the same way, a new lieutenant of the 20th Massachusetts received his money from his family, writing on 8 August 1861:

'I have just got the pistol. I am extremely obliged to you for it. I find it carries remarkably well, better I think, as you say, than Allen's. The case that comes with is very pretty & what is of more importance very convenient indeed. In fact it is just the thing that is desirable, and just what every man wants... I suppose [Shrine?] & Brown have sent in the bill for the sword & sash. I might have got each $2 cheaper, but the articles for that price were of a very much inferior quality... There was also a sword suspending strap that I bought at the same place of $.75.'[7]

George was paid $50 a month with $1.20 a day extra for food. Most officers participated in a company officers' mess fund and one individual, often an enlisted cook, obtained and cooked rations for them. 'We officers live on what we can get, buying milk, eggs, and lots of pies; (peach & apple price – 12½) now getting meat & again not,' wrote a young infantry company officer home in May 1861.[8]

Once the 8th was mustered in, dressed and equipped, it began learning the basics of fighting a mid-nineteenth-century war, first at Camp Morton in Indianapolis, and then on 1 June, as the camp grew more crowded, in Camp McClellan eight miles east of the city. The standard texts used then were generally *Hardee's Rifle and Light Infantry Tactics,* and *Infantry Tactics* by Silas Casey, although other versions of the drill were also available. It would not be until 11 August 1862 that the War Department officially adopted Casey's system as the standard. Generally speaking, the drill systems were similar. A company of four sections (two sections to each platoon) would form in line two deep, the captain on the extreme right of the line and in the front rank. George's post would be behind and centred on the extreme left-hand platoon. From there he would observe the firing and obedience to orders. Once in line the men would count off in twos and on the command 'right face', the even-numbered men would step up and to the right, so that the company would now be in a column of fours, the captain on the front and left of the column. Marching would be done in column, while fighting would be done in line.

In many regiments, after the men had finished their drill, the colonels would have officers gather to study more advanced material. George and his fellow officers had a great deal new to learn not only from the tactics manuals but also from the *Revised Regulations for the US Army* and H. L. Scott's *Military Dictionary.* Lessons often continued long into the night.

Drill commands, different uniform styles and segregation for meals represented a great change for Americans from small towns who were accustomed to seeing each other as equals. Wrote one Maine private of the time shortly after his regiment began its training: 'We began to be conscious of the immensity of icy space between the officers and the rank and file. Friendly neighbors in civilian life, one spreading manure and the other cleaning fish, were now immeasurably apart.'[9] An old acquaintance, now a private in the ranks, could not simply approach George in a group, slap him on the back, and say, 'How's things going, George?' It was now a salute and 'sir'.

In many cases, too, new officers quite failed to earn the respect of their men. 'We are greatly in need of well drilled officers,' wrote a new Michigan recruit in his diary in June 1861. 'It is amusing & at the same time painful to me to see our Capt. at battalion drill.'[10] Nor was it just drill in which many new officers fell down on the job. 'Officers must learn to take care of their men

15

and to make the men take care of themselves, and of one another. The officers of our regiment got new gold-mounted uniforms, and most of them swelled around without any thought that they had any duties or responsibilities,' recalled an Iowa recruit. 'Other companies fared as we did. There were a few good, conscientious officers, but only a few.'[11]

Aware of the problems with many new officers, the War Department issued its General Orders No. 49 on 3 August 1861 that provided for a mechanism for the army to rid itself of poor officers. Every separate department or army was authorised a board of five officers whose duty it was to examine the 'capacity, qualifications, and propriety of conduct, and efficiency of any commissioned officer of volunteers within his department or army who may be reported to the board or commission; and upon such report, if adverse to such officer, and if approved by the President of the United States, the commission of such officer shall be vacated...'[12] This order may have caused some of the changes that would occur in the 8th when it came to be reorganised in late August. George, however, must have been at least acceptable, since he would continue to serve for some time to come.

The new officers of the 8th Indiana would not have had long to learn their business, for on 17 June the regiment boarded a train that would take it eventually to Clarksburg, Virginia. On 23 June the new soldiers found themselves on a mountain top behind that town, awaiting an anticipated attack. After spending three days there, the men joined a column heading for a Confederate position at Rich Mountain in what would be one of the first Union victories of the war. On 10 July the regiment approached Rich Mountain. The regimental surgeon-historian recalled the battle there afterwards:

'During the night Gen. Rosecrans having learned from a citizen named Hart, that the left flank of the rebels could be turned, the General secured his services as a guide, and at 5 a.m. on the morning of the 11th, we took our line of march, our regiment in advance, and after a circuitous march of twelve miles, we came up with the enemy, strongly posted behind rocks and temporary breastworks; and after a fiercely contested fight of two hours, succeeded in routing them, capturing 1,500 stand of arms, 5 guns and 1000 prisoners, and all their camp equipage. Our regiment lost 9 men killed, and 20 wounded. This being our first fight, and unaccustomed to the horrors of the battle field, and the sufferings of the wounded, we felt very sorrowful for our brother soldiers, notwithstanding we were flushed with victory...'[13]

Typically, those who faced their first Civil War battles said later that they were terrified before getting into battle and wished they had not enlisted so quickly. Once, however, the first shots were fired and habits learned on the drill field took over, they settled down and pretty much lost their initial fears, at least for the time being. Not until afterwards, when they sat back and reflected, did the shock of battle hit them.

The regiment had received more of a blooding than most three-months' regiments and when it mustered out on 6 August back in Indianapolis the men were still excited about their triumphant service. Officers asked if the men would return to reform the regiment for service for three years or the duration of the war, should that turn out to be shorter. Overwhelmingly the troops agreed, and headed home for a short furlough before returning on 20 August to muster into the regiment for a second time. Changes occurred as officers, either unable to bear the demands of field service in the wet and cold, or having proved themselves inefficient, were shaken out. George found himself with a new company commander, Captain F. S. Wysong, replacing the ailing Captain Lacy. As well, Silas Colgrove, who had been the lieutenant colonel of the three months' regiment, became colonel of the three years' regiment.

The regiment mustered in on 20 August 1861 and received new, improved weapons – 0.58 calibre Springfield rifled muskets with an accurate killing range of 500 yards. Now they would be the equal of virtually any enemy unit they might meet on the battlefield. On 10 September they all boarded trains to St Louis, Missouri, where an army was being formed to clear the state from Confederate influence. Once there they marched from town to town in cold, wet weather. George, along with many others in the 8th, became sick enough to have to be sent to hospital.

Such widespread disease in a new regiment was common. Many men from rural areas had never been exposed to common childhood diseases such as chicken pox, mumps and measles. While in Missouri, some 140 men of the thousand in the regiment were in the regimental hospital at the same time suffering from measles. Indeed, many died from the disease. Furthermore, new volunteer regiments failed to maintain clean camps, helping infection to spread. Bad water and insanitary eating conditions would kill more Federals than would Confederate bullets. In all, 249,468 men in the Union army died of other than gunshots, the majority from disease. Most common of all were diarrhoea and dysentery, of which some 711 men out of every thousand died during the war. The 8th's regimental surgeon reported that on 23 September the regiment was due to march but had to remain in camp 'suffering very much from dysentery and diarrhea, with but few deaths; but a vast number were sent to the hospitals of St Louis, and other places, until October 14th...'[14]

As it turned out, however, the surgeon reported 'but few deaths' from these two ailments. George was one of the survivors and returned to duty within the month. As it was getting late in the year and the weather was getting rather cold, the 8th went into winter quarters near Otterville, Missouri. These camps contained better accommodation, as the men were permitted to build small log cabins in place of mere tents. A Pennsylvania officer noted in his diary how he 'put up the stonework of our chimney – then John & I built up the "stick" part – daubing it with clay &c. and put on the roof – tent covers – and got things in fair shape to sleep in by dark –and our chimney draws very well....'[15] Other cabin builders used barrels with the tops and bottoms knocked out and thickly covered inside, with mud for chimneys.

Generally, the two company lieutenants would room together in one hut. A New Jersey officer described how inside his quarters the two men had their beds 'heads together, the stove towards the door and table as you see at the foot of my cot with three pipes, two whiskey bottles, two tin cups, a box of cigars and writing material on it. The floor is constructed of damp ground and if anything drops it drops in the dirt.'[16]

The men had lived in tents while building huts. 'It being the custom of the soldiers at night to place in their tents their camp kettles filled with live coals to keep them from freezing, a private of Co. A, was poisoned to death, and several others severally injured by the generation of carbonic acid gas from the coals, in new, close tents.'[17] Other than that incident, things went smoothly enough. The regiment was ordered out of its winter camp on 24 January and sent in terrible cold and wet weather towards Springfield. One soldier actually froze to death on the march. Finally, after having to halt several times on the way because of conditions, the regiment reached Lebanon on 7 February where it joined a force under Major General Samuel Curtis, who drove the Confederate army into Arkansas. Following the rebels to Sugar Creek, Arkansas, the 8th went again into winter quarters from 17 February until 3 March when it moved out once more against the Confederates.

Learning that a large Confederate force was approaching, the 8th then fell back with the rest of the army to Pea Ridge, Arkansas, where they held against a fierce rebel attack in desperate fighting. The 8th lost thirty-eight men from its left wing alone. But on 8 March the Federals were in command of the field. However, the 8th was exhausted by this campaign. The regiment had been forced to burn its tents in the march from Otterville and had marched off with rations on hand for only fifteen days. Mud and ice took their toll on officers and men alike. The regiment moved off on a diversion towards Bentonville, falling back to Cross Timber where they finally went into camp to receive new clothing and supplies and to recuperate.

On 6 April the 8th marched towards Forsyth, Missouri, moving then to Sulphur Rock where it went into camp for two months. 'Towards the last of our stay here, the commissary of our Regiment issued to each man for daily allowance, *four ears of corn,* which, with meat, constituted all the rations.'[18] While there, too, the regiment's colonel was promoted, and the lieutenant colonel, David Shunk, was named new colonel in his place.

On 23 June the 8th left camp heading for a march through Missouri, skirmishing almost daily with Confederates who would hide in the canebrakes, fire a volley or two, and then flee before the advancing Hoosers. By 13 July they reached the Cache River, after marching almost a thousand miles in a seven-month period. Much of the time they were cut off from supplies and had to forage. 'The sufferings endured by our brave army, on account of the scarcity of water and rations, and the excessive heat, and want of proper clothing, can be but feebly expressed,' wrote the regiment's surgeon.[19] The regiment was to remain on the Cache for three months, with a side excursion to Laconia, Arkansas, where one Indiana man was killed in a small skirmish. Disease ran rampant in the regiment, but this time George remained unaffected.

On 11 October the regiment boarded trains for Ironton, going on from there to Black River, arriving on 24 November. Now attached to the so-called Army of South East Missouri, which lacked trained engineers, regimental pioneers were ordered to build a bridge across the river. Floods from a ten-day-long rainstorm, however, carried the bridge away and almost washed over the regiment's camp. Only quick thinking by a picket who noticed the rising water allowed the officers and men time enough to pull up their tents and take to higher ground.

The regiment resumed its wanderings, this time destined to join the army being put together by Ulysses S. Grant to take Vicksburg, a major blocking point on the Mississippi River. The men reached the gathering place for this force, Milliken's Bend, on 26 March 1863. Here the brigade that included the 8th and 18th Indiana, 33rd and 99th Illinois, and 1st Indiana Battery, was put in the 14th Division, assigned to the XIII Corps. At this stage George had to give up the trunk that officers were entitled to have transported on a company wagon. The regiment was ordered to leave behind all its baggage, tents and regimental and hospital property as it set off down the Mississippi, to land south of Vicksburg and drive northward on the well-fortified city. Previous attempts at the city from the north had ended in failure, and Grant was now gambling on a southern approach.

On 31 April the 8th landed near Port Gibson. The men advanced towards that city during the night and ran into southern defenders around midnight. At dawn the next day, the regiment was ordered forward, one of the lead regiments in the attack. The ground was poor, with canebrakes on either sides of narrow roads, deep ditches and ravines cutting up the ground. Still, overwhelming Federal numbers bought victory and the regiment camped on the ground that night as the Confederates fled back to Vicksburg. The regiment had lost thirty-two killed and wounded in the fierce fighting.

The following day, finding the bridge towards Vicksburg burned, regimental pioneers built a replacement bridge while the remainder of the regiment rested. Next day the men moved forward as the Union high command suddenly learned that a strong Confederate force was on its way to reinforce Vicksburg. Grant sent some of his men towards Jackson, the state capital, to block this move. There they met and drove off the Confederates and expected to be allowed to take a couple of days' break. Instead the rebels rallied and returned, to be met by the Federals at Champion Hill. The division in which the 8th was held in reserve, saw action only after the Confederates were soundly defeated and fleeing, when the regiment was sent in pursuit. On 17 May the Federals caught up with the Confederates at Black River and, after a five-hour fight, soundly defeated them yet again, taking a number of prisoners and cannon.

Then Grant and his army dug in, surrounding Vicksburg. Wishing to win quickly, Grant ordered an assault on the Confederate works. The 8th, supported by the 33rd Illinois, was given the target of a fort on the left of the railroad. The approach was over elevated ground, swept by rebel guns dug in at three different points. Even so, the men dashed forward, the colonel of the 33rd falling early in the assault and the regiments becoming intermingled by the terrain and fire. Some of the men dropped into safe pockets on the approach, seeing immediately that the attack was doomed. Others actually reached the walls of the fort and leaped in, but in short time they were almost all killed or captured.

Colonel Shunk sent for reinforcements, but none were available until nearly sundown. Before the attack could be renewed, much to the relief of all, it was called off, The survivors fell back to the trenches. The regiment had lost 117 officers and men, including Captain Wysong, George's commander. On 1 July George was promoted to the rank of captain to command Company D. He would now get $50 a month along with extra pay for four rations a day.

A regular siege began after the unsuccessful attack. On 4 July, out of supplies and with no hope of reinforcements, the Confederate commander of Vicksburg gave up, surrendering his army. The regiment looked forward to a restful time following the formal surrender ceremony and paroling of the Confederates, but it was not to be. Instead, it was part of a command that, on 5 July, marched out of the trenches towards a spot where a new Confederate force had been gathered near Canton, Mississippi.

On 10 July, skirmishing with pickets all the way, the Federals reached Jackson where they found the Confederates well entrenched. Again they dug in for a siege, cannon opening up and shelling the southern forces until, after six days, the Confederates gave up the city and fell back again. The regiment also was sent to Byron's Station to destroy railroad equipment there during this interlude. On 24 July it was back in Vicksburg, camping on the river bank, just below the Marine Hospital.

There the men rested until 20 August when they were sent aboard the steamer *North America* for a three-day trip to Carrolton, Louisiana. While the rank and file slept mostly on the decks, officers such as George had staterooms and ate in the dining room. Once in Louisiana, it was back to marching throughout the countryside until 12 November when the regiment embarked on the steamer *St Mary* for another three-day trip to Texas.

The regiment, part of the Coast Expedition, landed on Mustang Island in the evening of 16 November, marching to Aranzas Pass where on the 17th it surprised and captured a small Confederate garrison. That evening one of those driving cold rain and hail storms called 'northers' came up and, the regiment's camp equipage still aboard the steamer, all the men suffered greatly. Not until 20 November was the baggage landed and the men able to make a proper camp.

From that point they headed to Fort Esperanza, attacking that post on 27 November. Initially the Confederates held, but the Federals persisted in the attack. That evening, fearing the loss of the fort, the rebels retreated, first setting fire to the stores and magazine. Seeing the flames, the Federals rushed into the fort to see what could be saved, but the magazine exploded with a tremendous explosion before much could be saved except a small amount of food and nine heavy cannon. Then the regiment went into camp.

George, however, would not remain long there with his company. On 1 December he was named acting assistant commissary of subsistence on the staff of Brigadier General Fitz-Henry Warren, the brigade commander. He was now responsible for getting the men their proper rations, either by buying locally or receiving from army stores elsewhere. He also had to make sure that these rations, before being issued, were properly stored and cared for, and all properly accounted for. The job involved a sea of paperwork with a plethora of forms designed for different purposes. Moreover, as a period manual advised, 'A conscientious administrator should acquaint himself with the peculiar properties of different kinds of food, their relative nutriment, and the differences of food best suited to promote health under the various circumstances incident to field-service.'[20] What the exact rations were to be, however, was carefully spelled out in army regulations.

While George was serving on staff, his regiment was given the option of renewing its service for the remainder of the war, as the enlistments were drawing to a close. If the men accepted the extended tour of duty, they were entitled to a thirty-day furlough and the right to wear half chevrons on each cuff indicating that the regiment was now a 'Veteran Volunteer' regiment. In all, 417 men of the 8th, out of 515 in the regiment at the time, voted to accept; George, along with the rest of the regiment, was officially re-mustered in as a veteran volunteer regiment on 1 January 1864. Although officers were not officially allowed to wear veteran volunteer chevrons, George had a pair put on his generally non-regulation uniform coat anyway. Indeed, it was while wearing this coat that he had himself photographed by S. Anderson, on 61 Camp Street, in New Orleans.

In fact, the men who re-enlisted remained in camp, but since the army was so short-handed, it was not until April and May when they were sent on their furloughs. When they came together again, George, no longer on staff, rejoined his company.

The proud veterans gathered once more in LaFourche, Louisiana, where they remained on garrison duty until July. In the meantime, General Grant had arrived in the Eastern Theatre, having ordered one of his generals, Philip Sheridan, to clear the Valley of Virginia of Confederate forces, for which purpose men from across the country were assembled. The 8th was called from its sleepy Louisiana town to reboard a ship to sail to Washington, DC, thousands of miles away.

A sight of the unfinished capital city was bound to be a treat for Hoosers, many of whom had never been east at all. As their ship steamed up the Potomac River they crowded the rails to get a glimpse of the tomb of George Washington and his home at Mount Vernon. Undoubtedly the men would have liked to have gone sightseeing in the city itself, but time was limited. A Confederate raid on the capital had just been turned away by the line of fortifications surrounding the city, and the rebels were now falling back. Sheridan was on his way after them into the Valley.

The 8th found itself in a Fourth Brigade of the Second Division, XIX Corps, along with two other western regiments, the 24th and 28th Iowa. Initially, they were brilliantly successful, driving Lee's men in the Valley back at the battles of Berryville, 2 September and Opequan, 19 September. Then they rested near Cedar Creek.

The nights were getting colder now, and George bought himself a cavalryman's overcoat from the army quartermaster for $10.55. By regulations, officers were supposed to wear dark blue overcoats with a lace pattern on the cuff that indicated rank; a captain would wear his loop with two rows of lace. The men, on the other hand, were issued sky-blue overcoats. The colour difference made targets of the officers, many of whom began to wear enlisted men's overcoats in self-defence as early as 1861. By the time George bought his coat, Union officers had adopted the style of small circles, bordered in gold embroidery, of the branch of service colour, which was sky-blue for infantry, with the officer's rank insignia in the centre of the circle, on each sleeve just above the cuff.

George was not allowed a long rest, for the Confederates saw a chance of striking the Federals near Cedar Creek by surprise in an attempt to repeat their Valley victories of 1862. In the early morning hours of 19 October, in a heavy fog, they smashed into the Union camps. The Federals were taken unawares. Battle lines were hard to form in the fog and, moreover, the grey mist that hung over the ground hid the grey-clad enemy formations. The 8th and the other regiments in the brigade held on for a few minutes, giving time for a Rhode Island artillery battery to pull off all but one of its guns. But the price was high. Lieutenant Colonel Alexander J. Kenny, then in command of the regiment, fell with a grievous wound. Finally the men fled into the mists, the same grey clouds that hid the enemy now shrouding them as they made towards the rear.

Hearing gunfire, Sheridan mounted his horse and galloped towards the front. As he rode forwards, he rallied the men, most of whom were trudging slowly towards the rear. Many of the Confederate formations had fallen apart as the hungry and cold men stopped to loot the Federal tents of food and clothing. This gave Sheridan the time he needed. Basing his line on the VI Corps, which had managed to retain its formation and had fallen back to a firm defensive line, he ordered a counter-attack. The assault fell on weary Confederates whose units had been badly disrupted by looting, casualties and the general fog of war. The rebel line quickly fell apart, and the Federals dashed forward, giving the southerners a tremendous crushing.

The survivors of the Confederate forces retreated and were hit again. Needed in Petersburg, where Grant's troops were steadily draining Lee's defences, and unable to accomplish anything further in the Valley, the rebels abandoned the area. Most of Sheridan's troops followed, joining Grant's men at Petersburg. George's regiment was left as garrison in the Valley.

It was not terribly pleasant duty. There was little love lost between residents and soldiers. One southern family who lived in the Valley recalled how the Federal troops there destroyed 'everything before them. Hogs, sheep, cattle, & c. were shot down and left to rot and horses were taken and carried away, whether needed by the army or not. Springdale was left like a wilderness, almost every living animal on the place either being driven off or else killed and left in sheer deviltry and wickedness.'[21] While on this duty, on 28 December 1864, George was given command of Company E of the 8th.

On 6 January 1865 the 8th was ordered out of the Valley and sent to Baltimore, Maryland. Although many residents were southern sympathisers, the city on the whole was a friendly place. The Hoosers of the 8th must have felt much more comfortable in a town where people hung American flags from their windows because they wanted to. But the regiment was not to stay there long. On 14 January the men again went aboard a steamer, this time with the destination of Savannah, Georgia, arriving on 20 January. That city had fallen to Sherman's troops marching south from Atlanta only a month before. Some of the companies, however, were detached and sent to various other points along the coast of Georgia and South Carolina. George's company was sent to Darien, Georgia, once an attractive village along the coast which, several years earlier, had been needlessly burned in an earlier Federal raid. The attitudes of locals towards George and his men must have reminded the soldiers of life in the Valley of Virginia.

In July George was named to special duty as Assistant Provisional Judge for the post and sub-district based in Hawkinsville, Georgia. With a break-up of civil authority in the south (for positions held under a seceding government were not considered legal), the area came under martial law. The army provided the court system, and George would now find himself mired in all sorts of civil matters from domestic disputes to tax debts.

It was not uncommon for an infantry officer to perform such duty. 'A captain's duty to be filled properly requires a diversity of talents,' wrote a Massachusetts captain to his wife. 'He ought to be a good clerk, also be somewhat posted in military law, besides his other military requirements.'[22] For George, this was the way the war ended. In mid-August came word that the regiment was to be mustered out shortly, each company where it was, as other occupation troops would take over. On 28 August 1865 George W. Adams was mustered out of Union service.

NOTES

1 War Department, *The War of the Rebellion: A Compilation of the Official Records of the Union and Confederate Armies* (hereafter *ORs*), Washington, 1899, Series III, Vol. 1, p. 70

2 Todd, Frederick P., *American Military Equippage, 1851–1872, State Forces,* Vol. II, New York, 1983, p. 775

3 Baxter, Nancy N., *Gallant Fourteenth,* Indianapolis, Indiana, 1980, p. 8

4 Todd, op. cit., p. 780

5 *ORs*, op. cit., p. 89

6 Rieger, Paul E., and David E. Roth, 'James Theaker Joins The Army,' *Blue & Gray* Magazine, February-March 1985, pp. 40-1.

7 Scott, Robert G., *Fallen Leaves,* Kent, Ohio, 1991, p. 38

8 Howe, Mark De Wolfe, ed, *Touched With Fire,* Cambridge, Massachusetts, 1946, p. 6

9 Small, Abner R., The *Road to Richmond,* Berkeley, California, 1939, p. 13

10 Sears, Stephen W., ed., *For Country Cause & Leader,* New York, 1993, p. 14

11 Ware E. F., *The Lyon Campaign In Missouri,* Topeka, Kansas, 1907, pp. 92-3

12 *ORs*, Series III, Vol. 1, p. 383

13 Bigelow, James K., *Abridged History of the Eighth Indiana Volunteer Infantry, from its Organization, April 21st, 1861, to the date of Re-enlistment as Veterans, January 1, 1864,* Indianapolis, 1964, p. 8

14 ibid, p. 10

15 Mohr, James C. ed., *The Cormany Diaries*, Pittsburgh, Pennsylvania, 1982, p. 394

16 Olsen, Bernard A., *Upon The Tented Field,* Red Bank, New Jersey, 1993, p. 187

17 Bigelow, op cit., p. 11

18 ibid, p. 14

19 ibid, pp. 14–15

20 Scott, H.L, op cit., p. 577

21 Colt, Margaretta Barton, *Defend the Valley,* New York, 1994, p. 340

22 Howard, William F., 'Letters From The Front,' *Camp Chase Gazette,* December 1982, p. 14

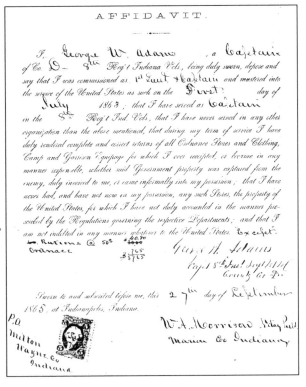

Right: George Adams had to sign this affidavit that he was elegible for discharge before he could become a civilian again. (National Archives)

2

David Alva Barnett

Sergeant, 99th Pennsylvania Infantry Regiment

There is a little town named Peach Bottom just inside York County, Pennsylvania, above the Maryland state line. It is an area of rolling hills and wide, green farmlands. By 1861 it had not changed much from when the first Scots/Irish settled there in the eighteenth century.

David Alva Barnett worked in this town as a blacksmith, helping to care for his mother. Barnett, in 1861, was twenty years old, and stood five feet nine inches tall. He had brown hair and grey eyes, his complexion being described as 'fair'.

Life loomed long and unchanging in small towns in America like Peach Bottom, and the firing on Fort Sumter raised not only patriotic indignation, but also thoughts of travel and excitement. Young women fawned over those men who said they were going to go off to war. Veterans of previous wars were trotted out and spoke at town meetings where companies were raised for the purpose of showing the southern rebels who was to be boss, to punish them for firing on the old flag. It was hard not to go to war then. As another young northern lad wrote in years after the war:

'When Fort Sumter was fired into by the Rebels under Genl. Beauregard from Fort Moultrie in Charleston Harbor, my military spirit along with the rest of the people in the Northern States rose to the boiling pitch, but being at the time bound down as an apprentice to learn the carpenter's trade, it was out of the question for me to enlist. The only way that I could show my military ardor being in helping to swell the crowds on the side walks, who had assembled to see the regiments off to the front.'[1]

David, too, had to stay home when the first wave of volunteers for three months gathered farther north, in Harrisburg, to get ready to march south and put down the rebellion. He may have had commitments to do with his blacksmithing trade; he may have not wanted to leave his mother alone. She may not have wished him to go. But, if he were like the vast majority of American men, his age, on both sides, he was determined to join up.

The first northern volunteers, however, did not succeed as they had expected. On the banks of a small Virginia creek called Bull Run those green volunteers met an equally expectant southern army and were thrown back, a beaten, running mob, to Washington. The three months' regiments, having reached the end of their enlistments, were disbanded. Authorisation came for new regiments, of a more serious stuff, to be organised for terms of three years or the war. One of these was to become the 99th Pennsylvania Volunteer Infantry Regiment.

The first 99th began to organise in Pennsylvania's largest city, Philadelphia, in late July 1861 as the 32nd Pennsylvania Volunteers. Hardly had its first companies been completed, when they were sent to Washington, on 8 August, to become the basis of a new 32nd regiment of Pennsylvania companies in that city. The remainder continued to organise into another new regiment which was now renumbered the 99th. Two of the companies that went south, B and D companies, were replaced by new volunteer companies raised in Lancaster County, recently arrived in Philadelphia.

Finally, David was able to break free of the ties that kept him back. He crossed the Susquehanna River that separates York and Lancaster Counties and joined one of these new Lancaster companies, Company B. On 31 July 1861 he was mustered into Federal service.

One of the first things any new volunteer company did was elect its officers. They then appointed the non-commissioned officers, from the company first sergeant to the eighth corporal. David was among those singled out as being a better than average soldier and was mustered in as a corporal. In fact, a corporal's pay was only $13, the same as a private's, so the grade did not allow him to send any more money home than he would have done otherwise. Nor did the higher grade greatly affect his social status among the privates in his company, since there were no such privileges as special messes or accommodations for non-commissioned officers. Even so, since many of the others in the regiment had seen service previously in one or another of the three-months' outfits, David's appointment was a distinction that marked what his company commander saw as his potential ability. Then the new soldiers began to learn their business. As one recruit from the 76th Pennsylvania later recalled:

'We had it all to learn from the primer class up. Nearly all of us made a grievous mistake in coming into camp clothed as we were. Some were arrayed in the best they had because they did not properly realise the rough usage their finery would have to endure. I was among this number. Others had too much faith in the ability of the Government to array them in uniform the moment they arrived in camp. They went to the other extreme and wore about the worst clothes they had. Consequently we were an odd looking crew, something like a crazy quilt outfit. And you can depend on it we did not improve as time went by. We never saw our uniforms for six weeks after entering camp, and it can be imagined what an unkempt lot we were.'[2]

Even when the first uniforms did arrive, most recruits agreed they did not look much more military than before. One recruit recalled:

'My first uniform was a bad fit; my trousers were too long by three or four inches; the flannel shirt was coarse and unpleasant, too large at the neck and too short elsewhere. The forage cap was an ungainly bag with pasteboard top and leather visor; the blouse was the only part which seemed decent; while the overcoat made me feel like a little nip of corn amid a preponderance of husk. Nothing except "Virginia mud" ever took down my ideas of military pomp quite so low.'[3]

A soldier in the 38th Pennsylvania wrote home in July 1861 that he had received :

'1 Over Coat, 1 Pr Pants (heavy duck) to scuff around in, 1 dark Blue Blouse, 1 Pr Shoes, 1 Shirt. That is all the Good we have drawn so far but expect to draw another pair pants drawers and stockings. I forgot to mention the Cap which is like that one I got from the Garrison before I left. The Over-coat is like the Regulars and as thick as thin board if you know how thick that is. It will turn the Rain for two weeks.'[4]

They had yet to draw dress frock coats, the sky-blue woollen trousers that were regulation standard issue, and dress hats. David would also have to draw the two sky-blue tape chevrons sewn to a dark blue wool backing that he would wear on his sleeves, points down, to mark his grade. As well, his grade was marked by a half-inch-wide dark blue stripe down each trousers leg.

Weapons were even slower to arrive. Eventually, however, the unit received British-made copies of the P1858 rifled musket, a single shot, rifled 0.577 calibre weapon with a triangular bladed spike bayonet. In addition, they received black leather cartridge boxes that held 40 rounds of ammunition and hung on the rear right hip. A black leather percussion cap pouch was worn on a waistbelt on the right front hip, while the bayonet was suspended from the same waistbelt on the left side. Each soldier learned to carry his rations in a black painted haversack suspended from the right shoulder, worn on the left side over the bayonet. He carried his water in a tin canteen covered with wool that was suspended from the right shoulder and worn on top of the haversack. His clothing went into a black knapsack, with a woollen blanket and a ground cloth coated on one side with rubber. He was permitted to pack a greatcoat strapped to the top of the knapsack, but many troops left their greatcoats behind when they went into the field, preferring to wrap up in a blanket on cool nights.

David had to learn the job of the corporal right away. The author of a standard enlisted man's manual of the period wrote:

'The duties of a corporal are simple, and they depend for their successful performance mainly upon his capacity to control and direct soldiers in the performance of their duty. They take charge of the smaller details for fatigue and police duty in camp and garrison duty: their most important duty is that of Corporal of the Guard. They frequently succeed to the responsibilities of sergeant in his absence, and should therefore be familiar with his duties.'[5]

According to the most used period drill manual, David and the other corporals had to know 'the School of the Soldier [i.e. basic drill movements], and such regulations as prescribe their duties in garrison and in campaign.'[6]

The company, and then the regiment, also embarked on the hours of close order drill that turned it from a mob of civilians into a finely honed fighting machine capable of confronting and destroying an enemy by fire and the final bayonet charge. Company B, the second company in the regiment, was always posted on the extreme left flank of the regiment in line of battle. It would, therefore, be the last company in line of march – not an enviable position since its men would get the most dust on their faces on dry roads and tread the deepest mud on wet ones.

Each man had a fixed place in the ranks. According to the standard drill manual of the period:

'The corporals will be posted in the front rank and on the right and left of platoons, according to height; the tallest corporal and the tallest man will form the first file, the next tallest men will form the second file, and so on to the last file, which will be composed of the shortest corporal and the shortest man.'[7]

Under fire, of course, the first rank would generally consist of the most dependable men, this being the most dangerous place.

The 99th had sufficient time to learn its job well, more time than many similar regiments, since it was not until 18 January 1862 that the entire regiment was organised and mustered in. In fact, the regiment itself would not be formally mustered into United States service until December 1862. In the meantime, the men lived better than they would for the rest of their enlistment. A private in the 35th Pennsylvania wrote home from the regiment's first encampment, 'We have good rations here, such as coffee, cookies, potatoes, rice, beans, beef, pork, ham, crackers, and first-rate bread.'[8] This variety would quickly disappear, however, so that although David would not go hungry, he would find his diet mostly consisting of 'stale beef ... rusty, unwholesome pork ... [and] "hardtack" ... a piece of petrified bread honeycombed with bugs and maggots...'[9] Coffee, too, was a basic staple. From time to time he would receive some vegetables such as potatoes, rice, or split peas as well as dried apples, and purchases from civilian sources also helped vary the diet.

David was further able to supplement his diet with items from his regimental sutler. Sutlers were civilians authorised to accompany specific units as a type of mobile general store. The 99th had two sutlers during its existence, E. Z. Collins and J. W. Starr. They sold items that the army did not issue, but soldiers actually needed. These included canned food, tobacco, cheese, cards, handkerchiefs, towels, stationery and writing equipment, patent medicines, suspenders, candlesticks, neckties, mirrors, shaving brushes, and, when they could get away with it, alcoholic drinks. The soldiers generally saw the sutlers as price gougers, taking advantage of their monopolies to get much higher prices for everything than other civilians charged.

Finally, in January, the regiment was ordered away from Philadelphia, down to Washington to help garrison the forts that had been built to ring the nation's capital city. But the regiment had no opportunity to visit the still unfinished Capitol building and the President's home in the White House. The Army of the Potomac – a mighty armed force – was being assembled. Major General George B. McClellan had planned a sweep by sea to the east, to land where a peninsula of land jutted south and east from the enemy capital of Richmond. The 99th was named a part of this force.

The regiment joined the army at Harrison's Landing on the 86th birthday of American independence, 4 July 1862. Instead of the large tents they had formerly used in permanent camps, they now slept in small shelter halves. One soldier later wrote home:

'We have been provided with shelter tents, which are made of two peices [sic] of light canvas about 6 ft square each which button togather [sic] in the center and make one tent to accommodate two men, they are very good on account of the heavy dews we have here, and for a shade, but as the two ends are open they are not much use in a storm. When we move the occupants of a tent each take half roll it and tie it on their backs so we always have our houses with us and can make ourselves at home wherever we stop.'[10]

The newly arrived regiment was immediately assigned to the 2nd Brigade, 1st Division, III Corps, in company with 62nd Pennsylvania, 14th New York, 4th Michigan, and 9th Massachusetts. In this organisation they would spend most of the war. Many might have considered the assignment a lucky one, since they saw no action in the bloody Seven Pines or later Seven Days battles where the army was checked by a series of Confederate punches – blows which, although not damaging enough to save Richmond, nevertheless demoralised McClellan badly. So badly, in fact, that he gave up any further attempt at aggressive action.

Back in Washington, the government was not prepared to give up just because its premier general had lost his nerve. The War Department cobbled together a new force from troops already around the capital city and assigned it to a general who had been victorious in the west, Major General John Pope. Pope received marching orders to drive overland due south, following almost the same track used by the army that met defeat at Bull Run in 1861. At the same time, McClellan was ordered to release many of his troops to Pope's command and, indeed, follow up with the rest to join Pope in this final campaign. The 99th was one of the first to be so released. It saw service in both the disastrous Second Battle of Bull Run and the little defensive encounter at Chantilly that finished the campaign with a smell of victory, even though it cost the life of one of the Union's better generals, Philip Kearny.

The 99th managed to miss the single bloodiest day of the war, at Antietam, when Lee's Army went on the offensive, raiding into Maryland after the Bull Run campaign. But the regiment was included when the Army of the Potomac, under its new leader, Major General Ambrose Burnside, again headed south directly from Washington. There it came to a halt along the Rappahannock River, awaiting the pontoon bridges that should have been ordered up from Washington long before. It was December before the army was ready to cross the river. By that time Robert E. Lee had assembled his forces along the heights just beyond Fredericksburg, where Burnside planned to cross, and dug them in, placing his men and guns so well that one Confederate officer claimed that even a chicken could not live on the field once they opened fire.

Burnside, unable to come up with a quick alternative plan, did not agree with the Confederate assessment. He decided to go ahead and make a frontal assault on Lee's lines anyway, with the intention of taking a road he believed ran behind enemy lines, and cutting the Confederate army in half.

The 99th was among the regiments assigned to cross on the left of the Union front. Major General William B. Franklin was overall commander on the left, and described the line David and his men had to cross:

'The ground upon which the troops were disposed is, in general, a plain. It is cultivated and much cut up by hedges and ditches. The old Richmond Road traverses the plain from right to left, about 1 mile from the river and nearly parallel to it. This road is bordered on both sides by an earthen parapet and ditch, and is an exceedingly strong feature in the defense of the ground, had the enemy chosen to hold it....The plain is bordered by a range of high hills in front, which stretches from Fredericksburg to the Massaponax... In front of and nearly parallel to the old Richmond Road, and about 500 or 600 yards from it, at the foot of the range of hills, is the railroad... The enemy had artillery on the hills and in the valley of Deep Creek, in the wood near Reynolds's right, and on the Massaponax, so that the whole field was surrounded by it, except the right flank. His infantry appeared in all directions around the position.'[11]

Into this hail of crossfire charged the Union troops. On the left they were partially successful, much more so than in the central attack, but they could not hold on and had to fall back. The regiment had been assigned to what Burnside designated the 'Center Grand Division', which was essentially held in reserve. Nonetheless, once the battle started the regiment was sent forward on the left to support the 2nd Maine Battery in time to see some fighting against Confederate counter-attacks. In all, the 99th lost sixty officers and men killed and wounded, including its colonel, at Fredericksburg. 'The proud reputation of the State of Pennsylvania will always be sustained by the Fifty-seventh and Ninety-ninth,' reported Brigadier General J. H. Hobart Ward, the brigade commander, in his report on the fighting.[12]

The army recrossed the river under a bleak December sky. Burnside started yet another offensive, this time swinging his army to the right to try to turn the Confederate flank. Heavy rains, however, turned Virginia's soil into the thickest imaginable mud. Wagons and cannon sank up to their axle hubs. Mules were reported to have sunk so deep that only their ears showed. Mocking Confederates posted signs with slogans such as 'Burnside: Stuck In The Mud along the Federal route'.

After this fiasco, the army fell back again to winter quarters, where the troops built small cabins that held five or six men together. They used tents for roofs, logs for walls, and mud-lined barrels for chimneys. Major General Joseph Hooker replaced Burnside in the army's game of commanders' musical chairs. Hooker, at least, did not dash straight off on another campaign, but waited to rebuild his army, plagued with low morale. He took immediate steps. First, he gave many men, particularly those who were married, and thus not including David, furloughs to go home. He also ordered a system of cloth badges to be worn on cap tops and sides that identified to which division each officer and man belonged. Those in the 1st Division, III Corps, including the 99th, were to wear a red 'lozenge', or diamond.

After the casualties of Fredericksburg and sickness had taken so many others out of the ranks, a number of promotions were made. On 1 March 1863 David was named a sergeant and replaced his two chevrons with three, and his trouser stripes with others an inch and a half wide. David's new position, which paid $17 a month, enabling him to send more money home, required additional knowledge. According to the drill manual, the sergeant's 'theoretical instruction should include the School [i.e. drill] of the Soldier, the School of the Company, and the Drill for Skirmishers. They should likewise know all the details of service, and the regulations prescribing their duties in garrison and in campaign.'[13] Furthermore, as another period manual writer said:

'It is difficult to draw the line between the duties of the corporal and those of the sergeant. There is really no great difference in their duties. Sergeants generally have larger details under their charge, and have corporals under their direction to assist them. They are usually intrusted with more responsible duties, and they are supposed to have greater experience, and to approach nearer the commissioned officer in a knowledge of all military matters.

'The most important duty of sergeant is that of file-closer. Posted in the rear of the company when paraded, it is his duty to see that the men pay attention to their duty, preserve order, march properly, and keep closed.

'In time of battle, it is his duty to keep the men in ranks, not to allow them to fall out on any pretext, and to prevent them from misbehaving before the enemy. He is even required to shoot men down when they attempt to run away in times of danger.'[14]

In line of battle the most junior sergeant in the company, the fifth sergeant, was posted opposite the second file from the right of the first platoon.

With the spring rains and new green shoots popping out all along the Rappahannock, Hooker finally got his revitalised command under way. He, too, proposed an overland route towards Richmond. However, his priority was to make a further demonstration towards Fredericksburg, where Burnside had seen so many of his blue-clad men fall. The main part of the army, though, would head west, upriver, cross at the many fords along the way, swing around and either trap Lee between the two forces at Fredericksburg or compel him to come out into the open where Hooker was confident he could beat the rebels.

Towards the end of April Hooker got his men on the march and, indeed, appeared to have succeeded in his plan. No Confederates opposed him in any force at the fords; their strengths along the heights above Fredericksburg seemed unchanged. 'It is with heartfelt satisfaction the commanding general announces to the army that the operations of the last three days have determined that our enemy must either ingloriously fly, or come out from behind his defenses and give us battle on our own ground, where certain destruction awaits him,' he declared to his army. [15]

Lee had a different idea. After meeting his trusted subordinate, 'Stonewall' Jackson, he left a masking force at Fredericksburg, while he hurled one entire corps, Jackson's men, around the Federal flank. The rebel flank march being undiscovered by the Federals, Jackson burst on XI Corps and routed it. Hooker, stunned when a cannon ball glanced off a pillar against which he was leaning, was demoralised. The Army of the Potomac stopped dead in its tracks.

III Corps was not among the advance troops, following instead in the wake of VI Corps. David and the other the men of the 99th were camped some four miles south of the river when suddenly they heard gunfire off to the front through the heavy underbrush. As dusk fell, the brigade was called into formation and hustled off towards the sound of the guns. That night they lay nervously on their weapons. At daylight they moved off to the right where they met survivors of XI Corps. Towards the afternoon, however, they learned that the entire brigade had been cut off from the rest of the army. Brigadier General J. H. Hobart Ward, brigade commander, determined to cut his way back to safety. At 11.30 he ordered the brigade out in line of battle to break through the defending Confederate line hidden within a line of woods. Despite the drama of the moonlight charge and blessed by surprise, Union losses were light. Poor visibility, and probably the unexpected timing of the attack, affected marksmanship. The 99th lost but one enlisted man dead on the field, with another sixteen wounded. and nine missing. Once again, David came out unharmed.

Lee's magnificent victory was marred by two things. Jackson was mortally wounded and the Army of the Potomac was not. Still, it had been battered and now, partly to carry the war to a north that had been relatively untouched and partly to relieve pressure on the western town of Vicksburg now under Union siege, Lee decided to drive north through Maryland and into Pennsylvania. In June his troops took to the road, followed, when the move was discovered, by the Army of the Potomac. On the march Hooker lost his commander's musical chair, and Pennsylvania native Major General George G. Meade became the army's new commander.

Both forces passed west of Peach Bottom where David's mother awaited news of him. The 99th reached Emmitsburg, Maryland, a little below the Pennsylvania line, and there learned that the armies had collided just to the north of them, at a crossroads town named Gettysburg. Through the hot summer weather, up and down rolling hills that seemed never to end, the 339 officers and men of the regiment marched to reach the field in the evening hours of 1 July. There they camped close to the Sherfy house near Little Round Top on the left of the Union line, deploying there into battle line in mid-morning, 2 July. Later the regiment was moved forward down a slope towards the west branch of Plum Run, below the Round Tops, to support the green-clad men of Berdan's Sharpshooters. They did not know it, but they were exactly where Lee planned to launch his attack on that day.

Finally, in the afternoon, howling Confederates came straight at them through the Rose Woods in which they were posted. The rebels were the best the south had to offer, men of the 1st Texas and 3rd Arkansas, of the famed Hood's Texas Brigade. The Union line held, and the 99th was pulled out of its position and sent towards Devil's Den where Confederates were beginning to drive a wedge between the Union line there and up on Little Round Top. The regiment's major, John W. Moore, looked back at his line and yelled, 'Up and charge!' The men following shouted, 'Pennsylvania and our homes!'[16] With this they swept forward against the troops from Alabama and Georgia who held the position.

Quickly, however, the Confederates counter-attacked. The 99th held out for a half an hour against tremendous enemy fire that ended up driving the regiment from the ridge they had taken. Moore ordered the 99th to fall back slowly, covering its rear. One of the regiment's corporals, James Casey, remained in the rear as it fell back, smashing abandoned muskets so they could not be used by the enemy. Moore called out to him to hurry up and join the rest of the regiment, but Casey could not resist firing a loaded musket he had found. As he fired, he was hit. Moore and Sergeant Robert Graham ran back to carry Casey off, but he told them to leave him behind and save themselves as the Confederates were too close. Unable to carry him, the two left the wounded man behind. His body was never found. Four officers and 102 enlisted men – over a third of the strength of the 99th – had fallen in this brief, sharp scrap. David, again, was not among them.

The regiment bivouacked in the rear, moving back to its original position on 3 July. But the fighting that day would be elsewhere. Gettysburg was history for David and the men of the 99th.

Lee's men, stopped all along the line, began to pull back, followed slowly by the Army of the Potomac. Much to the disgust of President Abraham Lincoln, the bulk of the Confederate Army escaped into Virginia. The 99th was among the following force, taking part in a small skirmish called Wapping Heights before going into camp near the foothills of the Blue Ridge Mountains.

Meade, the victor of Gettysburg, now transferred his army south to test his abilities of manoeuvre with Lee. On 10 October the 99th packed and moved off again, again heading south. On 7 November the 99th was in position near Kelly's Ford, on the Rappahannock, arriving shortly after noon.

There they found an entrenched enemy, with rifle pits overlooking the river and the ford, backed up by artillery. The Federals also brought up artillery, including Henry Sleeper's battery, and opened fire on the Confederate guns. Then the commanding Federal general ordered his infantry, including the 99th, to cross the waist-deep river in a column, deploy into line, and drive the Confederates off to allow the rest of the army to pass. The Confederates were unable to halt the overwhelming Union assault and fell back, inflicting only a few losses. In all, only forty-three officers and men were killed or wounded in the brief action. A New York surgeon, who accompanied the attacking infantry, wrote:

'It is amazing for me to think *how few* of us were killed or wounded in this affair. Not because they were silent, for an incessant fire was kept upon us, not because we were too far off, for we could hear officers give the word to their men – not because of their *love* to us, for we have too many counter assurances from that; but because we were too close; the balls passing over our heads, instead of falling short.'[17]

At least one southern bullet, however, was fired low to the ground, or perhaps high enough to drop into the ranks if the unit was sufficiently far from the front line, for David was hit in the knee during the charge. The first people to his aid, save, perhaps some of his platoon, would have been members of the Ambulance Corps. Marked by green half chevrons on each sleeve and a green cap band, these men followed the infantry forward to help wounded men get back to the regimental field hospital. While they were not extensively trained in medical aid, they did carry extra water and such items as tourniquets, one of which was probably used on David. A knee injury is one of the most painful types of injuries, yet he may have been able to hobble back to the advanced dressing station, usually posted near the front in a hollow or behind trees for protection, by himself or helped by one of the Ambulance Corpsmen. Private Lewis Metcalf, also shot in the leg, recalled after he was wounded, 'During the whole day I had suffered scarcely any from pain. The force of the ball which had broken my leg had so benumbed it that when I lay still I felt no inconvenience.'[18]

At the dressing station David would have been attended by his regimental surgeon. Since he was at this point only interested in immediate measures to save lives, the surgeon would have given David some liquor, probably whiskey, a procedure frowned upon today but considered standard practice at the time. He would have checked on the tourniquet, or if this had not been applied, put one on. He would have given David an opium pill or a small amount of morphine, to counteract the pain. Then he would have had David sent on to the field hospital for more intensive treatment.

The field hospital was set up just out of artillery range behind the lines with several surgeons and hospital stewards – enlisted men in charge of pharmacies and paperwork – on hand. Cooks there prepared food for the wounded. Tables, often made of doors laid across barrels, were set up for field operations.

Most serious wounds, such as David's was, required immediate operations. According to accepted medical practice, it was considered vital to operate within twenty-four to forty-eight hours after wounding, before infection had set in. Doctors had seen that slow-moving, heavy musket bullets, usually 0.577 or 0.58 calibre, smashed and splintered bones to such a point where they could not be put back together. Veins and arteries were torn, along with muscle and everything else in the way of the rambling bullets. Filthy uniform cloth was driven deep into wounds. The quickest way to make everything as right as could be was simply by cutting away the severely damaged limb. Because the causes of infection itself were unknown, these operations were, in a modern sense, filthy affairs, with scalpels and saws sponged off in bloody water between uses and the black ponchos laid over the table splashed off at intervals with polluted water. The doctors themselves wore their dirty wool uniforms, especially in the cool of a northern Virginia fall evening, while they cut away.

Luckily for David, casualties were so few that he probably did not have to spend much time lying in the straw spread for patients outside the field hospital before he was hoisted up on the operating table. The surgeon looked him over and decided the leg from above the knee down had to go. So, after applying chloroform to put David mercifully to sleep, he cut away. The next thing David knew was that he was lying on the ground, his leg missing.

'The night was a cold one, with keen freezing air from the North,' the New York surgeon recalled.[19] Usually a patient was assured of staying at least one night on a stretcher or straw at the field hospital, so that the surgeon could check that his stitches had not come out and the stump was appearing to heal. The cold and shock, along with the opium or morphine administered earlier, may have prevented David from feeling much pain, although he must have shivered from the cold all night. Fatigue and shock probably combined, however, to bring him some sleep. 'The toil and excitement of the day at last asserted their power,' Private Metcalf recalled of the evening after he had been shot, 'and I fell into a sound sweet slumber.'[20]

The next day, after being checked, David would be loaded, along with the other soldiers unfortunate enough to be wounded, into an ambulance for a trip to a rail head. The standard four-wheel ambulances were no joy in which to ride. Lacking soft suspensions, they bounced along deeply rutted roads, banging the soldier's wounded leg into the side of his stretcher. Many times ambulances had to be stopped when wounds reopened and the accompanying surgeon sewed them up again. Men cried to be put out of their misery, begging to be shot and left behind.

Finally, however, they reached a rail head where the men were jolted down off the ambulances and up on to specially designed hospital rail cars, fashioned from box cars and passenger cars with the seats removed, with bunks or posts from which stretchers could be hung. Other cars in the medical trains contained kitchens, operating rooms and storerooms. Even the relatively smooth iron rails could not prevent the pain as patients were buffeted as the trains passed over rickety tracks.

After some hours, David's train reached Washington. Medical personnel meeting the train at the depot assigned David to the Douglas Hospital in that city for his recuperation. Although many of the city's military hospitals had been built especially for the purpose, Douglas Hospital was not one of those, but was one of many civilian buildings turned into a hospital to handle the crush of Union wounded. The four-storey brick building on the corner of New Jersey Avenue and I Street had originally been built as three upper class homes. The late Stephen A. Douglas, one-time Democratic presidential candidate, had lived in the house on the corner, while Vice President John C. Breckinridge, now a Confederate general, owned the central one. The third home was owned by a former senator from Minnesota. All three buildings had been converted into the hospital bearing the Douglas name. Although spacious, the three mansions were not large enough for all the casualties sent there, and a sea of wall tents, each warmed by its own stove, was built behind them.

David had probably never been in a hospital before. In those days hospitals were used only by transients and the poor and homeless. After all, there was little that could not be done, and usually done better, at home than in a hospital for virtually any disease then treated. But David would not have much chance to explore his new environment, for the surgery that attempted to save his life would now end it. Soon he was diagnosed by Assistant Surgeon W. F. Norris at the hospital as suffering from pyemia – literally 'pus in the blood' – from which recovery was rarely expected. As one surgeon described it:

'Many a time have I had the following experience: A poor fellow whose leg or arm I had amputated a few days before would be getting on as well as we then expected – that is to say, he had pain, high fever, was thirsty and restless, but was gradually improving, for he had what we looked on as a favorable symptom – an abundant discharge of pus from his wound. Suddenly, over night, I would find that his fever had become markedly greater; his tongue dry, his pain and restlessness increased; sleep had deserted his eyelids, his cheeks were flushed; and on removing the dressings I would find the secretions from the wound dried up, and what there were were watery, thin, and foul smelling, and what union of the flaps had taken place had melted away. Pyemia was the verdict, and death the usual result within a few days.'[21]

David was doubly unlucky. Not only was he one of such a small number to get wounded at Kelly's Ford, but he was among that one per cent of wounded men to contract pyemia, which had a 97.4 per cent mortality rate.

In trying to save David's life, the usual treatment would have been stimulant drugs, which were dilute sulphuric acids or quinine; large amount of alcoholic beverages; and a diet of beef tea, milk, and eggs. In the majority of cases, even these remedies proved ineffective. Indeed, David died on 26 November 1863, one of 113 enlisted men in the 99th to die of wounds during the war.

NOTES

1 Donald, David H., ed., *Gone For A Soldier*, Boston, 1975, p. 3
2 Chisman, James A., ed, *76th Regiment Pennsylvania Volunteer Infantry Keystone Zouaves*, Wilmington, North Carolina, 1988, p. 4
3 Goss, Warren Lee, *Recollections of a Private*, New York, 1890, pp. 3–4
4 Flower, Milton E., *Dear Folks at Home*, Carlisle, Pennsylvania, 1963, p. 1
5 Kautz, August, V., *Customs of the Service*, Philadelphia, 1864, p. 103
6 Hardee, William J., *Rifle and Light Infantry Tactics*, Philadelphia, 1861, p. 14
7 ibid, p. 6
8 Janeski, Paul, ed., *A Civil War Soldier's Last Letters*, New York, 1975, p. 2
9 Billings, John D., *Hardtack and Coffee*, Glendale, New York, 1970, p. 110
10 Loving, Jerome M., ed., *Civil War Letters of George Washington Whitman*, Durham, North Carolina, 1975, p. 70
11 *ORs*, Series I, Vol. XXI, pp. 449-50
12 *ORs*, Series I, Vol XXI, p. 369
13 Hardee, op. cit, p. 14
14 Kautz, op. cit., pp. 116-17
15 Furgurson, Ernest B., *Chancellorsville 1863: The Souls of the Brave*, New York, 1992, p. 111
16 Pfanz, Harry W., *Gettysburg The Second Day*, Chapel Hill, North Carolina, 1987, p. 196
17 Greiner, James; Janet L. Coryell; James R. Smither, eds., *A Surgeon's Civil War*, Kent, Ohio, 1994, p. 156
18 Metcalf, Lewis Herbert, manuscript, private collection
19 Greiner, James; Janet L. Coryell; James R. Smither, *ibid.*, p. 157
20 Metcalf, op. cit.
21 Adams, George W. *Doctors In Blue*, New York, 1961, p. 123

3

Jerry J. Benson
First Lieutenant, US Marine Revenue Cutter Service

Ohio may not be regarded widely as a seafaring state, but her northern border touches one of the great lakes, Lake Erie. Many of her sons have shipped out as sailors on this lake which is the size of many of the world's small seas.

One of these was Ohioan Jerry J. Benson, who received a commission as a 3rd Lieutenant in the US Revenue Marine Bureau, often also called the Revenue Marine Cutter Service, on 6 March 1843. The service to which Jerry now belonged had been created on 4 August 1790 when the Secretary of the Treasury launched his own fleet of ten armed revenue cutters whose job it would be to end smuggling. Each cutter was assigned a specific part of the coast and its offshore waters to watch. However, as the service's founder, Alexander Hamilton, warned:

'To fix yourself even generally at one position would in great measure defeat the purpose of the establishment, and allow full scale to fraudulent practices everywhere else... One of the most extensive cases of illicit trade is that of unloading goods before the arrival of a vessel into port, in coasters and other small vessels, which convey them clandestinely to land.'[1]

This maritime service came into being almost eight years before Congress gave approval to a United States Navy. However, on 2 March 1799, the Congress authorised the President, at his discretion, to place the older service under orders of the Secretary of the Navy in times of emergency and war. Perhaps as a sop to the Revenue Marine, however, the same legislation authorised a unique flag for revenue cutters that consisted of 'an ensign and pennant consisting of sixteen perpendicular stripes, alternate red and white, the Union of the Ensign to be the Arms of the United States in dark blue on a white field.'[2]

Relations between the two services, indeed between the Navy and Treasury Departments above them, were not smooth. Secretaries of the Navy had an alarming habit of taking over revenue cutters for emergencies such as the quasi-war with France and then not returning them. Moreover, naval officers objected to Revenue Marine officers resembling them by wearing dark blue uniforms with gold epaulettes. Indeed, in 1834, after a Revenue Marine cutter captain arrived at a ball given in honour of Commodore John Downes in his navy-like uniform, the Secretary of the Treasury, who had earlier been head of the Navy, changed the uniform to grey cloth with black braid and buff waist-coats. This was too extreme for the Revenue Marine officers, and only two years later the grey coats were tossed aside officially in favour of dark blue again, but with black braid.

In 1842 Congress had passed a high tariff with the result of a great increase in smuggling. The Revenue Marine, which had been declining in numbers after a major tariff reduction in 1833, suddenly had to be enlarged. It was precisely during this enlargement programme that Jerry received his commission for the lowest rank in the service. He soon discovered that the service he had entered was expected to do a great deal more than simply stop smuggling. In 1837 cutter captains were ordered to assist scientists as long as their work did not interfere with revenue collection. They now began helping out in projects dealing with ichthyology, geography, medicine, oceanography and biology. Another area in which Revenue cutters would shortly become involved was in enforcing immigration laws. These were largely directed to ensure that immigrants, both Chinese coolie labour on the Pacific and Euro-pean steerage immigrants on the Atlantic, had the space, sanitary facilities and food required by US law.

In addition, on 23 December 1837 Congress ordered that 'public ves-sels adapted to the purpose' should patrol the coastline during the 'severe por-tion of the Season' to help vessels in distress.[3] With the advent of faster sailing vessels that made their trips regardless of weather, the number of nautical mishaps increased annually. By then, on average, ninety American ships were wrecked every year. The navy declined rescue work as not suitable for its ships, which were basically designed for combat, and the job fell to the Revenue Marine. This meant venturing out in rugged weather in small boats and then engaging in the dangerous business of helping survivors from sometimes sink-ing boats in swelling waves.

Indeed, the Secretary of the Treasury issued orders to revenue cutters in Boston, New York, the Delaware Bay, Baltimore and Norfolk, to get out to sea during the winter seasons and not to return save for repairs or resupplies. Once they put into port they were to 'immediately report to the Department the causes of such return to port'.[4]

Jerry's first assignment on 17 April 1843 was to the *Erie*, then based at Erie, Pennsylvania. This would have been a relatively easy mission, as the waters of Lake Erie would certainly not have been as rough generally as the North Atlantic. But it was not to last, for little more than two years later, on 23 July

1845, he was ordered to New Orleans. After a leave of absence to visit his Ohio home he reported on board the *Woodbury* there on 9 September of the same year. His new cutter was a sailing vessel, rather than one of the newer steam cutters the Revenue Marine had obtained. This meant less time ashore. Steam cutters were often in a state of disrepair and had to remain in port while their engines were being worked on. Crews of the sailing cutters had no such excuse.

New Orleans was then a hotbed of excitement. Texas, which a decade or so earlier had won its independence from Mexico, had been offered statehood by a new Democratic administration in Washington. Worse, in terms of future peace, the Texans had accepted it and now American troops passed through New Orleans to man a disputed border along the Rio Grande River.

But the Mexicans were not keen to allow a small buffer state between them and their gigantic northern neighbour to disappear. At least, they wanted the borders they felt were right, north of the Rio Grande. There was fighting in the disputed area and, on 2 May 1846, Congress declared war on Mexico. Much of the Revenue Marine immediately came under naval control. Some of the Revenue Marine cutters, however, actually fell under army command. The *Woodbury* had already seen action landing supplies for the American forces under Major General Zachary Taylor, being assigned to blockade the mouth of the Rio Grande.

For some reason Jerry was reluctant to serve, for he submitted his resignation from the Revenue Marine on 30 May 1846. The actual letter is not in his files, so his reasons cannot be known today. It may have been conscience about the cause itself. Certainly not everybody automatically thought it was a just war. Young Second Lieutenant U. S. Grant, declared, 'The Mexican War was a political war' and even 'unholy',[5] yet he was to fight in it. Many others, including Congressman Abraham Lincoln, felt the same way. At the outset, it was far from being a wholly popular course of action.

Despite such doubts, New Orleans was crowded with free enterprising individuals with an eye to making a quick dollar. Virtually all supplies for the armed forces serving in Mexico and Texas passed through the city, and many there made fortunes. A bright young man who was acquainted with the city's merchants, as an officer of the Revenue Marine certainly would have been, could well have joined in such an enterprise and made a pile of money. Jerry may have shipped as an officer, at much higher pay than his service salary, on a merchant ship. Perhaps he had a chance to join one of the volunteer army units that originated or passed through New Orleans, expecting to see more action than he would have done as a blockader or on a troop transport.

At any rate, his resignation was accepted on 3 July 1846, and Jerry Benson disappears from history – until the Civil War.

The years between were not kind to the Revenue Marine. The entire bureau was abolished by Congress in 1849, as a cost-saving device, with command of the cutters being passed to a Commissioner of Customs. Congress also cut costs by refusing pay increases and eliminating personnel. Many of the best service officers resigned for the civilian maritime service. Cutter officers were encouraged to become involved in on-shore politics. The only positive thing that happened was that the service launched one of the most modern ships in the American maritime of the period, the *Harriet Lane,* in 1858. By 1861, when war broke out, the Revenue Marine had only twenty-four cutters to patrol many thousands of miles of coastline, both along the Atlantic and the Pacific Oceans as well as on the Great Lakes.

When the Confederates formed a new government in early 1861 they demanded that the Federal government surrender all its property within state boundaries. This included forts, post offices, arsenals, armouries, buildings – and the cutters of the Revenue Marine. Southerner Captain James J. Morrison surrendered his cutter, the *Lewis Cass,* in Mobile, Alabama, to state officials. The rest of his crew, however, moved north to serve on other Federal cutters. Captain John G. Brushwood, a native of Louisiana, promptly gave his cutter, the *McClelland,* to state authorities at New Orleans. The *Dodge,* a cutter in Galveston, Texas, was turned over to Confederate authorities in Austin. The *Duane,* in Norfolk, Virginia, was captured when the navy yard there was seized. The Secretary of the Treasury suddenly discovered that the Revenue Marine no longer had any vessels under its command south of North Carolina, and that the remaining eleven cutters would have to be rearmed.

Under ordinary circumstances, this number of cutters might have been enough. But these were not ordinary circumstances. Not only was a war under way, not only had many of the Revenue Marine's cutters and officers joined the enemy in that war, but the service would from now on see more duty than ever. In 1857 the country had experienced a major economic panic. Stock prices had fallen, companies were ruined and people thrown out of work. In an effort to avoid this happening again, on 2 March 1861, Congress passed the first of what were known as the Morrill tariffs on foreign-made products, designed to protect American manufacturers. The high tariffs also encouraged smuggling from foreign ports, especially, after the South left the Union, from Canada.

As war continued, and the government's expenses rose, at times reaching an unprecedented million dollars a day, American manufacturers paid increasing taxes. However, to offer them continued protection and afford them a level playing field with foreign manufacturers of the same products who were not subject to such high war taxation, Congress passed additional tariffs in 1862, 1864 and 1865. Tariffs now reached unprecedented levels. The Revenue Marine collected $39.5 million in 1861 and $102 million in 1864. At the same time, the amount of contraband increased alarmingly. The Revenue Marine – which reached a peak of fifty-seven cutters with 219 officers in 1865 – would be busier fighting smugglers than ever before in its history.

When Lincoln learned this he wrote the Secretary of the Navy asking 'what amount of naval force you could at once place at the control of the revenue service, and also whether at some distance of time you could so place an additional force, and how much and at what time?'[6] Navy Secretary Gideon Welles replied that a dozen navy vessels could immediately go to the Revenue Marine, but more would depend on the number of men the navy was permitted to recruit. In fact, the Revenue Marine never did acquire any navy ships, and had to scramble to get replacement vessels from any sources it could. It did manage to obtain nine small steamers from the US Coast Survey Department, but these were considered too small for permanent cutter use and would be purely stop-gap measures.

The service also desperately needed more men. In addition to losing officers who went south, the top levels of the Revenue Marine, which, like the navy, offered no pension system, was getting too old for active service. Captain William A. Howard, who had been appointed to take general charge of revenue vessels, reported on 18 May 1861, that out of nineteen captains in the service, 'Six of the Captains are in my opinion unfitted by age, sickness, and otherwise for service.... Such is also the case of several of the First Lieutenants... On top of that, there was a "want of Esprit du Corps", caused by 'the curtailment of crews and everything that gave efficiency or circumstances was taken from them – no Service could be expected, none was attempted, the material in some degree is there, and the assurance already given, has rekindled the Hope of being again a corps worthy of the confidence of the Government.'[7]

Replacement officers were required, and again Jerry offered his services. His application was accepted, and he was commissioned a second lieutenant, a grade higher than his previous rank, on 21 November 1861. Some individual in the Treasury Department, however, took some exception to his appointment, noting in his official record, 'I question the validity of this Benson receiving this commission with the above G[eneral] H[istory, i.e. his resignation at the outset of the Mexican War].'[8] Despite such concerns, Jerry was ordered to the *Walter*

B. *Forward*, named for the Secretary of the Treasury when she was built, which was then stationed in Philadelphia. His salary would be $1,200 a year.

From this he would have to buy his sword, a unique model used by Revenue Marine officers, and his uniforms. The service wore slightly dated tailcoats of dark blue with plain dark blue trousers. Jerry's rank was indicated by three buttons around the cuff worn parallel to the edge of the sleeve and a gold epaulette on his left shoulder.

Jerry reported on board the *Forward* on 26 December 1861. He found his new ship to be the oldest cutter in service with the Revenue Marine in 1861. Built in 1842, the 1,395-ton schooner was some 90 feet long. There were six berths for officers off the wardroom and main cabin, which was also fitted out with a small library, Queensware service for the officers, along with a stone wash basin for each officer, and a stove in the main cabin for warmth as well as cooking. Her commander was a native Pennsylvanian, Henry G. Nones, who had earned his commission in 1838.

While Jerry was so assigned, the service updated its uniforms making them look more like those of the navy. Now Jerry had a double-breasted navy-style coat with a pair of gold-edged shoulder straps marked with a gold bar at each end. Otherwise his coat was perfectly plain.

Duty would be generally pleasant on the *Forward*. She did not venture into the Atlantic, but patrolled the Delaware River and Bay from Philadelphia to the Delaware Breakwater, far from scenes of conflict. At the beginning of the war, however, the *Forward* was withdrawn from revenue duties and armed for combat. Specialised combat drills had become the order of the day. Her crew now included men assigned to handle small arms, called 'infantry', and launch crews drilled as 'rifle men'. She was to be ready to serve with the navy's Atlantic Blockading Squadrons at a moment's notice.

Jerry, however, would manage to miss blockading duty, for on 15 September 1862 he was ordered to Detroit, Michigan, to help combat smuggling on Lake Erie between the United States and Canada. His new assignment was to the crew of the *John B. Floyd*, a 63-foot-long cutter launched in 1857 and originally posted to Lake Huron. Although officially at sea, in fact, he would spend most of the winter on shore in the city of Detroit, the cutter having been taken out of the water until Lake Erie thawed next spring. Indeed, there was so little to do that a Treasury official stationed in Milwaukee, on Lake Michigan, had written to the Secretary of the Treasury, 'As to the service of a Revenue Cutter on this lake, candor requires me to say that it affords no aid to commerce, and its *only* use seems to be to deplete the Treasury.'[9]

After careful consideration, the Department decided to take this report to heart and transfer six cutters on the Great Lakes to the Atlantic coast in late 1861. The *Floyd*, however, was transferred from her old post on Lake Superior to Detroit, and the previous cutter in that city, the *Jacob V. Thompson*, sent to the Atlantic. While Jerry was still considering whether to rejoin the service, Department officials worked out plans to send six cutters by canal then up past Montreal along the St Lawrence to the sea. The trip took five weeks. In 1864 the Department sold the *Floyd* to private concerns. Before that happened, Jerry spent the winter of 1862/3 on land in Detroit. With Canadian settlements right across a narrow river from Detroit, the ground was ripe for smuggling on small boats at night, and Jerry should have been fairly busy there.

At the same time, things were getting hotter in the naval war on the North Atlantic, with Confederate cruisers picking up prizes almost within sight of land. Between October 3 and 21 1862, the rebel cruiser *Alabama*, sailing in the Newfoundland Banks, captured and burned or ransomed sixteen northern ships. New England ship owners were becoming panic-stricken, as were the insurance companies whose firms paid out large sums to replace the destroyed merchantmen. The navy was hard pressed both to blockade all the southern coast and search out and destroy Confederate cruisers in the northern seas. The Revenue Marine cutters would have to do more to protect northern shipping.

Therefore, Jerry cannot have been surprised to receive orders sending him to the 63-foot-long *Isaac Toucey* on 10 January 1863. The *Toucey* was one of those cutters that had been previously stationed on the Great Lakes, her previous home port being Michilmackinac, Michigan, before passing through the St Lawrence to the Atlantic the earlier winter. Now she was based in Castine, Maine, where she had been posted under command of a veteran captain, Rufus Coffin, since August 1862. While there, Jerry's status as an officer and a gentleman in the service of the United States became official. On 4 February 1863 Congress authorised the President to appoint the commissioned officers of what it now designated 'the United States revenue cutter service', with the advice and consent of the Senate, the same procedure as for commissioning officers in the other branches of the armed forces.[10] Before that, such officers did not necessarily consider Revenue Marine officers their social equals. Now they would have to.

While Jerry was in Maine, war struck nearby Portland, Maine, where the cutter *Caleb Cushing* was stationed. A Confederate cruiser, originally a captured northern vessel, sailed into Portland's harbour on 27 June 1863. That night a boarding party in a longboat from the Confederate ship pulled alongside the cutter. Her men dashed aboard the cutter, capturing the crew, before taking her out to sea. The next morning, when the cutter was discovered missing, a makeshift fleet under a Revenue Marine lieutenant from Portland set out after the *Cushing*. In an exchange of cannon fire when the Federals caught up with the *Cushing*, the Confederates abandoned the cutter, setting her ablaze when they made for the launches. The Confederates were captured and the Revenue Marine crew freed, but Portland, a major port, lacked a cutter.

The *James C. Dobbin*, a 100-foot cutter launched in 1853, was ordered from her station on the Delaware River to replace the *Cushing*. On 8 August Jerry was detailed to meet her there to become part of her new crew. He reached his new home port on 12 August and had to wait a day until the *Dobbin* actually arrived. As he stood at the dock, he watched as the cutter sailed in, Revenue flags on her peak and her cutter number painted on the mast-head. Suddenly two guns from Fort Preble, which commanded the harbour entrance, fired, one cannonball splashing in the water near by. The cutter's captain hove to and sent first lieutenant John A. Henriques ashore to say they were friends and not a Confederate vessel. The fort's officers, meeting him on the shore line, apologised, but said that they had not been informed of the cutter's arrival and, after the loss of the *Cushing*, were taking no chances with strange boats.

The *Dobbin* then docked and Jerry went aboard to report to his new commander, Captain John A. Webster, Jnr. Webster was a professional who came from a New England Revenue Marine family. The senior Webster had been one of the most popular captains in the service in his time.

Jerry would now see some active duty. His cutter was ordered to sea in late August to find two of the Confederates who had captured the *Cushing*. They had been imprisoned in Fort Warren, in Boston Harbor, but had managed to escape. The *Dobbin* actually found the two, on board a schooner off Cape Porpoise, and returned them and their boat to Boston. Then, in late 1863 Jerry had his first chance at command when Captain Webster and the cutter's first lieutenant were ordered to leave the *Dobbin* behind and go aboard the Navy ship USS *Agawam*, along with twenty-four Revenue Marine sailors, to hunt for the steamer *Chesapeake* which had earlier been captured by Confederates. Jerry's crew was completed with sailors from the USS *Acadia* and soldiers from the local garrison.

An icy harbour and high winter seas kept the cutter tied up to her dock for many days during the winter of 1863-4. Jerry found living cold and miserable in the cramped cabin of the small cutter. He took advantage of the time ashore to do a little visiting, leaving the cutter's petty officer in charge. Unfortunately for him, his absence was reported, and he received an official reprimand on 12 January 1864 for leaving his vessel without a commissioned officer aboard her. Smarting, Jerry remained on board for early 1864, and then put in for his first leave of absence since the war began. On 23 April 1864 he was granted a month's leave.

Jerry had now been serving continuously since the beginning of the war. Although the Revenue Marine had been expanding fast, he remained a second lieutenant. Finally, however, on 11 July 1864, he was promoted to the rank of first lieutenant. Now his salary would jump to $1,400 a year. His new rank would be indicated by a gold stripe on each cuff, parallel to the sleeve end, and two bars and a single fouled anchor over a shield on his shoulder straps. This insignia would again be changed on 20 August 1864, when Jerry's rank would be signified by three gold stripes on each cuff with a gold-embroidered Treasury Department shield above them.

But the war was drawing to an end. With the closing of all the southern ports on the land and destruction of their cruisers, naval ships were able to return to their normal duties. The Revenue Marine would be less busy and, just over a year after his last furlough, Jerry managed to get another month's leave of absence on 28 September 1865. Now the war was over but Jerry had found a home in the Revenue Marine. On 15 November 1865 he was ordered to the *Sunnyside*, stationed at Waldsboro, Maine. He would spend the rest of his career there. That career, however, was not to be all that long, for a reforming Secretary of the Treasury, George S. Boutwell, took office in 1869, determined to improve the service. He re-established the Revenue Marine Bureau, appointing a new chief, Sumner I. Kimball. Kimball set about to raise both morale and discipline in the service, instituting a board to examine all the service's officers. Determined to weed-out inefficiency, the board got rid of thirty-nine cutter captains as well as lower-ranked officers. Jerry, having failed his examination, was dismissed from the service on 14 April 1871.

NOTES

1 Bloomfield, Howard V. L., *The Compact History of the United States Coast Guard*, New York, 1966, p. 8
2 ibid, p. 14
3 ibid, p. 38
4 ibid, p. 39
5 Grant, U. S., *Personal Memoirs of*, New York, 1952, p. 20, p. 56
6 Kern, Florence, *The United States Revenue Cutters in the Civil War*, Bethesda, Maryland, 1976, p. 5
7 ibid, p. 6
8 Benson, Jerry J., Service Record, National Archives, *Revenue Marine Journal*, p. 189
9 Kern, Florence, op. cit., pp. 6–7
10 Kern, Florence, op. cit., p. 1–2

4

Franklin S. Case,

Captain, 2nd Ohio Cavalry Regiment

The disaster to the cause of the Union at the First Bull Run in July 1861 showed that the southerners were determined to fight – and fight well – for their independence. It would take more than a burst of enthusiasm as demonstrated after the firing on Fort Sumter to restore the old Union. And it would take determined soldiers, willing to serve at least three years, to do the job. On 29 August 1861, William Dennison, governor of Ohio, issued a proclamation to the people of that state reading, in part:

'The Federal Government again calls upon you for soldiers. The late disaster at Manassas, serious as it was in many respects to the rebels, has added to their audacity and insolence. Encouraged by apparent success, they have augmented their forces, and enhanced the necessity for vigilance and power at Washington, in Western Virginia, and in Missouri.

'Twenty-nine regiments of infantry, together with a proportionate force of artillery and cavalry, are now being organised in your State.

'As the Executive of the State, it becomes my duty to appeal to you to perfect these organisations as rapidly as possible.'[1]

In answer to the governor's plea, in late August 1861, men began to gather at points in Cleveland and at Camp Dennison, Ohio, to form a new regiment of cavalry, the state's second. It was not a rapid process. Indeed, it was not until late September and early October that the last volunteers were formed into companies. Unlike an infantry regiment, each volunteer cavalry regiment was to consist of four, five or six squadrons, each made up of two companies. Each company had, at a minimum, a captain, a first lieutenant, a second lieutenant, a company quartermaster sergeant, four sergeants, eight corporals, two buglers, two farriers and blacksmiths, a saddler, a wagoner and fifty-six privates. At a maximum, and it would be rare, indeed, to muster in with a maximum force, the company would have seventy-two privates.

Company H was finally mustered in on 8 October 1861 at Camp Wade, in Cleveland. Aaron K. Lindsey was elected the regiment's first captain. At the same time, twenty-two-year-old Franklin S. Case, called Frank by his friends, was elected the company's second lieutenant. Frank had been in camp in Wellington, Ohio, since 15 August, starting a three-year enlistment. Unlike many cavalry recruits, he could ride, for before joining up he had been a farmer in Wellington, Ohio. He was five feet seven inches tall, with blue eyes and brown hair and a fair complexion.

Not until the company had been formally mustered into Federal service, however, would Frank begin to draw his pay. Pay for cavalrymen was set a bit higher than pay for those in the artillery and infantry as it was accepted that the service was more demanding. Frank, as a second lieutenant, would get $53.33 a month, as compared to the $45 drawn by similar officers in the other combat arms. He would also be paid for four rations, or meals, a day and forage for one horse. Finally, he would be allowed one servant.

While waiting for the company to recruit enough men to be officially mustered into Federal service, young Frank and the rest present each drew a horse and equipment on 9 September 1861. As well, they drew their first uniforms, which were provided by the state rather than the Federal government. Frank, being an officer, would have to buy his uniform, which consisted of a dark blue, single-breasted frock coat with a standing collar, dark blue trousers with a yellow welt down each leg, and headgear. Frank chose a black, broad-brimmed felt hat, with a gold and black intermixed cord, rather than the regulation cap. This would be typical of both cavalrymen and western troops. His rank would be indicated by a yellow shoulder strap edged in gold on each shoulder.

Frank would also be responsible for supplying his own weapons. He would need an officer's sabre, similar to that issued to the men but featuring an engraved blade and a rather more ornate hilt, and a revolver. Generally, Colt revolving pistols were favoured. They came in two calibres, 0.44 'Army' and 0.36 'Navy'. Cavalrymen generally preferred the heavier Army models. The men of his company were issued these revolvers, as well as pistols of the same calibre made by the Starr Arms Co., and M1840 sabres. Known as the 'old wrist breaker' for its awkwardly heavy grip and hilt, the sabre was none the less an excellent weapon. Its design formed the basis for the slightly lighter M1860 cavalry sabre that was the more modern style used by the Regular Army. Arms for the men arrived so slowly that the regiment had to borrow weapons from another regiment when it first took the field on scouting duty.

The mere receipt of their uniforms and equipment made the men feel like soldiers. As a New York cavalry volunteer wrote when his regiment received its equipage:

'Each man has now a new care and pride to keep his saber bright, and his entire outfit clean, that he may wear them with pleasure to himself and honor to his comrades. This morning of the 24th [of August 1861] was spent in saber exercise, with which we were all delighted. This is the first development in us of the cavalry element as such, and we getting to feel our individuality.'[2]

Then, armed and equipped, they began the long process of learning to become effective cavalrymen. This would not be as easy in the 2nd as it was in a regiment that had appointed West Point graduates as commanders ever since Colonel Charles W. Doubleday had been made colonel simply on the basis of some experience dating from a 'filibustering' expedition in Nicaragua – hardly a sufficient qualification. Luckily, Doubleday resigned soon after the regiment was organised. The regiment's members then elected Major Henry Burnett to fill the post. Major George Miner wrote to the governor that Burnett had been elected unfairly – apparently plying the officers and men with liquor – and Burnett's election was overturned. West Pointer and Mexican War veteran August V. Kautz was appointed the unit's colonel.

With this appointment, serious studying of the manuals began. According to cavalry drill manuals, Frank, as a second lieutenant, would have command of the company's second platoon when the company served with the battalion, moving up to command of the first platoon when the company acted independently.

When the war began, the Regular Army, then on duty protecting settlers in the west, was called back east to fight Confederates. Volunteers took up the slack in the west, and the 2nd was sent immediately on scouting duty to Fort Scott, Kansas, serving in the Army of the Frontier until April 1863. The regiment's first fight, however, was not against native Americans, but against pro-southern guerrillas, led by the daring and ruthless William Quantrill in Independence, Missouri, on 22 February. One man of the 2nd was killed and another three wounded, while the guerrillas lost five killed, four wounded and five captured. Then the regiment moved on to Fort Scott where, on 10 March 1862, Frank was promoted to the rank of first lieutenant, marked by a single gold bar on either end of his shoulder straps. The promotion, however, brought no increase in pay. When the company acted independently, as was often the case in the west, he would no longer command a platoon, his new position being 'in rear of the center, in the rank of file closers'. When the company was part of the battalion, he commanded the first platoon. When in line of march as a regiment, his post was 'at the head of the 1st platoon, *one* pace in advance of the first files, having the particular guide of the right on his right'. [3]

Duty in the west, though not heroic, was wearing. The plains were hot in summer, frigid in winter, with both water and shade scarce. A cavalryman was always on the move. Recalled a veteran of the 1st Ohio Cavalry:

'The life of a cavalryman in time of war is one of constant activity – hard and dangerous service. During the winter season, when the main army is snugly ensconced in winter quarters, the cavalry are the most active and have the hardest service to perform, as they are kept constantly patrolling and scouting... The cavalry outpost duty was a hard and dangerous service and they were required to furnish the advance sentinels, when not confronted by entrenched lines... Marching always in silence and on the approach of the enemy to fire and fall back on the reserve, by routes selected during the day... All these movements of the cavalry arm of the service required vigilance, secrecy, energy, promptness and dash; and whether the command was composed of a Brigade, regiment, squadron, Company or Platoon, the commander must not halt or hesitate, but act immediately and supply by strategy what he lacks in numbers.'[4]

The 2nd saw action at Independence, Missouri, on 22 February 1862; at Horse Creek, 7 May; at Grand River 6 June; at Fort Gibson 18 July; and at dozens of other small places, skirmishing with both native Americans and guerrillas. The tiring duty resulted in many of the men becoming sick, and Frank was one of them, sent home on leave on 28 August 1862. While there, according to his orders, he was to be in charge of recruiting duty. Typically, rather than setting up recruiting offices manned full-time by regimental representatives, regiments would send home for a short time a small group made up of an officer and a couple of enlisted men, to open an office, have fliers printed up calling for volunteers, and swear in as many able bodied men as they could find. When their time was up, they would bring their new recruits back to the regiment. One cavalry officer sent home to recruit in October 1861 recalled:

'Though recruiting offices could be found on the principal streets of our cities and villages, yet a good business was done by them all, such was the enthusiasm which prevailed among the people. War-meetings were frequently held, and addressed by our best orators. The press, with few exceptions, poured fourth its eloquent appeals to the strong-bodied men of the country to range themselves on the side of right against wrong... On the fourth of December I returned from recruiting service, bringing with me all recruits who had not been previously sent to the regiment.'[5]

Frank would report back, fit for service again, with his recruits on 17 September 1862. However, he was not to remain long in the west. Shortly after his return, both officers and men were probably delighted that in December they were ordered back to Columbus, Ohio, from where they were sent on to Kentucky to serve against regular Confederates.

The 2nd was part of a force that included the 7th Ohio, 1st Kentucky Cavalry, 2nd Tennessee Mounted Infantry and 45th Ohio Infantry, stationed near Steubenville, Kentucky, on 9 June 1863. Commissary Sergeant H. W. Chester recalled coming out of some woods to behold a line of enemy infantry:

'Lieutenant Frank S. Case was in command of the Company and said, "Chester, you take charge of the horses." When Cavalry fight on foot the horses of the men numbers one, two and three tie the halters of their horses to the halter of number four so that the man on number four can look after them and move them about just the same as thought [sic] the men were on their horses, all being kept in the same relative position as when mounted. Lieut. Case took the dismounted men right back into the woods, together with all the rest of the force that was available, the larger part of which had passed on several miles towards the crossing of the river. Then the fight opened in earnest, all on both sides being dismounted.'[6]

In the course of what was nothing more than a small skirmish that would not make the history books, during which both sides drove each other back and forth, Frank fell badly wounded, shot through his right lung. Sergeant Chester recalled, 'I came up just as Lieut. Case was being put into an ambulance, he having been shot through the right lung.'[7] Such a wound, made worse by the pieces of dirty fabric pushed into the wound by the soft lead bullet, was quite dangerous. The surgeon at the nearby field hospital, would usually probe with a finger or rubber catheter (although metal probes were sometimes used) to make sure the ball passed through the chest cleanly and all foreign bodies were removed. Then broad bandages were wrapped around the chest to keep the patient's chest immobile. A wounded Michigan cavalry officer recalled having his wound probed and bandaged:

'My own wound gave little annoyance except when the surgeon ran an iron called a probe into it, which attempt met with so vigorous a protest from his patient that he desisted and that form of treatment stopped right there, so far as one cavalryman was concerned. The wound was well bandaged and plentiful applications of cold water kept out the inflammation.'[8]

Thereafter Frank was transferred to a general hospital for rest and a light diet. It was the kind of wound only nature could cure; doctors could do nothing to repair lungs. The great fear was of haemorrhaging, infection and pneumonia, although the last complication was comparatively rare. Even so, death resulted in 62 per cent of cases of chest cavities that had been penetrated by bullet, shell or edged weapon. Frank, however, was one of the lucky ones. Once in hospital, he slowly healed. But he would not recover sufficiently to return to duty until 1 October 1863.

Meanwhile, however, he was not forgotten. On 18 July Frank was rewarded for his services with the two gold bars of a captain, the rank to which he was promoted to replace A. B. Nettleton who had risen to the rank of major. Frank now received $70 a month. When he returned, he would be company commander of H Company, and be entitled to ride, according to the manual, 'in front of the centre of the squadron, the croup of his horse 4 paces in advance of the heads of the horses in line'. On the march his position was 'on the side of the guides, and 8 paces from the flank and abreast of the center of their squadrons'.[9] When his company was acting independently, his post would be 'in front of the center, *one* pace distant from the rank flank'.[10]

When Frank finally returned to duty on 10 October he found the 2nd taking part in Burnside's campaign in East Tennessee that lasted from 16 August to 17 October. Indeed, he arrived just before a skirmish at Blue Springs, and his men were delighted to have him back. 'We were all glad to have him with us again as he was a fine officer and leader,' recalled one of his troopers.[11] Constantly on the move and seeing action, they arrived back at Knoxville on 4 November, taking part in that campaign that lasted until 5 December. Frank, however, was to have no relief after the campaign, as he was detached from duty with the regiment on 31 December, when his company's enlistments were officially up, to serve on detached duty. It was, however, 'light duty', since he had yet to recover fully from his wound.

His regiment would also be kept busy as it would not go into winter quarters, remaining in the saddle until the men's enlistments were up in January 1864. Then they were offered the chance of staying together as a unit, ennobled by the title of 'Veteran Volunteers', each enlisted man receiving a bounty and advance of $402 and a thirty-day furlough. But this would happen only if enough men volunteered to serve an additional three years or for the length of the war to maintain a full regimental status.

The 2nd managed to retain enough men who re-enlisted to become such a veteran volunteer regiment, and promptly headed back to Ohio to recruit as many men as would be needed to fill its ranks completely, while allowing re-enlistees a much-deserved holiday. While on leave, on 2 March 1864, Frank married Clara Burr in Brighton, Ohio. They would not have long together, for on 20 March the furloughs came to an end. The regiment reformed and headed off for a new post in Annapolis, Maryland. Frank, still officially on detached duty, was released on 18 April to rejoin his company.

If it was hard for soldiers to be separated from their women, in many ways it was even harder for the wives, trained from birth as they way to depend on their husbands virtually for everything. One wife wrote to her soldier husband, a sergeant in a heavy artillery regiment stationed in Maryland:

'How it does make me fairly chafe when I think of your being in the army. At times it comes over me with tenfold fury, just as it does tonight. I can feel the very scowl on my forehead, my teeth and lips are shut so tight one would think I was fairly enraged, and without slackness the hold on my pen I shall be tempted to believe I am getting in a passion. Do you wish to know what has caused this outburst of wrath? Well, I have just been looking at your pictures. It makes me *swearing* (if you'll allow the expression) *mad* to think I cannot get to you.'[12]

When regiments were in fixed posts, such as garrisons in cities or in winter quarters, officers were often able to have their wives join them. Indeed, one New York cavalry officer criticised his fellows for this practice, writing, 'I must here say that I have noticed in too many of our officers a weakness for taking their wives and families to the war with them. I can imagine no greater incumbrance, or indeed anything that can work so much injury to the service.'[13] In more cases than not, however, wives and families had to remain home, and this put strains on marriages since the prototype mid-nineteenth-century marriage, with the man firmly in control of household affairs, could not be managed. Suddenly independent women realised their own strengths and abilities, and this conclusion did not always come easy to either party.

But Frank would be too busy with his company to reflect much on this. New recruits had been added to the regiment in great number and the veterans had been softened by their long leaves. As a cavalryman in the veteran 1st Ohio Cavalry recalled after their veteran furloughs:

'A large number of recruits had enlisted in the regiment during the veteran furlough and the regular routine of drill and guard duty was inaugurated with strict discipline, much to the disgust of both veterans and recruits. Dismounted drill, manual of carbine, pistol and saber, kept up continuously until April 18th, just one month, and at this date the regiment received their horses, much to the delight of men and officers.'[14]

The 2nd received horses previously assigned to the 22nd New York Cavalry, the latter regiment considered unfit for the field and therefore needing horses less than the veteran Ohio men.

The regiment also had to get accustomed to the very different ways of the eastern Army of the Potomac. Wrote one veteran:

'We felt almost like strangers in a strange land. Everything was so different from what we were used to. There were many young staff officers that appeared to want to do something, but they did not appear to know what to do but to make some fuss. They would gallop about with an orderly behind them, giving orders about anything and everything, and creating confusion... When ...[they] came about the 2nd Ohio ... cursing with their "whoop-em-up" orders they were received with remarks and looks of contempt. They soon became scarce in that locality, and we could now see why the cavalry of the Army of the Potomac had fallen into bad repute.'[15]

The 2nd was caught up in Grant's great move against Lee's Army that began with the Wilderness in May 1864. It took part in much of the action of that summer's campaign that ended up in Petersburg, serving at Gaines' Mill, Salem Church, Cold Harbor, Haw's Shop, Totopotomoy, Long Bridge, White House Landing and Smith's Store. That the regiment saw heavy fighting can be judged by the comment of its lieutenant colonel in his report on fighting of 31 May that the army should provide ordnance sergeants or detailed men to keep ammunition coming to the front since the typical cavalryman would fire sixty to eighty rounds in a few hours and then be out of ammunition.

Here Frank did what so many soldiers did; he wrote a description of his regiment's activities to his newspaper back home, in effect becoming an unpaid reporter in the field. His letter, describing a skirmish at St Mary's Church, was published in the *Lorain County News* on 6 July 1864, Frank signing himself as 'Spurs'. Since most smaller papers could not afford to send reporters to distant places, soldiers often either wrote directly to the papers or relatives brought in letters from the front for publication. In this way the smallest newspaper managed to print war news of community men at the front, maintaining home ties.

The regiment took part in a raid in June 1864 on the Petersburg & Weldon Railroad. The raid, under the command of Brigadier General James H. Wilson, destroyed track for miles south-west of Petersburg, meeting little opposition since most of the Confederate cavalry was busy chasing Union cavalry near Lynchburg. But the northern troopers were halted at the Staunton River Bridge near Roanoke Station by a mixed bunch of local militia and Confederate infantrymen. In the meantime, returning Confederate cavalry smashed them at Stony Creek Station on 28 June. Outnumbered and almost surrounded, the Federals abandoned wounded, wagons and cannon, heading to safety as quickly as possible. It was at Ream's Station, Virginia, in a fierce firefight with Confederate cavalry, on 29 June, that Frank's luck ran out. The regiment had been left, along with an artillery battery and the 5th New York, to hold off attacking Confederates while the overall commander sent several other regiments to check Confederate infantry from bagging the Union troopers. Although the movement was successful, it was not without cost. Frank was slightly wounded and captured in the fighting and sent on to prison camp in North Carolina. He was one of five 2nd Ohio officers and a hundred men of the regiment killed, wounded or missing in the raid.

One of his men wrote home on 16 July:

'During the last raid of General Wilson, Company "H" again passed the fiery ordeal losing some of its bravest and best. They are as follows: Capt. F. S. Case... All but the latter [Stephen Babcock] were left on the field in the hands of the enemy, it being impossible to get them off, Capt. Case being one of the best Officers in the Regiment is missed very much. Although suffering somewhat from the effects of the wound received in Kentucky last summer, he continued to do his duty and remained in command of his Co. when many others would have had their names on the sick list.'[16]

Frank could not have been captured at a worse time. Early in the war most prisoners of war only stayed in prison camps for a relatively short period before they were exchanged for enemy prisoners of equal rank or paroled back to their own side to wait a legal exchange. But after the Federals began recruiting Afro-Americans as regular soldiers, the story had changed. Since the Confederates considered such men not as regular prisoners of war but as men to be sold into slavery, and refused to exchange them, the Federals declined to authorise exchanges as previously. One man held at Salisbury, North Carolina, military prison, one of the larger southern prison camps, in November 1864, recalled:

'Our prison was like the tomb. No voice from the North entered its gloomy portal. Believing we had been unjustly neglected by our government, wondering if we had indeed been forsaken by God and man, we seemed to lose all human interest, and to care little whether we lived or died.'[17]

At the same time the blockade had cut off supplies of needed medicines and the like from reaching the south, while a lack of industrial ability had caused a breakdown in the railroads, so that transportation of foodstuffs was difficult. Consequently, Confederate prisoner-of-war camps, never exactly picnic sites, were terrible places by 1864. Bad rations and unsanitary water gave most men intestinal diseases, many of which proved fatal. A Pennsylvania cavalryman held in the prison camp in Salisbury, North Carolina, in late 1864 recalled his issued rations:

'The ration that was served seldom varied, and if there was a change at all, it usually was less in quantity and inferior in quality. It consisted chiefly of six ounces of sour corn bread, baked from corn meal ground with cobs and kernels, which was so hard that it was almost impossible to break it; about two ounces of condemned meat of some kind; and, about twice a week, a little rice or bean slop unfit to eat.

'The ration was usually brought into camp in the afternoon and thrown from the wagon, somewhat after the manner that a farmer feeds his cattle. Frequently the corn meal would be issued unbaked. With hardly any cooking utensils and no wood, ofttimes the corn meal was simply stirred in water and used in that way. Some would eat it raw.'[18]

Finally, on 21 March 1865, Frank was taken to Wilmington, North Carolina, where he was exchanged and returned to his own side. But his health could not have been improved by his prison experience. Nor was he the only one. Walt Whitman, the poet, received a letter from his mother about his brother George, a captain exchanged in early 1865. 'George says there was 20 yesterday died at anapolus [Annapolis, Maryland, where exchanged prisoners were sent to recuperate],' his mother wrote, 'some died eating they were he says like hungry woolvs had got so famished...'[19]

Frank, however, was in better shape than that, and soon rejoined his old company. The 2nd was then with Sheridan's troops around Petersburg, where Grant's Army lay besieging Lee's army. That siege ended, as anyone could have foreseen, with Lee's ragged men fleeing west, forced out of their lines by overwhelming numbers. The 2nd was part of the pursuit that ended at Appomattox Court House on 9 April. The war in the east was virtually over.

Frank and his men participated in the grand review of the two major Federal armies through the streets of Washington on 23 May. The regiment was then ordered to St Louis, where the men did duty until 12 October 1865 when they were finally mustered out. Frank, still in poor health, was honourably discharged on 26 May 1865 and returned to Ohio. He would never fully recover his health, however, his doctor reporting in March 1868 that because of the wound to his lung he 'cannot endure active exercise [and] feels slight pain with ketch on coughing & nervous disturbance'. The latter comment suggests the mental condition known today as post-traumatic stress disorder, in which the sufferer relives his experiences through nightmares, often reacting to loud noises by having flashbacks to his life-threatening experiences.

In April 1868 Frank received a pension of $5.66 a month, post-dated to 23 May 1865. His pension was increased to $30 a month on 25 August 1886, when his doctor reported his suffering from 'congestion of the lung and hemorrhage resulting from gunshot wound received while in service'. By then he was in very bad shape, with 'impairment of power in right arm and bronchitis and dropsy and paralysis of right side of body,' as a Pension Bureau official reported.[20] He did not have long to collect his increased pension. Frank died on 9 August 1887, as a result of his war-time wound.

NOTES

1 Official, *Message of the Governor of Ohio to the Fifty-fifth General Assembly*, Columbus, Ohio, 1862, p. 50
2 Glazier, Willard, *Three Years in the Federal Cavalry*, New York, 1874, p. 29
3 Patten, George, *Patten's Cavalry Drill, and Sabre Exercise*, New York, 1861, pp. 45, 46, 49
4 Curry, W.L., *Four Years In the Saddle*, Jonesboro, Georgia, 1984, p. 19
5 Glazier, op cit., pp. 45–6
6 Chester, H. W., *Recollections of the War of the Rebellion*, Wheaton, Illinois, 1996, p. 48
7 ibid, p. 48
8 Kidd, J. H., *Personal Recollections of a Cavalryman*, Ionia, Michigan, 1908, pp. 192–3
9 Cooke, Philip St. Geo., *Cavalry Tactics*, Philadelphia, 1862, p. 5, 12
10 Patten, op. cit., p. 49
11 Chester, op. cit., p. 67
12 'Janie,' letter to Sgt Merritt Williams, dated 5 April 1865, author's collection
13 'A Cavalryman,' *A Trooper's Adventures in the War for the Union*, New York, 1894, p. 146
14 Curry, op. cit., p. 163
15 Gause, Isaac, *Four Years with Five Armies*, New York, 1908, pp. 221–3
16 Chester, op. cit., pp. 93–4
17 Cooper, George, *Lost Love*, New York, 1993, p. 67
18 Moyer, H. P., *History of the Seventeenth Regiment Pennsylvania Volunteer Cavalry*, Lebanon, Pennsylvania, 1906, pp. 168–9
19 Loving, Jerome M., *Civil War Letters of George Washington Whitman*, Durham, North Carolina, 1975, p. 25
20 Case, Franklin S., pension records, National Archives

5
David H. Cole
Artificer, 50th New York Volunteer Engineer Regiment

David H. Cole had probably seen the posters around his home in Sauger-
ties, New York, seeking volunteers for enlistment in an unusual type of
military organisation: an engineer regiment. 'Wanted, a few able bodied first-
class men ... Mechanics, Carpenters, Farmers, and ordinary Laborers', the
posters read. 'This Engineer Regiment is to be one of the best in the service, and
as the principal duties in this Corps will be of a professional character a position
in it is more desirable than one of equal rank in ordinary Infantry Regiments.'
In addition, proclaimed the poster, 'Men attached to this Regiment, will receive
extra pay when engaged in professional duties as an Engineer Corps.'[1] Combine
that with a bounty and a conscription breathing down one's neck, and the deal
sounded too good to pass up, even for a thirty-six-year-old man such as David.

As 1863 drew to a close, on 29 December, David made his decision
and enlisted in the 50th New York Volunteer Engineer Regiment for three
years. The 50th, like its partner the 15th New York, had a unique organisational system. According to General Orders 177, dated 31 October 1861,
each volunteer engineer regiment was to consist of 'One colonel, 1 lieu-
tenant-colonel, 3 majors, 1 adjutant (not an extra lieutenant), 1 quarter-mas-
ter (not an extra lieutenant), 1 chaplain, 1 surgeon, 2 assistant surgeons, 1
hospital steward, 3 quartermaster-sergeants, 3 commissary sergeants'.
Beyond that, it would have a dozen companies, each consisting of, 'One captain, 2 first lieutenants, 1 second lieutenant, 2 musicians, 10 sergeants, 10
corporals, 64 artificers, 64 privates'.[2]

David was mustered in as a labourer, noted above as a private, on 2 January 1864, and assigned to Company E. Then he was sent to the Engineer
Depot located in the Washington Navy Yard, where the two regiments of volunteer engineer regiments, the 50th and 15th New York, were stationed. It was
a busy place, where the men built components for pontoon bridges to be used
in the upcoming campaign. As well, a detachment of the 50th, under Lieutenant Colonel Ira Spaulding, was at work at Rappahannock Station. The men
were engaged, Spaulding reported on 31 January, 'in work upon winter quarters, fencing and flooring corrals, corduroy roads, and repairs and renewals in

pontoon trains'. Later, he hoped, the engineers could 'resume our drills in infantry tactics and sapping and mining'.[3]

David would have been welcome, as recruiting was slow and many of the intelligent, skilled men of the 50th were assigned to details outside the regiment. A sergeant from Co. I of the 50th wrote home on 5 March 1864, 'I am afraid we will not fill the company up. It seems that most of the men that have been enlisted for the company have been coaxed away. We have now 109 men in the company.'[4]

David would draw his uniform and equipment there. He would receive a standard foot soldier's single-breasted frock coat, piped in yellow, the engineer branch of service colour, with a black dress hat bearing the brass castle that indicated his branch of service, along with a yellow hat cord. The brass castle was worn proudly, although members of the Regular Army's single battalion of enlisted engineers were initially so annoyed at the fact that volunteers also assumed the right to wear the badge that for some time they refused to wear the castle symbol themselves. Additionally, David would receive a blouse of dark blue wool, fastened down the front with four brass buttons for fatigue wear. Engineers also had a unique uniform item issued for working in the field – a pair of canvas overalls that were described in regulations as 'of white cotton; one garment to cover the whole of the body below the waist, the breast, the shoulders, and the arms; sleeves loose, to allow a free play of the arms, with narrow wristband buttoning with one button; overalls to fasten at the neck behind with two buttons, and at the waist behind with buckle and tongue'.[5] His trousers for all occasions were plain sky-blue.

Engineers were likewise considered capable of serving as infantry and hence they were also supplied with the accoutrements of that corps. David would soon learn how to care for all his new equipment, for the 50th held a formal inspection on the parade ground at Washington on 23 January 1864, with the brigade commander himself acting as inspecting officer. These inspections were both formal and complete. The men stood in ranks, spaced far enough apart to allow the inspecting officers to pass between. David would be fully equipped, opened knapsack at his feet, resting against his infantryman's overcoat. The inspector would check David's weapon, a unique, British-made pattern of 1855 Royal Sappers & Miners Carbine, to see that it was clean and worked smoothly. He would then check the contents of David's cartridge box and knapsack.

David would duly have to learn the unique jobs performed by the engineers. According to a period manual, engineer enlisted men 'are expected to know all the garrison and field duties of soldiers of the line, and, in addition, the practical duties involved in the construction of fortifications, bridges, &c.'[6]

His days were busy. One sergeant in the regiment wrote home on 18 March: 'We are having a little more to do of late than [is] common, such as drilling, Squad drill from 8 to 9 a.m., company drill from 10 to 11.30, battalion drill from 1.30 to 3.30 p.m., dress parade at 4 p.m., guard mounting at 4.30. So you see the greater part of the day is occupied.'[7]

Although there was plenty to learn, drill to be practised, and much work to do, the close proximity to the capital city, with its attractions ranging from the national Capitol Building to a busy red light district was a constant distraction. Finally the brigade commander, Brigadier General Henry W. Benham, issued his brigade's Special Orders No 30, which read:

'Some irregularity having existed in regard to passes for men to leave camp for short distances, the following will in future be the rules governing the issue of passes. Commandants of Companies may allow two or three men at one time to leave camp to visit in its immediate vicinity for not over two hours at any one time between Guard Mounting and retreat and not after the last named hour, but men so absent must always have the written pass of the commandant of their Company.'[8]

On 29 February David drew his first pay. Because of their unique abilities and the type of work they did, the Corps of Engineers had a slightly different pay structure to the rest of the army. It had two grades of privates, Privates of the First Class, or Artificers, and Privates of the Second Class, or Labourers. David was a second-class private, and hence drew $13 a month. In a short time he would be promoted to the first class, at which time his pay went up to $17 a month, an amount equal to that paid to an infantry sergeant. Much of David's money probably went to A. H. Tower, the regimental sutler, who sold needed items on credit and took his share of the men's money as they were paid.

As the weather improved in the spring, the men, who had been assembling bridging equipment in the depot sheds, could move outside for drill. On 6 March 1864 the brigade commander issued his General Orders No. 8, which read:

'The Ponton drills of this command will be resumed at once. These will be a drill by successive Pontons on Monday, Wednesday & Friday mornings at the usual hours for drill (9.30 to 11.30) when as many of the old men as can be spared from their other duties will be distributed among the recruits to assist in instructing them.

'On Tuesday & Thursday at the usual hour (2 to 4) there will be ponton drill by battalion under the direction of a Field Officer of each regiment when practicable – when the whole of each regiment will be out – except the

Guard and such number of mechanics & as may appear to be necessary to complete the barrack within the week.

'The drills as infantry will be continued at the hours above named, whenever practicable without interfering with the ponton drills above directed and with as large a portion of each regiment out as can be spared from the fatigue duty required for arranging the barracks and drill grounds. The new recruits – being excused from this fatigue duty, will be drilled at least six hours a day – the hours other than those named above to be designated by the Regimental Commander.'[9]

In the course of pontoon drill the men practised assembling the large pontoon bridges used to cross the many rivers that bisected Virginia. Using a manual written by a regular army officer of engineers, Captain J. C. Duane, who was by then the chief engineer of the Army of the Potomac, the 103-man company, divided into eight sections each with its own specific duties, would assemble the bridge. A member of Co. A, US Engineers described the process:

'Four or five with spades and other implements improvised a wooden abutment on the shore; another party rowed against the stream, moored a scow, and let it drift down until it was opposite the wooden abutment; then a party of ten advanced, each two men carrying a claw-balk, or timbers fitted with a claw, one of which held the gunwale of the boat, the other the shore abutment. Twenty men now came down on the left with planks [called chesses], one inch thick, six inches wide, and fifteen feet long, narrowed at each end; these they laid across the five joists or balks, and returned on the right.

'Another party meanwhile moored another boat, which dropped down-stream opposite the one already bridged; five joists, each twenty feet long, were laid upon the gunwale by five men; these were fastened by those in the boat, by means of ropes, to cleats or hooks provided for the purpose on the side of the scows, which were shoved off from the shore until the shore end of the balk rested upon the shore boat. These were covered with planks in the same manner as before; side-rails of joists were lashed down with ropes to secure the whole. So one after another of the boats was dropped into position until a bridge several hundred feet long reached from the Maryland to the Virginia shore, for the passage of artillery and every description of munitions for an army.

'Owing to the force of the current, a large rope cable was stretched from shore to shore fifty feet above the bridge, and the upper end of each boat was stayed to the cable by a smaller rope.'[10]

There were several different model pontoon boats. Some were simply wooden barges. Others were made of wooden frames 21 feet long, 5 feet wide, and 2½ feet wide around which canvas was lashed. When soaked, canvas would become water-tight. The advantage of such canvas pontoon boats was that they could be taken apart when not used so that a great many more of them than wooden boats could be carried on each wagon. Moreover, canvas pontoon boats could be carried by thirty-six men quite easily for fairly long distances, while wooden pontoon boats had to be launched into the river directly from the wagons. The downside, however, was that canvas boats were both less durable and buoyant. On the whole, the commander of the Engineer Brigade reported on 25 January 1864, 'I have no hesitation in recommending for future use the canvas pontoon trains for the general service of our armies, the wooden boats being retained, or constructed only for special cases where they are manifestly indispensable and will not require much land transportation.'[11]

In practice, by 1864, the typical plan was to position the canvas boats near the front during an advance, where they could be quickly laid down for infantry to use. Then, wooden boats from the rear would be brought up as bridges for artillery and wagons.

These bridges could be quite long. The engineers built one pontoon bridge across the mouth of the Chickahominy in 1862 that was 1,980 feet long. And, with well-trained engineer soldiers, they could be built quickly. In May 1863, at the start of the Chancellorsville campaign, Army engineers built a pontoon bridge 390 feet long in an hour and ten minutes. Roughly figuring, however, the norm was a hundred feet of bridging an hour.

The engineers got ready to move out with the rest of the army as a new general from the west, Ulysses S. Grant, joined the Army of the Potomac and prepared it for its final battle against the army of Robert E. Lee. The remaining men of the 50th back at the Engineer Depot were ordered to join the engineer camp near Rappahannock Station on 28 March. Once there, the regiment was prepared for action, the Army of the Potomac's chief engineer ordering, on 9 April, that three companies from the regiment be assigned to duty with the headquarters of each corps of the army.

On 22 April the brigade held yet another inspection of all ranks, especially making sure that everybody had a shelter half. On the next day a number of men from the 50th were sent to VI Corps to be assigned to their Ambulance Corps. Signs were everywhere that a big push was due. On 9 May, brigade General Orders No. 19 set up a new, busier-than-ever schedule:

'Until further orders the calls for the different duties of this command will be sounded as follows.

Reveille	5 a.m.	Dinner	12 noon.
Police	5.30	Drill	3 to 5 p.m.
Breakfast	6	Recruit Drill	3 to 6
Sick Call	6.30	Dress Parade	6
Recruit Drill	6.30 to 7.30	Supper	6.30
Guard Mounting	8	Tattoo	8.30
Drill	8.30 to 10.30	Taps	9. [12]

In the meantime, the entire Army of the Potomac opened its final campaign, heading across the Rapidan River into the tangled area known as the Wilderness. The engineers were busy. One regimental officer wrote that his company, 'On the 4th May, bridged the Rapidan at Ely's Ford at daylight. Took up bridge at ten o'clock (after a good portion of the 2nd Corps having crossed) and went on. Stayed the night at Chancellorsville where we left the train and went the same night with arms and ammunition to the front.'[13] With a limited number of bridges available, as soon as the rest of the army had crossed one, the engineers had to go to work to tear it up, pack it back on the wagons, and then press to the head of the column to be ready to lay it down over the next river.

The next day, the Federals clashed with Lee's troops, hurriedly sent to fight in the brush and trees where the overwhelming Federal numbers would count for less than on open ground. The engineers, including David's company, saw their first fighting of 1864 here. A company officer wrote home:

'On the morning of the 6th at daylight, we went into the line of battle, front of the old Wilderness Tavern, where we remained twenty-four hours in rifle pits back of the first line of battle. There were no casualties in Company I. One man of Company E was hit with a piece of shell in the head, did not kill him. The fighting raged in front of us all day. We had a good position which we made better during the day by throwing up rifle pits, etc.'[14]

David's company had now been blooded, with its first casualty of the campaign.

Overall casualties in the Wilderness were heavy, with almost 17,700 dead, wounded or missing. Grant sent back to Washington for reinforcements. And then, on the morning of 7 May, he sent his army south, not north as so many stalemated Union generals had done previously, towards Spotsylvania Court House. The tired troops of the 50th were withdrawn from their post in the line, and brought back to headquarters. Lee quickly realised what the Army of the Potomac was up to, and reacted by racing his troops towards that vital position.

Late that evening the 50th returned to its old post in Chancellorsville, and then began to follow the infantry in its forward move. Six companies of the 50th, under Spaulding, were acting as infantry, assigned to the V Corps, and had been posted to the left of the 2nd Brigade, 1st Division, V Corps, just south of the Orange Turnpike. The rest of the regiment was scattered in detachments between that post and Washington, where some of its members still worked in the Engineer Depot.[15]

Through its service in the Wilderness, the New York Engineers had proved their value, both as workers and fighters. Army headquarters now decided to bring them all down into Virginia. On 13 May Benham was ordered to move the remaining men of the Engineer Brigade to Belle Plain to build and repair roads between there and Fredericksburg. The brigade was to bring some of its bridge train to construct more floating wharves to facilitate the loading of stores and embarkation of the wounded. Only sufficient men needed to guard equipment at the Engineer Depot were to be left behind.[16]

Benham's brigade marched to the wharf at the end of Sixth Street, in Washington, where they boarded boats heading for Belle Plain. They arrived there on the afternoon of the 15th, joining a 15th New York Engineers company in a crowded, confused scene. At the same time, Brigadier General R. O. Tyler was sent to Belle Plain to organise the chaos that had developed at that point. He was directed to gather fit men into brigades to be forwarded to the front as quickly as possible.

According to Benham, the roads from Belle Plain

'... will probably be put in very good order, as to all the worst places, in the course of two or three days, which my own reconnaissance confirms, although, perhaps, while they are being much used, it may be expedient to continue a company or part of a company in the care of them, or some pioneer workers from the infantry here, if the engineers are needed elsewhere.'[17]

On 17 May, as lines of supply trains developed to cross the one bridge south at Fredericksburg, in what became yet another major bottleneck, Benham received orders to get another bridge built at that point. He was also told to bring the 15th back to Washington once the work around Belle Plain was done. Colonel William H. Pettes, of the 50th New York, back at the Engineer Depot in Washington, was ordered at noon on the 17th to fit out and be ready to send a train of twenty-four pontoons on to Belle Plain.[18]

On 17 May the 50th arrived at the army's headquarters near the Spotsylvania Court House. The next morning the regiment broke camp, moving two miles to the right, except for Company I, which was left behind until noon to build a corduroy bridge before rejoining the regiment.[19]

On 21 May Benham reported as follows from Belle Plain to the army's chief of staff, Major General A. A. Humphreys:

'The roads are now essentially in very good condition between this and Fredericksburg, and I expect to withdraw the command from them to-morrow, except one large company for the care of the bridges and the repairs of the roads. The bridge received from Washington on the 19th for that place was sent over as early as it was possible to procure transportation from the quartermaster's department, the last half of the animals only being supplied at 4 a.m. to-day. I ordered the bridge to be laid (to replace the pontoons from the front) this fore-noon, and I doubt not that it was so laid.'[20]

There were still more rivers to cross. The men of the 50th completed building a bridge across the North Anna at Jericho Mill between 4 and 4.30 p.m. on the 23rd. As soon as the last baulk was secured, the V Corps artillery chief, Charles Wainwright, ordered six batteries – twenty-four 12-pounder cannon, each weighing two tons – to cross, which they did successfully. Brigadier General Lysander Cutler's division followed, putting three-quarters of V Corps across in a successful beachhead.[21]

Benham was then ordered, on 26 May, to move from the Engineer Depot in Washington to Fortress Monroe with all the bridging material available and there to be ready to move up the James River at short notice.[22] He left behind Pettes and a number of men from the 50th New York to continue building more bridging material, such as pontoons and barges. The new equipment was sent on to replace older material that was fast wearing out through steady use. On 1 June a 50th company officer wrote home that he finally could take a break: 'Time afternoon, 31st May, our bridge is on the wagons ready to move. There is a wooden ponton bridge here now. The weather is fine. Nearly every day since I last wrote there has been a hard battle fought.'[23]

The depot back in Washington managed to keep up with the front-line engineer requirements. By 12 June Benham was able to report that his equipment at the fortress included 155 wooden pontoons, enough for 3,100 feet. He was short of chesses, but ordered the troops in Washington to make more and forward them as quickly as possible.[24] All told, in May and June 1864 the men of the 50th laid thirty-seven bridges across seven different rivers in support of the army's drive. The bridge across the Chickahominy at Cole's Ferry was 1,240 feet long. It was an exhausting campaign for the 50th New York Engineers.

On the same date that Benham was reporting on the engineer equipment, David's Co. E was ordered to march southward with VI Corps, carrying the corps' entrenching tools. On this march, the Army of the Potomac finally swung around Lee's left south of Richmond, but failed to grab the important railroad west of the city that ran through Petersburg. Confederate engineers had ample time to prepare an elaborate line of defences at Petersburg and southern infantry defended that line well. Now both sides dug in. On 18 June the elements of the 50th with the main army halted near Old Church, about two miles from City Point, the main headquarters and supply point of the Army of the Potomac. There they parked all their trains and set up camp. They could tell that the war had slowed down when they read the brigade's General Orders No. 22 which were dated 29 June 1864:

'I Commanding Officers of Regiments and Detachments of this Brigade, will muster their men for pay on the 30th inst.

'I.I: The Infantry and Ponton drills of this command will be resumed at once & be continued whenever practicable.

Gen Orders No. 19 of May 9th from these Head Quarters are modified as follows.

Drill	8.30 to 9.30 a.m.
Do	4 to 6 p.m.
Dress Parade	6.30 p.m.
Supper	7.' [25]

Garrison life became even more evident by the brigade's General Orders No. 24 dated 18 July:

'Hereafter except otherwise specially ordered, the drills of this command will be as follows.

'A ponton drill from 8½ a.m. each morning - Sundays excepted - to continue two hours or until the designated practice is completed. A Company drill on Monday, Wednesday and Friday afternoons, for abut two hours from 4 p.m. and a Battalion drill on Tuesday and Thursday afternoon at the same hours. Dress Parade will be had each day at 6.30 p.m.

'At all such drills and parades all officers of the command will be present acting and directing according to their respective ranks or grades unless specially excused in writing by the Surgeon – or from these Head Quarters or unavoidably detained by other duties – excepting only the actual officer of the Guard – the officer of the Guard for Ponton drill, and the field officers from company drills – for which his general supervision it is expected will be sufficient.'[26]

Not all the elements of the engineer brigade were at City Point, some companies having been sent to assist the cavalry corps. It was not until 10 July that all the battalions of the 50th finally were united 'as one detachment for engineering operations in front of Petersburg,' Spaulding reported.[27]

An officer of the 50th wrote home 24 August:

'We are still laying quiet near City Point. Nothing of any importance has taken place here except that we have had some considerable rain which has in a measure rid us of our active and troublesome enemy, the fly. One that has not been here and seen for himself cannot imagine what a pester this little insect is.'[28]

Bridging work was largely done for the moment; now the main effort was in building redoubts, batteries and rifle pits for the siege that would last for the rest of the year and into the next.

The men of the 50th also took over infantry work in the trenches around City Point. One 50th officer wrote home on 28 August that his company was 'in the rifle pits the other night and by the way that was the same night we had a scare here which was on the 25th of August'.[29] But things were not totally static. Grant had the infantry constantly moving, feeling out the Confederate positions, especially to the left, towards the Weldon Railroad line. The 50th, in late September, was sent out there both to tear up tracks and build fortifications. But by early October the weather had started to turn chilly. Thanks to having the tools and being suitably trained, David and his friends started to build decent winter quarters.

In late November the regimental headquarters left City Point to join its line companies near the Weldon Railroad. In December they moved again, this time to a place near Poplar Grove Church. 'We have a beautiful camp,' a regimental officer wrote home from there.[30] In mid-January the regimental log-cabin cantonment was further enlarged by the addition of a church. Weather slowed down much of the building, with hard rains in the winter leaving mud that was ankle-deep throughout the area. Even so, the engineers worked on. Finally, the finished church was complete with steeple and the castle insignia of the Engineers over its front door. Soldiers from other regiments toured the Engineer Brigade camp just to see its elaborate buildings. 'Even the quarters of the rank and file were remarkable ornate,' a jealous artilleryman recalled of one winter Engineer Brigade cantonment, 'and as cosy and convenient within as they were attractive without. Their streets were corduroyed, and they even boasted sidewalks similarly constructed.'[31]

As the engineers were improving their camps, the death rate continued to climb in the front lines. The war-weary Army of Northern Virginia was stretched nearly to breaking point. Lee authorised a desperate attack on the Federal lines, only to lose a large number of irreplaceable men. Then, Grant continued to drive on the Confederate right. Finally, on 1 April the Federals struck at Five Forks, and the Confederates dissolved. Lee knew that the only chance his army had was to abandon Petersburg, and therefore, Richmond, and to flee west, then south to try to hook up with the other major Confederate Army in the field, currently in the Carolinas.

The Confederates pulled out of their trenches. The Federals, however, were after them immediately, together with the engineers and their wagons of bridging and road-building supplies. But this campaign was not to last as long or be as wearing as the campaign through Virginia in 1864. On 8 April Lee and his forces were trapped, surrounded by Federal troops in overwhelming numbers. On 9 April the Army of Northern Virginia surrendered.

'We are all proud of this great and glorious event, proud that we are here and have participated in crushing out this wicked rebellion that came so near ruining our *glorious* and *noble government*. Thank God it is over now,' a 50th officer wrote home the day Lee surrendered.[32]

There would be little for the engineers to do now. Garrisoning a defeated south would fall to the men of the infantry and cavalry. The regiment remained in the area for a short time, making sure all the bridges they had built were in good shape. Then, on 6 May, the regiment was ordered to make one last march. Brigade General Orders Number 17 read:

'Col. W. Brainerd 15th N.Y. Engineers will march the two regiments of Volunteers of the Engineer Brigade by the routes which shall be directed from Head Quarters of the army of the Potomac at the head of the column of that army now moving to Alexandria, repairing roads and laying such bridges as may be required. On reaching that point unless otherwise ordered from Hd. Qrs. A-o-P or other superior authority, Col Brainerd will march the command and report to the Head Quarters of the Brigade at Engineer Depot of the Army of the Potomac, near the Navy Yard at Washington D.C.'[33]

Once there, the men used spit and polish for the formal victory parade of the Army of the Potomac through the streets of Washington. It was almost over. On 6 June the men were ordered to turn in their English Sappers & Miners carbines, with the accoutrements that came with these weapons, to the Corps of Engineers. Then, on 13 June 1865, David and the rest of his company were mustered out of the service at Fort Barry, Virginia.

NOTES

1 Recruiting poster, author's collection
2 *ORs*, Series III, Vol. 2, p. 705
3 *ORs*, Series I, Vol. XXXIII, p. 450
4 Floyd, Dale E., *"Dear Friends at Home..."*, Washington, 1985, p. 27
5 War Department, *Revised Regulations for the Army of the United States,* 1861, Philadelphia, 1863, p. 488
6 Kautz, August V., *Customs of Service*, Philadelphia, 1864, p. 66
7 Floyd, op. cit., p. 30
8 Brigade Order Book, author's collection
9 ibid.
10 Gross, Warren Lee, *Recollections of a Private*, New York, 1890, pp. 19–20
11 *ORs*, Series I, Vol. XXXIII, p. 414
12 Brigade Order Book, op. cit.
13 Floyd, op. cit., p. 38
14 ibid, p. 38
15 Matter, William D., *If It Takes All Summer*, Chapel Hill, NC, 1988, p. 13
16 *ORs*, Series I, Vol. XXXVI, Part 2, pp. 733–5
17 ibid, pp. 852–3
18 *ORs*, Series I, Vol. XXXVI, Part 3, p. 232
19 Floyd, op. cit., p. 25
20 *ORs*, Series I, Vol. XXXVI, Part 3, p. 67
21 Trudeau, Noah Andre, *Bloody Roads South*, New York, 1989, p. 230
22 *ORs*, Series I, Vol. XXVII, Part 3, p. 232
23 Floyd, op. cit., p. 42
24 *ORs*, Series I, Vol. XXVII, Part 3, p. 772
25 Brigade Order Book, op. cit.
26 ibid.
27 *ORs*, Series I, Vol XL, Part 1, p. 300
28 Floyd, op. cit., p. 51
29 ibid, p. 53
30 ibid, p. 66
31 Billings, John D., *The History of the Tenth Massachusetts Battery of Light Artillery*, Boston, 1909, p. 187
32 Floyd, op. cit., p. 82
33 Brigade Order Book, op. cit.

6

George Cole

Second Lieutenant, 2nd Massachusetts
Heavy Artillery Regiment

On 23 June 1864 Irish-born George Cole, five feet nine inches tall, with black hair and dark eyes, and a clerk by trade, stepped before a recruiter in South Hadley, near Boston, and swore allegiance to the United States as a new member of the then-being-organised 2nd Massachusetts Heavy Artillery.

Why did he join? Since he left no memoir we shall never know. Certainly at twenty-seven he was older than the majority of privates. Most rank and file in the Union Army, even allowing for under-age youths who lied to enlist, were around eighteen, followed by those who were twenty-one years old. There were a number of individuals older than twenty-one; in fact, the average of all members of the Union Army, from drummer boys to general officers, in July 1863, was 25.76.[1]

Although Irish by birth, George did not join an Irish regiment even though there were many of them around. Indeed, the Army of the Potomac had an entire Irish Brigade which included the 28th Massachusetts, the *Faugh a Ballagh!* [Clear the road] regiment. Moreover, the 9th Massachusetts Infantry was noted as an Irish regiment. Both these regiments were initially raised from the Irish citizens of Boston, not far from South Hadley. George presumably could have joined either of those or a similar regiment. Of course, there were many Irish in other than Irish regiments. The almost 150,000 Irishmen who joined the Union Army could hardly have been accommodated in uniquely Irish units. However, by the time George joined the Army, many Irish had become more interested in avoiding service than joining up.

The signing of the Emancipation Proclamation greatly distressed Irish members of the Democratic Party – and most Irish were Democrats – as they felt betrayed by the Lincoln government which until then had been fighting simply, they thought, to maintain the United States government. In the summer of 1863 Irish in New York rioted for several days against the draft, burning such buildings as a Negro orphanage and battling both police and eventually Federal troops until calm was restored. Nonetheless, there were no more new all-Irish regiments raised by the time George decided to enlist.

Although the war had been dragging on for a while, there were still some volunteers. 'I gave up my job at John D. Pringles & went home (at Dawson Ferry) for I have made up my mind to go to the army,' noted nineteen-year-old Daniel Chisholm in his diary on 25 February 1864. 'I did not feel that I was doing my duty to stay at home when nearly all my comrades and friends was leaving for the seat of the war.'[2] Although it is impossible to fathom George's motives for joining up, older men such as he rarely felt the same urge as did young Chisholm. On the contrary, for them the offer of a bounty for service in a unit that was likely to see little combat would be a strong incentive to recruitment.

There were Federal bounties, state bounties and local bounties and they all added up to what amounted to a great deal of money to people who could make a decent living on less than $20 a month. Federal bounties alone, after the Enrolment Act of 1863, offered $100 to every conscript and substitute, $300 to every man who enlisted for three years, and $400 for every man who enlisted for four years. Local areas added more money to get enough recruits in their areas so that their quotas would be full and conscription could be avoided. By the time George joined up, he could have received $677 – $302 from the US government, $75 from the state and $300 from the county – without having any prior military service had he enlisted in New York County. Veterans who joined up received a Federal government bounty of an extra hundred dollars. Indeed, George could have received as much as $1,500 in certain rural Mid-Western counties for a three-year term.

The type of regiment the recruit joined was as important as where he joined. It paid considerably less to join an established regiment in the field than one such as Company E of the 2nd which was just being raised. For example, a Philadelphian joining an established regiment drew a $50 bounty and a $6 premium from the local citizens' bounty fund. On the other hand, join a new regiment, and the recruit would get a total of $84 plus the first month's $13 pay in advance. As well, a recruit in an established regiment where the majority of men had joined before bounties became substantial faced considerable hostility about their bounty when they reached their new unit. One officer wrote about recruits joining his regiment in September 1863:

'Poor devils I fear theyl [sic] have a rather hard time in this Regt, for the troops that came out before the big bountys were given, seem to think themselvs [sic] a great deal better than all the big bounty men (as they call them.)'[3]

George was one of the first to enlist in Company E, and indeed had to wait around at Camp Meigs until the company received enough recruits to be mustered officially into Federal service. And, while waiting, he received $25 in bounty and $12 in advance pay when he enlisted.

There he was issued the uniform of a heavy artillery enlisted man, a single-breasted dark blue frock coat, with red piping around the collar and on each cuff, worn with brass shoulder scales and a stiff wide-brimmed hat with crossed cannon on front, a red hat cord and, for dress, a black feather. A pair of plain sky-blue kersey trousers worn for both dress and fatigue. The fatigue dress included a plain dark blue hip-length single breasted sack coat and a leather-peaked dark blue wool forage cap.

Heavy artillerymen were foot soldiers and therefore received infantry accoutrements and rifled muskets. George's first days would have been largely spent in drilling with these weapons. The main weapon of the foot artilleryman was the large cannon, mostly mounted in fortifications, especially on the sea coasts, for use against enemy ships or for defence of fixed positions. Such guns not being available, training emphasised infantry drill, with gun drill being reserved until the men reached their final assigned post. A great deal of specialised knowledge was required for heavy artillery duty, according to the advice to recruits given in a period manual:

'Service in the branch, in addition to a knowledge of the ammunition and implements of gunnery, requires a practical knowledge of the forces and appliances for handling and moving heavy guns. This kind of information is not easily acquired from books; and, moreover, the appliances that may be available at one time may not be on hand at another; and tact for applying make-shifts is an essential qualification.'[4]

For anyone who was not all that keen on heroic infantry charges, the obvious advantage to joining such an organisation was that members of heavy artillery units, for the most part, would have barracks or at least comfortable tenting and fairly safe duty. At that time, nobody knew that Grant would take the majority of heavy artillerymen from Washington's forts and hurl them at Lee's army as infantry in the forthcoming 1864 eastern campaign. Many heavy artillery units would suffer terribly. Indeed, according to one student, 'Of the 2,047 regiments in the Union Army, the First Maine Heavy Artillery sustained the greatest loss in battle. Not only was the number killed the largest, but the percentage of killed was exceeded in only one instance.'[5]

Units spent relatively little time in camps of instruction once they had been organised and mustered into Federal service. Company A of the 2nd had been mustered in as early as 28 July 1863, and most of the officers and probably many of the men, were eager to escape from the cold, damp New England air and the tedious rounds of drill and move on to their destination. George, however, put the time waiting for the regiment to be fully organised to advance himself. He let the new officers know of his experience as a clerk. As there were always dozens of forms to be completed, ranging from daily morning reports to returns of clothing and equipment to special requisitions and special recruiting forms, clerks who wrote with a clear hand were much in demand. George was put to work at headquarters.

This prevented him going to the front with his company, one of four companies sent from Boston to New Bern, North Carolina, 4 September 1863, another two companies following on 6 November. Obviously George got along very well with the regiment's field officers, Colonel Jones Frankle and Major Samuel C. Oliver, for on 16 November 1864 he was jumped over the heads of all the first sergeants in the regiment to be named the new regimental sergeant major, with $21 a month in pay. His uniform would now include three red chevrons and arc and a red stripe down each trouser leg. He was authorised to wear a red worsted sash and carry a straight-bladed, brass-hilted non-commissioned officer's sword.

'The sergeant major is the ranking non-commissioned officer of the regiment,' wrote August Kautz in his manual for enlisted personnel. 'His pay is twenty-one dollars per month, an allowance of clothing, and one ration.' His duties were largely clerical. He helped the adjutant in keeping track of all the office paperwork as well as supervising the regimental clerks in making out the various returns, rolls and reports required by the army. Every day the company first sergeants reported to him with their morning books, which he used to complete the regimental morning report, and pick up their orders for the day and details required from their companies. In keeping with this, the sergeant major kept the various rosters for guard, orderly and fatigue duties. If there were no drum major with the regiment, the sergeant major took direct control of the field musicians. He also had to be present at guard mounts and dress parades, where he served as left guide. When in battle the sergeant major served near the major, behind the left wing of the regiment; on the march he was positioned alongside the colours some six paces from the right of the column. Finally, he had the responsibility of maintaining standard time in the regiment.[6]

On the surface it may seem odd that an ordinary private should be picked from the ranks and made the senior regimental non-commissioned officer, over the heads of all the company first sergeants. However, since the job was strictly clerical in nature, such a move was not uncommon. Division clerk

Elisha Hunt Rhodes, 2nd Rhode Island Infantry, noted in his diary for 9 March 1862:

'Saturday while visiting the camp, Colonel Wheaton sent for me and informed me that I had been promoted to be "Sergeant Major" of the Regiment. Well, well, who would have supposed that this would ever have happened? To say that I was delighted would be very tame. Corporal William G. Bradford Co. "G" is to take my place as clerk at Division Headquarters. This morning my traps were brought out to camp, and I was mustered as Sergeant Major. I have received many congratulations from officers and men, and I am very happy. Tomorrow I shall receive my sash and sword. I shall mess with the officers by special arrangements... The former Sergeant Major George C. Clendennin has been made a Second Lieutenant.'[7]

George, too, could reasonably look for a lieutenant's shoulder straps in the future, as the sergeant major's position was a common launching platform for commissioned careers.

Eventually, in early January the regiment's headquarters received orders to pack up and board ships for Fortress Monroe. From there it would be assigned to garrison duty along the coast farther south. The departure date was set at 8 January 1864. George was then posted to regimental headquarters in Norfolk, Virginia, while other detachments of the regiment were stationed at Fort Macon, Newport Barracks, Fort Totten, Morehead City, and Plymouth, North Carolina. George's Company E ended up at Smithville, North Carolina.

In March George took sick and was sent to the garrison hospital. When he was released he apparently began serving with another regiment. This was certainly uncommon: not only did men usually prefer their own regiments, often going to great lengths to get back to them after getting out of hospital, but by regulation they would require a transfer to do otherwise. One wonders what George's reason might have been. Was it the location of the headquarters, away from North Carolina or a chance of further promotion? At any rate, the commander of the 2nd took quick steps to regain George. On 20 March Major George Perkins, at headquarters, then at 1st Division, District of Beaufort, New Bern, North Carolina, wrote the commanding officer of the 5th Rhode Island Artillery:

'Will you please inform me whether Sergt. Maj. Geo. Cole 2nd Mass. Arty. is able to return to his regiment for duty. He was sent to the field hospital for treatment about the 1st of March. The Comdg Officer of the 2nd Mass informs me that he has understood that Cole has been discharged from hospital and is now doing duty with your regiment. If he is able to do duty you will order him to report to the Comdg. Officer of his Regt. stationed at Riuston NC.'[8]

Several days later George was back with the 2nd. It appears, however, that his commander sweetened the deal to guarantee his return. On 29 March 1865, Second Lieutenant Robert B. Sinclair was promoted to first lieutenant and George traded in his enlisted man's uniform for the plain single-breasted frock coat of a second lieutenant of heavy artillery, with its red shoulder straps edged in gold and red welt down each sky-blue pants leg. His monthly pay leaped to $45.

But his war was coming to an end. Resistance was dying down everywhere. There was nothing more for the regiment to do but garrison duties, which it performed in companies assigned to places in Virginia and North Carolina. Finally, on 2 September, the regiment was reunited and sent to Galloupe's Island in Boston Harbor to await muster out. On 23 September 1865 George Cole was mustered out of military service, along with the rest of his regiment.

NOTES

1 Wiley, Bell Irvin, *The Common Soldier in the Civil War*, New York, 1952, p. 303.
2 Menge, W. Springer and J. August Shimrak, eds., *The Civil War Notebook of Daniel Chisholm*, New York, 1989, p. 3
3 Loving, Jerome M., ed., *Civil War Letters of George Washington Whitman*, Durham, North Carolina, 1975, p. 104
4 Kautz, August V., *Customs of the Service*, Philadelphia, 1864, p. 63
5 Fox, William F., *Regimental Losses in The American Civil War*, Dayton, Ohio, 1985, p. 125
6 Kautz, op. cit., pp. 172–4
7 Rhodes, Robert Hunt, ed., *All for the Union*, Lincoln, Rhode Island, 1985, pp. 57–8
8 Cole, George, personnel file, National Archives, Washington

7

Alister Macalister Grant
Private, Independent Battery Militia Light Artillery

The morning in June 1863 was already warm as young Alister Macalister Grant checked to see that the door of his house at 14 Merrick St., in Center City, Philadelphia, was locked, and then hurried off to a meeting of his battery members. Out west in Pennsylvania it was said that Lee's ragged army, victor of virtually every battle thus far fought with the Union forces, was plundering its way through the state towards its largest city. Grey-clad troops were already said to be in Adams and York Counties, only a day's train trip away. As Alister hurried along he passed dozens of posters stuck to gas-lamp poles: 'DEFENCE OF THE CITY OF PHILADELPHIA, I do hereby require Brigadier General A. J. PLEASONTON, Commander of the HOME GUARD, to order our (and into the service of the City of Philadelphia,) THE WHOLE OF THE SAID GUARD, for the preservation of the public peace AND THE DEFENCE OF THE CITY. And I hereby call upon all persons within the limits of the said City, to yield a PROMPT AND READY OBEDIENCE to the Orders of the said Commander of the HOME GUARD, and of those acting under his authority in execution of their said duties.' It was signed by the city's mayor, Alexander Henry.

The concept of the people turning out *en masse* to repel an invading force was part of the basic American soul. Back in 1790 George Washington, in submitting a plan to prepare for the national defence, wrote, 'An energetic national militia is to be regarded as the *capital security* of a free republic, and not a standing army forming a distinct class in the community.'[1] Even a veteran of the Civil War, Union Major General John A. Logan, wrote after the war that 'the volunteer soldier standing for and in place of a permanent army – that curse of monarchies, and despoiler of the liberties of the masses – is the Atlas upon whose broad shoulders are safely borne our republican institutions...'[2]

From the Revolution to the Mexican War, militia even won battles alone. As the country grew ever more industrialised, however, many state militia systems became moribund. People stopped bothering to drill or even to own required arms and equipment, which did seem somewhat useless in urban areas. Many Northern and Western state assemblies simply ignored their militia. Other states set up elaborate systems of regiments, brigades and divisions, but these were largely on paper and did little more than give innkeepers and clerks a chance to call themselves generals and colonels.

Eventually, there was little in the way of militia to call upon in case of emergency. Yet as the nation grew more prosperous, and people no longer had to spend all their time fighting for their livelihoods out in the wilderness, men began to reflect on the pleasures of part-time military life. From early days there had been some independent volunteer companies, and these continued their existence, largely as social groups who paraded on holidays such as Independence Day, to the cheers of their fellow citizens. By the mid-nineteenth century others began to form their own volunteer companies. Most of these were made up of infantry, as it was easier and cheaper to provide infantry weapons than horses or cannon.

So it was that at the outbreak of the Civil War the old militia system had virtually ceased to exist in many states, although volunteer companies filled the gap. The outbreak of war led to even more volunteer companies being formed. And when southerners fired on the American flag at Fort Sumter in early April 1861, most Philadelphians wanted to show their patriotic enthusiasm. One leading Philadelphian noted in his diary for 18 April:

'Went to town with Bet at 12. The streets are all of a flutter with flags, streaming from windows, hotels, stores, &c. The passenger cars are all decorated with them. Indeed, they are necessary to protect the houses of persons suspected of "secession" opinions from insult by the mob. Fortunately, the sentiments of the people are so generally loyal to the government that, tho we are to have the curse of civil war, we are not likely to suffer from the greater evil of partizen war among ourselves.'[3]

Many men who had previously formed the core of volunteer militia companies now chose to join active field units. But although some volunteer companies became inactive or even folded, the haphazard system of such companies forming the heart of local defence continued when the Civil War began. There were always men, unwilling or unable to take a more active part in the war, ready to replace those now at the front.

Thus on 19 April a group of the city's leading citizens met at the law office of Chapman Biddle on 131 South Fifth Street in Philadelphia to discuss plans for local defence in the forthcoming war. Biddle, a member of one of the city's most socially prominent families, proposed reviving an old volunteer company that had passed out of existence for lack of interest. It was unusual in that it was an artillery, rather than an infantry, company. The group agreed, electing Biddle the captain of what they designated Company A, 1st Pennsylvania Artillery. Alexander Biddle, another of the large clan and a stockbroker by profession, became the company's lieutenant. Charles E. Cadwalader, a member of another of the city's most famous families, signed up, as did others who became quite celebrated in later years. Frank H. Furness, for example, would become a leading architect, S. Weir Mitchell an important neurologist and novelist; and Isaac J. Wistar would earn a general's star and later found an important scientific institute.

Biddle knew and invited many of his fellow lawyers to this formative meeting. So many from the legal profession joined the new company that it was noted that while they might not be as expert in military affairs as other companies, they were 'great on papers'.[4]

Some of those who originally signed up for the company later left to join units that would take the field. These included T. C. Williams, who became a regular army captain; John M. Gries, who would become colonel of the 104th Pennsylvania Volunteer Infantry; Captain Charles Chauncey of the 2nd Cavalry; and Major A. G. Rosengarten of the 15th Cavalry. Both the Biddles, who joined this group, decided to become more active in the war for the Union, quitting to raise what became the 121st Pennsylvania Volunteer Infantry. Henry D. Landis, a pre-war member of the old Company I, was elected to command the company. Samuel C. Perkins, another lawyer whose office was at 6th and Walnut Streets, was elected the battery's first lieutenant.

Most of the unit's members, however, chose to remain in what was eventually known variously as the Independent Battery Militia Light Artillery; 1st Philadelphia Militia Light Artillery; 1st Artillery Pennsylvania Home Guard; and Landis's Philadelphia Battery of Light Artillery. Alister was among those who elected to stay.

Alister described himself by occupation as a 'gentleman' rather than a labourer, tradesman, or businessman.[5] Such men considered themselves well above the workaday world. As another Philadelphia citizen, Sidney George Fisher, noted in his diary about his role as a gentleman:

'Far superior in this to those of much of the flashy society in town and for this reason, that the family is, in position, fortune & education, what they have been all their lives & what their fathers were before them. They live on the estate which they *inherited*, & the furniture of the house, plain compared with modern luxury, belonged to those who lived there before them. They are not *parvenues*, & this one thing gives a man qualities which *nothing* else can. I always feel socially superior to a man who is not a gentleman by *birth*, and I never yet saw one who had *risen* to a higher position, whose mind and character as well as his manners did not show the taint of his origin.'[6]

It is not surprising that people feeling this way did not see fit to join the mob that was essentially the Union Army, and certainly not as an enlisted man.

It was the practice among volunteer companies to select their own uniforms. These were often quite elaborate affairs, with tailed coats known as 'claw-hammer' coats, fastened with three rows of buttons down the front, standing collars, and lavish amounts of gold lace everywhere it could be applied. Headgear often included tall shakos, almost hidden by towering plumes of various colours, and covered in front with metallic badges. Perhaps as an indication of the unostentatious way in which gentlemen of the period were expected to live, as indicated by Sidney Fisher, the men of the new company selected a plain, understated uniform.

The hat was a broad-brimmed light brown slouch hat, pinned up on the left side, with a US Army artilleryman's cap badge in front and red worsted hat cords knotted in front. The coat was a custom-tailored version of the US Army fatigue blouse, cut slightly longer than was the issue coat, and made with five brass buttons down the front instead of the regulation four. Trousers were a darker brown than the hats. Each man wore a black belt with an obsolete two-piece US Army belt buckle that had been worn between 1835 and 1851.

Busy members of the company could rarely meet to study the art of contemporary cannon usages. Yet to be an effective unit they had to be familiar with such a subject. Each man needed to know the drill of the entire gun crew, not just his own, in case men fell in action. Wrote an army officer in a manual for recruits:

'The peculiarities with which an artillery soldier in a field-battery must familiarise himself, in addition to most of the duties of cavalry and infantry, is the care of guns and harness, and especially the ammunition. He should understand well the principles in firing, and the peculiarities of the particular gun and the ammunition used in the battery. All the cannoneers should be perfectly familiar with all the different kinds of ammunition, their uses and application, and where they are to be found. They should understand the uses of the implements in the ammunition-chest; how to spike a gun, and how to remove a spike; how to blow up ammunition-chests, and render artillery unserviceable temporarily and permanently.'[7]

Civil War cannon were, for the most part, muzzle-loading weapons fired directly at their targets. Each gun required a relatively large crew, with each member known by the number of his post. Number 1 stood, when the gun was in action, on the left front of the muzzle, as one looked at it, with a ramrod in his hand. It was his job to sponge the bore of the gun out between firings with a wet sponge, on one end of the rammer, to prevent sparks from previous firings setting off a new cartridge prematurely. Then he would ram down the next cartridge for firing.

Number 2 stood on the other side of the muzzle. He received a cartridge from Number 5 as it was brought up, and placed it inside the muzzle of the gun so that Number 1 could ram it home. Number 3 stood to the rear of the gun, in line with Number 1. He covered the gun's vent with a heavy leather thumbstall to prevent air being drawn into the piece as it was being loaded, and possibly spark a premature explosion. Once it was loaded, Number 3 moved to the rear of the piece and moved its trail as indicated by the gunner who aimed the cannon. Once it was aimed, Number 3 stuck a long, sharp, iron rod into the vent to prick the material cartridge bag open so that the gunpowder would be exposed. Then Number 4 inserted a lanyard into the ring of the primer, stepped back, and prepared to fire on command. When the chief of the piece ordered 'Fire', he gave the lanyard a jerk, and the friction primer went off, sending a spark through the vent into the cartridge which then exploded, hurling the projectile out of the gun's muzzle.

The rest of the gun crew were involved in the loading process. Number 5 carried cartridges, one at a time, between the limber chest, in which ammunition was stored, and Number 2. Number 6 stayed next to the limber chest and prepared fuses to the correct time, according to orders from the chief of the piece, and then handed them to Number 5. Number 7 took cartridges from the limber chest and handed them to Number 6. It was vital that every single member of the crew do his job exactly, while under fire. This took quite some training, which was particularly difficult for a volunteer battery, staffed by busy civilians, to master.

In September 1862 Lee's army burst out of Virginia and into Maryland, a free state bordering Pennsylvania. Pennsylvania's Governor Andrew Curtin called up all militia and volunteers not already in uniform, and Alister's battery prepared for war. The company was hurried onto a train to Harrisburg, lacking any equipment. They were one of nineteen companies from the Home Guard Brigade and three sadly understrength Philadelphia Militia regiments that rode to Harrisburg to meet the call for recruits.

There they disembarked in a sea of volunteers who had also rushed to the state capital in the emergency. Almost none of them had equipment, many even lacked uniforms, and above all, there was no organisation to handle the flux of volunteers and militia. One such group called to Harrisburg received only one meal there, dry bread, cold ham and a cup of coffee at the railroad depot before being sent to sleep in the state's Capitol Building. 'We did not sleep much as the boys were singing and dancing just as if we were at some great frolic,' one recalled later.[8]

Some of the volunteers managed to get organised and on a train to Hagerstown, Maryland, which they garrisoned while Lee's men were holding off the Army of the Potomac at Antietam. But the Confederates had been so bloodied there that they had to retreat back into Virginia and the crisis was over. Alister's battery never even left Harrisburg before they were ordered back to Philadelphia, their chance at glory gone.

Alister and his comrades went back to their civilian lives, reading of the great battles at Fredericksburg and Chancellorsville into early 1863. Then, when least expecting it, the battery was given another opportunity to make its mark. In late June, Lee again put his men on the road north, and this time he evaded the Federal forces until he had passed across Maryland and was into Pennsylvania.

Philadelphia, which had a number of southern sympathisers in its midst, was strangely quiet during this crisis. One citizen reported 'the people as quiet and apathetic as if it was all a false report. Thousands of able bodied young fellows are ever parading the streets, but no enlistments go on with spirit.' Indeed, from the city government level, he wrote, 'There has been some little vaporing and quibbling in Councils, and that is the end of it. Not a spadeful of earth has been raised in the defence of Philadelphia.'[9]

Alister and his fellow battery members, however, were rushed to Harrisburg again. The 108 officers and men of the battery were mustered into the service of the United States on 18 June 1863, 'for the emergency', given equipment, and assigned to the defences of Harrisburg along the Susquehanna. They spent only a few days at Fort Washington, as the post along the river had been named, before marching off to counter Confederate probes towards Pennsylvania's capital.

Meanwhile the Confederates were on their way north. They were led by veterans of many a hard-fought battle, commanded by seasoned Lieutenant General Richard S. Ewell. On 21 June Ewell had asked Lee for permission to take his infantry corps northward into Pennsylvania. Lee approved, noting, 'Your progress and direction will, of course, depend upon the development of circumstances. If Harrisburg comes within your means, capture it.'[10] Ewell set off north, his march slowed by his requirement to gather horses, cattle and provisions from the locals. His men were also detailed to stop African-Americans and, if they could not prove they were legally free, have them sent south into slavery.

One private in Ewell's Corps, John Casler, recalled being camped at Middleburg on the state line between Maryland and Pennsylvania on 23 June: 'then on to Greencastle and Marion, and camped near Chambersburg, and remained there one day. Then through Chambersburg and Green Village, and camped near Shippensburg. On the 27th we marched through Shippensburg, Palmstown, Stowestown, Mount Rock, and camped near Carlisle. We lay in camp at that place the 28th, about twenty miles from Harrisburg, the capital of the State.'[11] This camp was made in one of the oldest military posts in America, the Carlisle Barracks, which had been built in the middle of the previous century. 'It is a lovely place,' Confederate topographical engineer Jedediah Hotchkiss wrote, 'and we enjoyed our rest there.'[12]

While Casler and his friends rested from their hard marching, Ewell sent units to probe north, towards the Susquehanna River and Harrisburg, to see what sort of defences lay before him. He was sadly lacking enough cavalry for this probe, the main body of Lee's cavalry under J. E. B. Stuart having some time earlier cut loose from the main army in a giant raid that would leave the Confederates badly lacking mounted scouts.

As the Confederates drew near, northern officials prepared to stop them. Governor Curtin had earlier ordered black railroad workers to join state militia in building fortifications to protect the state's capital in the Camp Hill region, west of the city and on the other side of the Susquehanna, and at suburban towns of Marysville, Lemoyne, Bridgeport, and Oyster Point. Now, with Confederates in Carlisle and almost on Harrisburg's doorstep, militia units that had gathered at Fort Washington and Camp Curtin in Harrisburg, Alister's battery among them, were ordered to man these new works.

It had started raining on 25 June and the rain lasted through the morning of 27 June. The roads were deep in thick mud, making travel slow for the heavy guns, their wooden wheels digging deep ruts through the sticky mud. The historian of the 22nd New York State Militia Regiment, with whom the battery served, later recalled seeing them leave:

'The battery as it left Fort Washington consisted of six 3-inch rifled guns (10 pounders) and five caissons, one caisson being left in the fort on account of the want of horses. There was no picket rope, no blankets, forage bags, whips, spurs, curry combs, or anything necessary for the care and comfort of the horses and drivers. No battery wagon, forge or blacksmith was attached to the command, though many of the horses wanted shoes and re-shoeing. The guns also were deficient of equipment; there was but one prolonge and two worms in the whole battery, while buckets, spare poles, shovels, axes, etc., were in many cases wanting. The supply of ammunition was also short.'[13]

First Lieutenant Rufus King, a regular officer of the 4th US Artillery Regiment, accompanied the battery which was in sore need of professional instruction. The volunteers were so unfamiliar with the involved leather straps that made up the rigging for the horses that they were unable to assemble them or take them apart. Their solution was simply to leave all the harnesses on the horses for two days. Finally, they had to let the horses loose, at night, after a long, weary day on the road. 'Try all the buckles and unbuckle those that work easiest,' was the order the volunteer officers gave. In fact, the harness was brand new and all the buckles worked easily. The men took all the harness apart and Lieutenant King spent all morning the next day reassembling the straps.[14]

On 28 June the battery was behind the works at Oyster Point along with the 71st New York State Militia, an infantry regiment also known as the American Guard, composed of native-born Americans from New York City. Hardly were their guns in position around late afternoon, when the dingy grey of Confederates appeared. They were men of Brigadier General Albert G. Jenkins's brigade of cavalry, sent out to scout the Union line, and were supported by horse artillery. The southern veterans advanced slowly, in open skirmish order, testing Federal defences rather than assaulting them. The Federals opened fire, which was returned by Confederate cannon. But it rained again in the afternoon and when darkness came the Confederates fell back.

The next day, 29 June, was essentially a repeat of the evening of the 28th, complete with rain in the afternoon. Again the Confederates moved out cautiously and again Federal fire kept them at bay. Then, that evening, the Confederates were gone. Word came, however, that more troops were approaching a Federal position at Sporting Hill. Alister, with the rest of his battery, hitched up their guns and caissons as best they could and moved off over deeply muddy roads, leaving the 71st to defend Oyster Point.

On 30 June, as the cloudy day broke, the battery behind two regiments of infantry, the 22nd and 37th New York State Militia, was at Sporting Hill, near Harrisburg, facing another line of Confederate skirmishers supported by their own artillery batteries. Again these were merely probing attacks, lacking the full infantry support Ewell could have thrown at the Union position. Still, Confederate fire was hotter than it had been at Oyster Point. One nervous Number 2 man, shaken by the Confederate counter-battery fire, started pushing the fused projectile for his three-inch rifle in backwards, fuse towards the charge. Had it been rammed home, the gun could have blown up, killing and wounding most of its crew. A horrified Lieutenant King leaped forward just in time, stopping the Number 1 from ramming the shell home.[15]

Finally the Confederate cavalry, having tested the Union line, fell back to Carlisle. The exhausted Union troops were fiercely elated at their victory and the fact that they had survived. Though they had held their ground, they had paid a higher price than at Oyster Point, with nine men wounded, none from the battery.

The victorious Federals remained in position until they saw that all the Confederates had withdrawn. Then they moved forward cautiously, for it was their first advance against an enemy. They did not know, however, that the situation ahead had changed considerably. On 29 June, under orders from Lee who had now found large contingents of Federal soldiers at Gettysburg, the raiding Confederate forces had started back in that direction. Stuart, who was out of touch with Lee, had reached Carlisle on his raid north and now it was southern cavalrymen who fanned out in front of the advancing Federal militia.

On 1 July, as the opening shots were fired of what would be the greatest battle fought on American soil, the New York militiamen and the Pennsylvania amateur cannoneers were brought up short by volleys from Confederate cavalry carbines. Firing grew quite sharp as the Federal infantrymen, supported by Alister's battery, advanced. Slowly, the Confederates, whose carbines were no match for the long-arms of the infantry, withdrew, fighting from house to house and fence to fence. By the end of the day the Federals were on the edge of the town, with the Confederates still holding the town centre. In all the Federals had casualties of a dozen men wounded. None of them were cannoneers.

On 2 July Stuart, finally learning of Lee's situation at Gettysburg, withdrew south. The Federal militiamen were in possession of Carlisle and were quite content to let Stuart's cavalry withdraw as they wished.

The battery remained in Carlisle as the fierce fighting continued to their south. On 4 July, a day after Lee had been fought to a standstill at Gettysburg, the battery was ordered to join the rest of the army around his lines. That night it rained again and movement was slow. On 5 July Lee began his withdrawal, the rain continuing on and off as it would for several days. A day later the Union Army of the Potomac began its slow pursuit. The battery followed, ending up at Hagerstown, Maryland, where it was halted.

On 28 July the battery was notified that it would soon be mustered out of service. A regular army officer inspected and signed for all its guns and equipment, and turned them over to another battery which had just arrived from Chambersburg without any equipment. Then the men boarded a railroad train for Harrisburg. They spent the evening of 28 July in Harrisburg, leaving for Philadelphia on 29 July.

The battery was mustered out of Federal service in Philadelphia on 30 July 1863, the men sent back to their homes. Alister apparently went directly to the photographic firm of Wendertoth & Taylor at Ninth and Chestnut Streets. There he had himself photographed as a fighting man, complete with mud on his trouser legs. He had done his bit, and probably bored friends at clubs such as the Union League for years with his war stories.

NOTES

1   Logan, John A., *The Volunteer Soldier of America*, Chicago, 1887, p. 130
2   ibid, p. 78
3   Wainwright, Nicholas B., *A Philadelphia Perspective*, Philadelphia, 1967, p. 384
4   Winey, Michael J., 'Landis' Philadelphia Battery of Light Artillery, 1863', *Military Collector & Historian*, Vol. XXVI, No. 4, p. 231
5   McElroy, A., *McElroy's Philadelphia City Directory for 1863*, Philadelphia, 1863, p. 299
6   Wainwright, op. cit., p. 150
7   Kautz, August V., *Customs of Service*, Philadelphia, 1864, pp. 61–3
8   Conrad, W. P. and Ted Alexander, *When War Passed This War*, Greencastle, Pennsylvania, 1982, p. 83
9   Weigley, Russell F., ed., *Philadelphia, A 300-Year History*, New York, 1982, p. 408.
10 Freeman, Douglas S., *Lee's Lieutenants*, New York, 1944, Vol. 3, p. 28
11 Casler, John O, *Four Years in the Stonewall Brigade*, Dayton, Ohio, 1994, pp. 180–1
12 McDonald, Archie P., *Make Me a Map Of the Valley*, Dallas, Texas, 1973, p. 155
13 Wingate, G. W., *History of the 22nd Regiment, N.G.S.N.Y.*, New York, 1896, p. 161
14 Winey, op. cit., p. 231
15 Nye, Wilber S., *Here Come the Rebels!*, Baton Rouge, Louisiana, 1965, p. 161

8

William Raymond Lee
Colonel, 20th Massachusetts Volunteer Infantry Regiment

While the bulk of all the fighting in the Civil War was done by amateurs – men torn from civilian life into the sudden ups and down of military existence – the top ranks were mainly filled by men who had been professional soldiers at some point before the war, trained at the US Military Academy at West Point, New York.

The Academy was unusual among service schools around the world in that its graduates were not only made regular army officers but also received the degree of Bachelor of Science in engineering after completing the school's four-year course. Engineering was initially emphasised to provide a new, growing country with engineers to build its canals, roads and tunnels, as well as its fortifications.

There were two cadets named Lee in the class of 1829 of the US Military Academy. One, named Robert Edward, graduated second in his class. The other was William Raymond Lee, Jnr.

The new cadets who entered the stone-walled Academy in 1825 were immediately marched off to get equipment and then onto what was known as 'the Plain', where they would spend several months in tents learning the basics of military discipline and drill, as well as practical tips such as using ashes from their fires to polish their brass belt plates and buttons until they shone like new gold. Discipline was harsh, designed to weed out those who could not stay the course. Many of the young men were away from home for the first time, and experienced a new feeling, homesickness.

On their return to the barracks in September they had to pass a physical examination and then be grilled by an Academic Board to determine if they were ready for the classroom work that would follow.

Once classwork began, life fell into a routine. At the frequent formations, every cadet had to be spotlessly turned out or face receiving a demerit. In a day of universally long hair, failure to get a haircut every month would earn such a demerit. Too many demerits bought the cadet a ticket on the next train to New York and back to civilian life. Meals were eaten formally, and were followed by classes that began at eight and ended at four on weekdays and noon on Saturdays. Class sizes were limited to some fifteen cadets, each of whom had to recite some part of the lessons every day.

On weekdays, classes were followed by infantry, artillery and cavalry drill. To learn leadership, the corps of cadets was divided into four companies, and cadets were appointed to the various responsible posts. Senior fourth-year cadets became the officers, including the adjutant and quartermaster. The third-year juniors became the sergeants, while corporals were taken from the second-year (sophomore) class. Freshmen, or 'Plebes' as they were called, were all privates. Not all classmen worked to obtain such an appointment. Jubal Early, a member of the class of 1837, wrote:

'I was not a very exemplary soldier and went through the Academy without receiving any appointment as a commissioned or non-commissioned officer in the corps of cadets. I had very little taste for scrubbing brass and cared very little for the advancement to be obtained by the exercise of that most useful art.'[1]

William T. Sherman, who later made something of a name for himself in the Union Army, had much the same experience as a member of the class of 1836:

'At the Academy I was not considered a good soldier, for at no time was I selected for any office, but remained a private throughout the whole four years. Then, as now, neatness in dress and form, with a strict conformity to the rules, were the qualifications required for office, and I suppose I was found not to excel in any of these.'[2]

Although classwork was centred around the two essential areas of engineering and military expertise, the range of subjects was broad. The cadets studied geometry, mensuration, trigonometry, geography, history, English, French, fencing, 'Natural and Experimental Philosophy' [physics], Spanish, 'moral science', chemistry, history of philosophy and logic, chemistry, drawing, civil and military engineering, law, history, mineralogy and geology, ordnance and gunnery, and practical engineering. Out of class, the cadets were taught riding, starting in the second year, and the purely military arts of infantry, cavalry and artillery drill.

For some cadets this course came relatively easily. Ulysses S. Grant, a member of the class of 1843, wrote:

'I did not take hold of my studies with avidity, in fact I rarely ever read over a lesson the second time during my entire cadetship. I never succeeded in getting squarely at either end of my class, in any one study, during the four years. I came near it in French, artillery, infantry and cavalry tactics, and conduct.'[3]

Others had a much harder time. Thomas J. Jackson was seen many hours after the sounding of lights out lying in front of his fireplace, face buried in a text book. Generally slow in learning and lacking a sound foundation of education before he arrived, he survived only by dogged determination – something he would later bring to the battlefield.

The four years at the Academy, however, did not entail an endless round of grinding work. There were diversions. Grant recalled spending many hours in the library, reading the latest trashy novels. Others strolled the many trails in the area. It became quite a tactical practice for small groups of cadets to sneak off Academy ground to a nearby tavern owned by Benny Havens for an evening of drinking and eating food not found in the mess hall. The summer of the sophomore year brought a furlough, the first time off for two years, and cadets who could not travel all the way back home often visited New York and the homes of fellow cadets. Summers also brought dances, called 'hops', in which daughters of officers on the post and ladies from New York spent pleasant evenings with the cadets. Relationships ending in marriage were often started at these hops.

There were close relationships, too, among the cadets, who had spent so many gruelling hours both in the classroom and on the parade field. William became acquainted not only with fellow classmate Robert E. Lee, but also with Jefferson Davis who was in the class above his own; with William Pendleton, in the class below, who would become the Army of Northern Virginia's chief of artillery; and with Andrew Humphreys, of the class of 1831, who would be on General George B. McClellan's staff. In a way, attendance at the Academy by leaders on both sides made the war something of an 'old boys' network'.

Shortly before graduating, however, William was forced to drop out of school. This was not unusual. In all, of the cadets admitted in 1825, forty-six were graduated and fifty-three failed to do so, dropping out earlier. There were a number of reasons why one might have to leave the Academy before receiving the diploma and commission as a second lieutenant. Some of William's class, for example, were involved in the so-called 'Christmas Eve riot' in 1826. One of those was Benjamin Humphreys who returned home to enter politics, becoming a US senator before the war and a Confederate brigadier general during it. Some cadets gathered too many demerits. Others failed to stay with the difficult academic programme. There was no disgrace in failing to last the course. Indeed, ex-cadets received a form of diploma stating that they had attended the Academy but had not graduated.

William's reason for dropping out of the Academy, however, had nothing to do with misbehaviour, studies or demerits. His father suffered what doctors of the time called a 'brain attack', something that today would be known as a mental breakdown, and disappeared. William resigned, only two weeks short of receiving his diploma and commission, in order to search for his father.

Some of those cadets who failed to graduate still managed eventually to get a commission in the regular army, while others proceeded to civilian occupations. Many went into professional life but still maintained some interest in the military. Others joined volunteer militia regiments formed by different state governments and served in action, especially in the Mexican War.

After locating his father, William actually returned to the army and saw service in the Seminole War. But his career was obviously damaged by his early departure from the Academy, and he soon left the regular army. He then went to work as a civil engineer and a railroad superintendent. In 1861, at the outbreak of the Civil War, he was fifty-six, older than most men who volunteered to serve in active campaigning units, and working in Virginia as a civil engineer.

When war was declared, William returned immediately to Boston, the capital city of his native state of Massachusetts. There he offered his services as a professionally trained soldier to the state's governor, as did so many ex-West Pointers. He was immediately given the job of raising and training one of the state's infantry regiments. On 1 July 1861 he was commissioned colonel of the 20th Massachusetts Volunteer Infantry Regiment, then forming in Camp Massoit, Readville. William was now earning a salary of $95 a month, plus six daily issued rations for himself and his servant, and forage for four horses.

William's uniform included a double-breasted dark blue frock coat with gold-edged shoulder straps featuring a silver eagle, its wings spread, on a sky-blue background. He sometimes wore a single-breasted company-grade officer's coat as well as the regulation model. Trousers were initially dark blue with a sky-blue welt, but following a change of regulations in December trousers were sky-blue with a dark blue welt down each leg. The dress hat was a wide-brimmed black felt hat with black feathers and a gold-embroidered infantry horn encircling a silver number 20 on the front and a gold-embroidered national coat of arms on the side. A dark blue wool forage cap with a black leather peak and chinstrap was worn for fatigue duties, officially with the same badge, although William wore his cap unadorned. His personal weapons were a 'general and field grade officers sword', which was slightly heavier than the company-grade model and featured the Roman letters US within its hilt.

The 20th, its cadre being mustered in on 21 July, slowly took shape under his experienced eye. It was the colonel, more than any other single individual, who moulded the regiment. He it was who would lead by example, inspiring both officers and men. The colonel was also responsible for teaching his novice officers basics of Army Regulations, infantry tactics and whatever else it took to run a regiment. In another volunteer regiment, the adjutant later recalled of its first camp:

'Schools of instruction for officers were organised and kept up at various periods subsequently during the term of service. The instruction for officers was mainly devoted to the school of the company, and occupied one or more evenings each week. The school for officers was conducted by Col. H. R. Guss, during the early period of the service, and subsequently by Maj. G. Pennypacker.'[4]

This training included not only material found in books but actual parade-ground practice. According to the standard infantry manual, 'The instruction of officers can be perfected only by joining theory to practice. The colonel will often practise them in marching and in estimating distances, and he will carefully endeavor to cause them to take steps equal in length and swiftness. They will also be exercised in the double quick step.'[5] William, with his West Point education, would have been a natural instructor for a bunch of green officers. One of his officers later recalled, 'Very strict discipline was enforced through the entire regiment, – it was demanded by Colonel Lee of all the officers, and by them of all the men.'[6]

William was nevertheless sufficiently intelligent to realise that he was in command of volunteers who would not put up with the harsh discipline of the period regular army, and he treated his men with respect. For example, one of his company officers wrote home:

'Col. Lee always wanted to be very liberal in religious matters. So he assembled the regt. & instructed them that prayers would be read every Sunday, but that nobody should be forced to go... Well, that worked very well for some time, till finally the audiences became very slim & dwindled down to about sixty. Still, my company all turned out because they knew their officers wanted them to. Finally there were 3 one Sunday who didn't fall in. Of course, one couldn't do any thing directly, after Col. Lee's order, so I made the 3 do all the water carrying during the services & for an hour or two afterwards. And since then nobody in my company has availed himself of the col's. permission to stay away from religious service...'[7]

Of course, it was possible for William to do because the 20th, nick-named 'The Harvard Regiment' because of the unusually large number of graduates from that college in its officer ranks, was of a higher quality than many other volunteer regiments. Its members were drawn from across the state, rather than just one location, with the exception of Co. I, which mostly consisted of fishermen and sailors from Nantucket Island.

The colonel would also make sure that the approved regimental sutler did not charge much above fair prices and did not sell items such as liquor which was not approved for sale in some places. His regiment had two sutlers at different times, Frank S. Ruggles and P. H. Griswald.

William's immediate task was to get the regiment ready for action, and that entailed drill, drill and more drill. Every man had his particular place in line and in column and was taught to act immediately on hearing appropriate commands. William, as well as his other officers, had to learn the correct command for every situation that might arise on the field. In battle the actions of up to a thousand men were entirely dictated by one man – the colonel. 'Every colonel will labor to habituate his battalion to form line of battle, by night as well as by day, with the greatest possible promptitude,' began the standard infantry drill manual of the day.[8] William himself was to drill the regiment while mounted and would ordinarily be posted some thirty paces to the rear of the file closers and opposite the centre of the battalion.

Because of the lack of time and need for immediate combat-readiness, the nuances of the complete drill manual were often ignored. A British Guards officer, observing the Army of the Potomac in late 1863, reported:

'They take evident pride in their drill, and do their best to show themselves to advantage in this respect; and though the movements I saw were slow, and always confined to marching past and deploying from a double column of companies into line and *vice versa,* they were more steadily executed than I expected, – quite equal, I should say to those of our own Volunteers at home.'[9]

Eventually the regiment was organised and both officers and men provided with at least a rudimentary understanding of company and battalion drill. On 4 September 1861 the 20th, although still one-third under-strength, marched out of camp and on to war. Its route was through New York, Philadelphia and Baltimore. Arriving at Washington on 15 September, it was forwarded to the Upper Potomac as part of a division led by Brigadier General Edward Stone. William now would be the second oldest officer in what was shortly to be known as the Army of the Potomac, junior only to sixty-four-year-old Brigadier General Edwin V. Sumner.

Captain Frank Bartlett, one of the company commanders, led the march to the new post along the Potomac. In a letter home he mentions the attention to detail and consideration for his men that William, as a good colonel, exemplified: 'I led the column at a smart step until the Colonel rode up and said that the men were complaining of having to march too fast, and asked for an easier gait. We slackened up.'[10]

Once in position, William had to acquire intelligence of the force that faced him across the river. Bartlett described how he did this:

'The Colonel was down at the river today with General Stone, and got one of our pickets to made advances to his neighbor opposite, and draw him into a conversation across the river. They kept in the background, and listened to the dialogue, which of course wasn't in a whisper. The rebel said they had two or three hundred cavalry there, and only one or two batteries. Of course their information goes for what it is worth. But it seems rather laughable, the whole thing.'[11]

The scouting had a purpose. The overall army commander, Major General George B. McClellan, ordered William's divisional commander, Major General Charles P. Stone, to make a diversion along the Potomac River. Stone ordered a brigade under Colonel Edward D. Baker, a politician with little military experience, to cross the river towards Leesburg, Virginia. Hearing reports that there was a Confederate camp near Leesburg, Baker sent the 15th Massachusetts across the river, ordering William to have a company of the 20th prepared to cover the 15th as it returned from its raid. William followed the 15th with Companies E and I of the 20th.

As it turned out, Union scouts were mistaken in their location of a Confederate camp. Moreover, their activities attracted Confederate notice, and soon an entire southern infantry brigade hustled out of Leesburg towards the 15th. Baker ordered the rest of his brigade forward, although with only a couple of small boats available, crossing the Potomac took time. It was not until half past noon, 21 October, that some 300 officers and men of the 20th, under William's command, were formed into line of battle along the bluffs overlooking the river. Before them lay an open field edged by heavy woods. The rest of the regiment was ordered to remain on the Maryland side of the river.

William was on the scene before Baker, who remained behind to oversee the river passage. Soon, however, William was told that Baker was on hand. He later recalled:

'I turned around, and a military officer on horseback presented himself, and bowed very politely, and said: "I congratulate you upon the prospect of a battle." I bowed, and said: "I suppose you assume command." I knew it was Colonel Baker.'[12]

Baker may have been an outstanding politician, but he lost any control of the battle almost from the beginning. He simply ordered the Federals to remain in line facing the woods as Confederate fire tore gaps in their ranks. At one point he rode up to William, whose regiment held the right of the line, and asked the Massachusetts man how he liked the battle. William replied that he expected the main battle would be on the Federal left. Making no reply, Baker rode off, soon to fall, mortally wounded. By then dusk was approaching. Seeing Baker dead and the entire Union force about to be overwhelmed, William told his company officers that he thought they should fall back.

Knowing that crossing the river on the two boats would be slow, William assembled a small force of men from the 20th, the 15th and the 71st Pennsylvania to form a line to cover the retreat.

Before this could happen, one of the other colonels assumed command and tried to move the troops to the right, in an attempt to reach a ford upriver. A Mississippi regiment soon blocked that move. The troops, many of them by now panic-stricken, ran back towards the river and tried to get across. William, lying partly protected by a dead horse, remained behind to organise a covering party. One company commander later recalled:

'I went to the Colonel and he was sitting behind a tree, perfectly composed. He told me there was nothing to be done but "surrender and save the men from being murdered". Most of the men had now got down the bank... When we got back to the bank we induced the Colonel to go down and try to escape. The Adjutant took his left arm and I his right, and we got him down to the bank unhurt. Here was a horrible scene. Men crowded together, the wounded and the dying. The water was full of human beings, struggling with each other and the water, the surface of which looked like a pond when it rains, from the withering volleys that the enemy were pouring down from the top of the bank. Those who were not drowned ran the chance of being shot. I turned back and left the Colonel, to collect the remnant of my company, and when I returned he was gone.'[13]

In fact, deciding that there was no safe way across the river, William and Major Paul Revere of his regiment attempted to work their way along the bank upriver to reach the ford where a crossing was feasible. However, they were spotted by a Confederate cavalry patrol and soon on their way to Leesburg where surviving prisoners of the battle were being gathered. At that early stage of the war captured enemy officers were still treated fairly well. William and his fellow officers relished a plate of beefsteak, with bread and preserves, and coffee – a meal for which they were duly charged by the hotel in which they were held. The next day they were marched south, reaching Richmond on 24 October.

The Confederates were generally unprepared for a major war, but were especially ill-prepared for large numbers of prisoners-of-war. Improvising, they rented an old tobacco warehouse, a large, three-storey brick building in Richmond, to house Federal officers. On arrival there, William was issued with a tin plate and cup, a cotton coverlet and five yards of brown muslin which he was to sew into a bag and fill with straw for a mattress. He would then find an empty spot on the floor to place his mattress. His captors also gave him the opportunity to buy a spoon, fork and knife. An officer of the 71st Pennsylvania, who was at Libby Prison at the same time as William, described the prison:

'In the center of the officers' floor is placed the machinery for pressing and preparing tobacco, dividing it into two equal sections, – the western end being used for eating and writing purposes, the eastern for promenading and sleeping. Ten mess-tables, made of rough pine boards, and a number of wooden benches and stools, occupy the main portion of the western division; and the floor is well covered in the eastern by bedsteads and cots of Southern and prison manufacture.'[14]

Days passed slowly. The routine included a roll-call at eight in the morning, followed by a great deal of nothing to do save wait for meals. This early in the war, there was still sufficient food in Richmond to allow William and his fellow prisoners adequate fare. Breakfast, served at nine, included fresh beef and five ounces of bread. Dinner was served at noon and also comprised boiled or roast beef with five ounces of bread. Supper, consisting of a further five ounces of bread, arrived at six. In addition, prisoners were allowed to buy such delicacies as butter, coffee, tea, molasses and potatoes, prepared by hired cooks. 'Lights out' was at nine. William was a favourite among the prisoners, as one of his fellows recalled:

'At the lower end of the room, we see the slight but agile figure of Colonel Lee, of the 20th Massachusetts Regiment, (taken at Ball's Bluff,) who is earnestly engaged in conversation with two visitors, one of whom is the Episcopal Bishop of Virginia, the other a divine of note from the same State. Colonel Lee has a warmth and an earnestness of manner which endear him not only to his brother-officers, but interest all who come within the sound of his genial voice. He is beloved by the junior officers of his command, – four of whom are prisoners here, having preferred to share his fate rather than desert him when the hard-fought field was lost.'[15]

William, however, was soon to become a pawn in period politics. On 6 July 1861 an armed vessel with a letter of marque, the *Jefferson Davis*, captured a northern merchant schooner off the coast of Delaware. That schooner, the *Enchantress*, was then manned with a prize crew and sent back south, only to be intercepted by the USS *Albatross*. The prize master and the rest of his crew were tried in Philadelphia on charges of piracy and sentenced to death. On 10 November, the Confederate government selected, by lottery, a number of Union officers held in Richmond to share the fate of the southern privateers. William, along with six other colonels and the 20th's Major Revere, were among this group. A first sergeant of the 20th, learning of William's sentence, asked him if there were anything that he could do. 'No, Sergeant,' William replied, 'all I want now is your best wishes.'

GEORGE W. ADAMS

Right: Captain George W. Adams, 8th Indiana Infantry, as photographed by S. Anderson, 61 Camp St., New Orleans. George wears a half chevron over his Austrian knot on each cuff, indicating his regiment's veteran status.

DAVID BARNETT

Below: Infantry moves up towards Kelly's Ford in this *Harper's Weekly* engraving. David Barnett is among them.

Left: David Alva Barnett photographed when still a corporal. He wears a private's be plate; he should, by regulations, wear a rectangular brass plate with a silver wreath on its front.

Below: A typical scene of an infantry company resting in the field. Within minutes some men would break out a deck of cards for gambling, while others would read letters or just chat quietly. (Library of Congress)

Left: This ward in the Armory Square Hospital in Washington was something like the ward into which David Barnett found himself after Kelly's Ford. Note the amputees, one in his wheel chair. Eli Nichols would have served at a Washington area hospital at some time while in the Veteran Reserve Corps. (Library of Congress)

JERRY J. BENSON

Right: Jerry J. Benson was photographed by F. Gutekunst, 704 & 706 Arch Street in Philadelphia, probably while assigned to duty on a cutter that patrolled the Delaware River.

FRANK CASE

Left: Clara and Frank Case were photographed by J. Fryder, 171 Superior Street, Cleveland, Ohio during his leave home after being promoted to the rank of captain.

DAVID COLE

Below: Soldiers from other than the Corps of Engineers admired the winter quarters laid down by Corps members which included corduroyed side walks. Note the black man, probably an officer's servant, who had acquired a soldier's cap and blouse. (Library of Congress)

Left: David Cole was photographed at the Beardsley Brothers' Gallery of Art, 73 Owego St., Ithaca, New York, with the standing collar of his frock coat turned down.

Right: David Cole's company of the 50th New York Volunteer Engineer Regiment spent most of its time in the 1864 campaign to Petersburg building pontoon bridges such as this one across the North Anna River. (Library of Congress)

Right: In a pinch, pontoons could be used as assault craft loaded, as here, with infantry and artillery. (Library of Congress)

Above: Engineers lay a pontoon bridge. It may have looked like mass confusion, but the well-practised volunteer engineers all knew what they were doing and could assemble such a bridge rather quickly.

Below: Once the active campaign of 1864 finished, volunteer engineers were put to work building lines of entrenchments facing Lee's men defending Petersburg. The large wicker baskets called gabions line the walls of Fort Sedgewick in that ring of fortifications. (Library of Congress)

GEORGE COLE

Right: George Cole was photographed wearing the chevrons and arcs of a sergeant major by Miller & Rowell, 335 Washington St., Boston.

A. MACALISTER GRANT

Left: A. MacAlister Grant had himself photographed by Wenderoth & Taylor, 912–196 Chestnut St., Philadelphia, right after returning from the Gettysburg campaign, complete with mud on his trousers.

WILLIAM RAYMOND LEE

Left: William Raymond Lee wears a single-breasted company-grade officer's coat and holds a McDowell-style forage cap with a plain infantry officer's badge, lacking his regimental number. Other photographs show him with the regulation coat.

WILLIAM P. McCANN

Below: Some of the officers and men of William McCann's ship, the U.S.S. *Hunchback*. Note the obvious social differences between enlisted and commissioned personnel. Naval crews were racially integrated on the enlisted level during the Civil War. (Library of Congress)

Right: William P. McCann wears the star of an executive officer over his rank badge on each cuff, as well as a boat cape in this photograph made by Silsbee, Case & Co., 299½ Washington St., Boston.

WILLIAM S. MUSE

Right: William S. Muse had himself photographed in Lima, Peru, while serving with the Pacific Squadron.

Right: While a corporal dusts off his first sergeant, probably preparing to go on duty, the other men in this scene of winter quarters spend their off-duty time in usual ways, cleaning equipment, chopping wood, cleaning up, playing practical jokes, or just sitting about. (Library of Congress)

Below: A company of US Marines at the Marine Barracks in Washington. Here William Muse would have received his commission, bought his first uniform and equipment, and learned the rudiments of his new profession.

ELI NICHOLS

Left: Eli Nichols was photographed by Baum & Burdine, 'near the Capital,' in Washington while in the Veteran Reserve Corps, whose sky-blue jacket trimmed with dark blue he wears.

MARSHALL F. PRICE

Right: Marshall F. Price, photographed by E. A. Stein in Ravenna, Ohio, wears the major's uniform authorised for surgeons, with an Old English U.S. within a gold wreath for a badge on his slouch hat. The hat cords are mixed black and gold.

CHARLES B. ROHAN

Far right: Charles B. Rohan presented this photograph produced by Port Hudson, Louisiana, photographer A. I. Blauvelt, to a friend.

HENRY SLEEPER

Above: This engraving of Henry Sleeper appeared in the 9 July 1864 edition of *Harper's Weekly*, along with a brief write-up of the man and his unit.

Left:: Henry Sleeper was photographed by R. W. Addis, 308 Pennsylvania Avenue, in Washington. Addis was one of the more active photographers of soldiers during the war.

Below: A sketch artist for *Harper's Weekly* caught the action at Kelly's Ford as Henry Sleeper's battery fires over the heads of David Barnett's charging infantry regiment.

WINSOR BRUCE SMITH

Right: Winsor Bruce Smith's father, Benjamin, photographed him in his corporal's jacket while he was on leave. Benjamin Smith's studio was at 91 Middle St., Portland, Maine.

Below: Winsor Smith's regiment, the 1st Maine Cavalry, was sketched in skirmish line. Out of every four men, three would advance on the firing line, while the fourth man took care of all four horses, holding them in the rear.

LYMAN B. SWEENEY

Left: Lyman Sweeney's photograph was a tintype, a direct impression on a piece of photo-sensitive plated iron which was then placed into a cardboard holder so it could be placed in an album. It was made, according to a notation apparently in his hand, when he was stationed near Winchester.

Below: An homage to the Signal Corps as it appeared in *Harper's Weekly*. The signalman waving the flag has one with a star, awarded to individuals who had demonstrated bravery in action.

Above: Northern publications such as *Harper's Weekly* certainly played up the miserable conditions in southern prison camps, such as at Belle Island here, but the death of Lyman Sweeney from starvation in Camp Lawton indicates they may not have been that far off the mark.

JOHN THOMAS

Right: John Thomas, seated, was photographed by Charles W. Higgs, 190 Fulton St., Brooklyn, New York, near the US Navy Yard there. His friend, standing, was Seaman Joseph Lang.

CHARLES J. TROTTER

Left: Charles J. Trotter was photographed by B. Moses whose studio was located on the corner of Canal and Camp Streets in New Orleans. He wear the rank insignia of a first assistant engineer.

Below: Charles Trotter's boat, the *Chillicothe,* was saved by an army officer when it was grounded by low water on the Red River. The soldier suggested building a dam, then releasing the boats unable to cross the bar when the water rose high enough. An artist from *Frank Leslie's Illustrated News* caught the scene as one of the rams floats to safety.

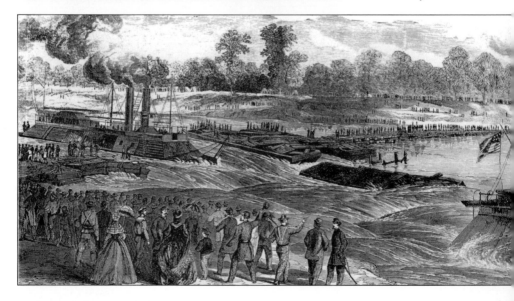

'You not only have my best wishes, but the best wishes of all the regiment,' the sergeant replied. William almost broke down, then cleared his throat and replied, 'Tell the men...' Again he had to clear his throat. 'Tell the men that their colonel died like a brave man.'[16]

It proved unnecessary. Faced with the difficult situation, the Federal government backed down and simply made the southern crew prisoners-of-war. William and the other hostages were returned to the general prison population.

The officers and men of the 20th missed William in his absence. 'I wish to God Col. Lee were back or Frank Bartlett had command,' one officer wrote home on 9 April 1862.[17] Another officer on returning from leave wrote home on 25 March, 'Don't like the look of things under [Lieutenant Colonel Francis] Palf.[rey] wish Lee was here.'[18]

William would not have to stay long in Libby. Fairly early on, the two sides began exchanging individual prisoners-of-war on an equal rank basis. On 23 February 1862 he was exchanged for the Confederate Colonel Robert F. Baldwin, 31st Virginia Militia Regiment, who had been captured at Romney, West Virginia, in February 1862. Oddly enough, William and Colonel Baldwin had been born in the same year. William returned to Boston, first on parole to await official exchange, on 28 February. On 1 May 1862 William finally rejoined his happy regiment. 'Didn't you jump up and clap your hands when you heard that Col. Lee had got back?' an officer wrote home on 8 May.[19] Later, on 18 May, the same man wrote home:

'Col. Lee is enormously popular with the regiment. He certainly has a charm of conciliating every body about him. All old cliques surrender to him unconditionally. Besides, it is so good to see the head officer work just as hard as his subordinates, always up before any body, & 3 o'clock in the morning is no joke for a man who, though not very old, has suffered so many hardships. Some days, too, he has been in his saddle all day long, so stiff at night that he can hardly get off.'[20]

William arrived just in time for the next major engagement of the Army of the Potomac – McClellan's Peninsula Campaign. The 20th had departed with the army on 27 March, before William returned, and was some five miles from Yorktown by 6 April. Outside Yorktown, where McClellan fell prey to his fears of enemy superiority, the Federals dug in for a formal siege. The 20th went into line, there to be joined by their missing colonel. On 4 May, the badly outnumbered Confederates retreated and the 20th entered their works. On 6 May the regiment was sent by water to a spot on the Pamunkey River above West Point, and then moved westward. It was brigaded with the 106th Pennsylvania, with William acting as brigade commander. On 31 May he led his troops across the Chickahominy by the Grapevine Bridge into the action later known as Fair Oaks.

The Confederates had driven back Federals ahead of the 20th as William led his men on through thick woods and thicker mud. 'Our men showed wonderful discipline, firing & ceasing to fire just as they were ordered,' a 20th company commander wrote home. 'The col. lt. col. & all the officers showed great presence of mind & gallantry.' William, mounted for the attack, led from the front, as colonels were expected to do, the officer adding, 'Over the fence we went, when the little col. bolted ahead, & I was afraid he would come to grief, but, thank God, he didn't.'[21] In the tangled underbrush and sloppy ground, however, William's horse fell, and he suffered bruises and sore muscles from the accident. The regiment halted where it was, darkness filling the woods with deep gloom, the men lying on their arms on the wet ground. The next day the regiment was placed in the reserve.

But the campaign, as far as a Union offensive was concerned, was drawing to a close. On 25 June Lee struck in what became known as the Seven Days Campaign. McClellan, psychologically if not physically beaten, withdrew to his base on Harrison's Landing on the James River, giving up his offensive. The 20th set up camp there.

The battle, the weather and the accident with his horse had combined to damage William's health. In order to recuperate, on 3 July he received a leave of absence of twenty days. His orders, dated 11 July, instructed him to 'report in person to the governor of Massachusetts to assist in raising new regiments of volunteers until his health is sufficiently restored to enable him to join his regiment'.[22] He was not alone in leaving the regiment: One company officer wrote home on 10 August 1862, 'We have, however, only 11 company officers & 1 field officer for duty....The small number of officers in the regiment has made the work too hard for them.'[23]

On 16 August the 20th left Harrison's Landing, reaching Newport News on 22 August. Three days later the men boarded the steamer *Collins* and sailed for Alexandria. They arrived there to form part of a force designed to assist John Pope's Army of Virginia on 28 August. From there they marched to Tenallytown, District of Columbia, and then south through Fairfax Court House. For two days they drew up in line of battle, a reserve for the beating Pope's army was getting at the Second Manassas. They watched as the rest of the army withdrew past them towards Washington, the 20th eventually receiving orders to retire back to Alexandria on 2 September.

Here, on 3 September, William finally rejoined the regiment. However, as senior colonel in the brigade, he immediately assumed command of the brigade and therefore did not have active charge of the 20th. This was not uncommon. Colonels often took over brigade command, while their brigadier generals were given division command or were otherwise absent. As a result, however, regimental colonels were often away from their regiments in combat situations. William, for his part, was able to return to regimental command after only a short time.

Now the Confederates went on the attack, crossing into Maryland. One wing of their army captured Harper's Ferry, while the rest passed near the small town of Sharpsburg near the Antietam creek. By a stroke of good fortune, a copy of Lee's marching orders fell into McClellan's hands. Working with what for him passed for remarkable speed, McClellan pushed his army towards Lee's divided forces. The 20th, again commanded by William, who felt he had recovered well enough for continued campaign life, had been assigned to the Third Brigade, Second Division, II Corps. The regiment pressed over the mountain around to the Union right, where McClellan had drawn up a vice around apparently trapped Confederates at Sharpsburg.

Yet again, however, McClellan mishandled the battle. His plans called for a general assault, which would have overwhelmed the thin Confederate lines. In fact, the attacks came piecemeal, hours apart, and Lee was able to use his interior lines to rush troops around from one threatened point to another. First to attack had been I Corps. To its left, II Corps was ordered to support the attack at 7.30 in the morning.

A wounded officer, on his way back to a field hospital, saw the corps, including William's men, on their way into the fray:

'A little further on and I saw lines of our men hurrying to the front; they were already deploying and preparing to advance to the fight "What troops are those?" "That is Sumner's Corps" was the reply. "Glorious" I thought "they know how to fight," but O, what a pity they were not on hand sooner! Now they must fight over a part of that field we had gained and have lost or are fast losing! that ghastly cornfield must be crossed again with bayonet charging! and thousands more must add their blood to the already reaking earth! "Hurry on" I said to myself. Every minute you lose is an hour to the rebels.'[24]

The Third Brigade, with the 20th second from the left in line of battle, moved out 75 yards behind the attacking line. Passing through some woods, the brigade came under sudden fire from the left that broke up many of the formations. The brigade commander, hit by a musket ball, had to retire, first leaving word to Colonel Norman J. Hall of the 7th Michigan to rally the troops and bring them back up. According to Hall:

'In a field behind the woods I found Colonel Lee with his regiment, Twentieth Massachusetts Volunteers, in perfectly good order and with very full ranks. I informed Colonel Lee that he was in command of the brigade, being my senior; but he positively declined to relieve me, and repeatedly desired me to give such orders as I saw fit, and he would obey them. I reported this immediately to General Howard, commanding the division, and he directed me to continue in command.'[25]

In the meantime, William received orders to send his regiment to the support of an artillery battery coming under infantry attack. He did so, the 20th effectively withdrawing from further offensive action with the rest of the brigade. There it came under intensive enemy artillery fire. The regimental surgeon was killed while helping the wounded; a number of other officers, including Oliver Wendell Holmes, Jnr, were wounded. William, however, managed to escape unhurt. The brigade commander was wounded, and William, on 18 September, again assumed command of the brigade that consisted of only 960 men after the fierce fighting.

But William's age and the wear and tear of campaigning life was getting to him physically. One of his officers later recalled:

'Colonel Lee suffered a great deal from the various illnesses of camp brought on by exposure to wet and cold, for he would not claim the privileges of age, and so avoid anything to which younger men might be exposed with impunity. He refused to shirk any duty or take a leave of absence, saying that if he could not do his whole duty he would do none, but would resign.'[26]

Worse, the strain appears to have affected him mentally. 'Col. Lee (strictly private) is undoubtedly very much shaken in his intellects, at any rate at times,' one of his captains wrote home on 20 November. The officer went on to describe an incident shortly after he took command of the brigade on 18 September:

'One of the col's. crazy things while in command of the brigade is rather ludicrous. Somebody came in & told the col. that one of [Brigadier General Willis] Gorman's aides accused this brigade of running shamefully at Antietam. The col. was raving. He exclaimed Gorman was responsible for his aides. He shall take back the calumny or fight me. Well, poor old Ropes (who was an aide of [the] col's.) was in an awful stew. The col. wouldn't listen to any remonstrances, but called for his horse, buckled his sword, to speed to Gorman's headquarters. Gorman, of course, denied the whole thing, saying in his own sweet way, "Sooner may the Lord tear my right arm from its socket & beat me about the head with the bloody stump, than allow me or my staff to say aught to tarnish the glory of the noble 3rd brigade." So the thing ended.'[27]

Such an incident suggests William was suffering from the condition known today (but then unknown) as Post Traumatic Stress Disorder, possibly brought on by the stress of command on a field such as Antietam, the bloodiest day of the war. It may well be, however, that in the light of family history, he was also prone to such mental problems. Another officer recalled a short excursion towards West Virginia on 16 October in which William again commanded a brigade:

'Poor, plucky Colonel Lee got into the saddle for this reconnaissance a sick man, passed two nights in rain and cold, without even a tent for shelter, and came back to camp dangerously sick, so that he was forced on the 21st to move into drier and warmer quarters in a house in town. He persisted in doing his duty, when he was physically unfit. He was so ill that his death was actually reported in camp on the 25th.'[28]

Finally, in October, William applied for leave of absence. Surgeon G. S. Palmer, the chief medical officer of his regiment's division, wrote a letter that accompanied his request:

'I hereby certify that I have carefully examined this officer, and find him suffering from bronchitis on account of which he is in my opinion unfit for duty. I further declare that in my opinion he will not be fit for duty in a less period than twenty days. And in order for him to prevent permanent disability it is best for him to go beyond the lines of this military district.'[29]

William returned to Boston where, on 4 November, he attended a dinner at Parker's, a well-known restaurant in the city, with other officers of the 20th recovering from various wounds or simply on leave. Less than two weeks later, however, he headed south again.

Even after this leave William still was not up to active command. He was examined by a medical officer in Washington and there received a medical certificate on 17 November 1862 that stated:

'He is suffering from *Bronchitis, Chronic Diarrhea*, and *General Debility*, following long confinement in the *prisons of the enemy*.

'Change of climate is necessary to recovery within a reasonable time.

And that, in consequence thereof, he is, in my opinion, unfit for duty. I further declare my belief that he will not be able to resume his duties in a less period than thirty days, without risk of permanent disability.'[30]

Although he returned to the army's camp near Falmouth, Virginia, by early December it was obvious that he could achieve little. Physically unable to command, he spent his time in hospital or his tent, turning over regimental command to others. Finally, Nathan Haward, the regimental surgeon, certified that William was 'permanently disabled'. Indeed, he was unable to lead the

20th in the useless assault on the Confederate defences at Fredericksburg, a captain commanding the regiment for the attempt. On 17 December 1862 William submitted his resignation: 'It is with great regret that I feel compelled, in consequence of ill health to tender my resignation, based on the above medical certificate.' On the same day Special Orders No. 60, Right Grand Division, officially noted the acceptance of William's resignation.[31]

The same officer who chuckled at William's mental condition wrote home on 21 December:

'Poor old Col. Lee is ... gone from ... us. It fairly made my heart ache to see the brave little fellow trying to do duty here. A single week of it would have killed him outright. He is certainly the model of a plucky English officer. When he went away he wouldn't have us officers told of it. He couldn't bear to bid us good bye. He fairly broke down & shed tears when he got into the ambulance which took him away. Holmes has written a very good address to him to express our feelings. I trust it will do something to comfort the gallant little colonel in showing him how much his officers love ... him.'[32]

Although gone, he was not forgotten by his old comrades in arms. On 22 June 1865, he received a commission as a brigadier general by brevet 'for distinguished conduct at the battle of Antietam, Maryland, and for gallant and meritorious services during the war'.[33] William lived until 1891.

NOTES

1 Early, Jubal A., *Narrative of the War Between the States*, Wilmington, North Carolina, 1989, p. xviii

2 Sherman, William T., *Memoirs of*, New York, 1990, p. 16

3 Grant, U. S., *Personal Memoirs of*, New York, 1952, pp. 14–15

4 Price, Isaiah, *History of the Ninety-Seventh Regiment, Pennsylvania Volunteer Infantry, during the War of the Rebellion, 1861–65*, Philadelphia, 1875, p. 76

5 Hardee, W. J., *Rifle and Light Infantry Tactics*, Philadelphia, 1861, Vol. II , p. 13

6 Bruce, George A., *The Twentieth Regiment of Massachusetts Volunteer Infantry 1861–1865*, Cambridge, Massachusetts, 1906, p. 18

7 Scott, Robert Garth, ed., *Fallen Leaves The Civil War Letters of Major Henry Livermore Abbott*, Kent, Ohio, 1991, p. 86

8 Hardee, op. cit., Vol. II, p. 5

9 No author given, *Montreal during the American Civil War*, Montreal, Canada, no date given, p. 56

10 Nielson, Jon M., ed., 'Debacle at Ball's Bluff,' *Civil War Times Illustrated*, January 1976

11 ibid

12 Lee, William, Testimony before the Joint Committee on the Conduct of the War, report of, 1863–6

13 Nielson, op. cit., pp. 32–3

14 Harris, William C., *Prison-Life in the Tobacco Warehouse at Richmond*, Philadelphia, 1862, p. 22

15 ibid, p. 51

16 Bruce, op. cit., p. 69

17 Scott, op. cit., p. 109
18 Howe, Mark De Wolfe, *Touched With Fire*, Cambridge, Massachusetts, 1946, p. 37
19 Scott, Robert Garth, ed., op. cit., p. 115
20 Scott, Robert Garth, ibid., p. 119
21 Scott, Robert Garth, ibid., pp. 127–8
22 Lee, William R., personnel record, National Archives, Washington, DC
23 Scott, Robert Garth, op cit., p. 134
24 Casey, James B., ed., 'The Ordeal of Adoniran Judson Warner,' *Civil War History*, September 1982, p. 230
25 *ORs*, Series I, Vol. XIX, Part 1, pp. 321–2
26 Bruce, George A., op cit., p. 177
27 Scott, Robert Garth, op cit., p. 143
28 Bruce, George A., op cit., p. 179
29 Lee, William R., op cit.,
30 ibid
31 ibid
32 Scott, Robert Garth, op cit., p. 154
33 Lee, William R., op cit.

William Lee's corps commander, the only man in the army older than Lee himself, was officially informed of the colonel's leave for twenty days with this letter. (National Archives)

9
William Penn McCann
Lieutenant Commander, US Navy

On 4 May 1830, in Paris, Kentucky, not far from Lexington, William Penn McCann was born to James Harvey and Jane R. McCann. Young William was not born to position or wealth. Although the land was rich, dotted with horse farms and old stone fences, most of its inhabitants were not. The most famous places in Paris were the Duncan Tavern, founded in 1788, and the Cane Ridge Meeting house, birthplace of the Disciples of Christ Church.

There were few avenues to an exciting life in Paris for a young man such as William, with his adventurous turn of mind. Finally he saw his chance in the Mexican War in 1846, when volunteers flocked to be mustered into the state's regiments. For some reason, however, William had decided on a naval career. At that time, there were two ways to a captain's stateroom on a warship. One, the traditional method, was to be appointed as a midshipman, and then ship aboard to learn the ropes. If lucky, he would accordingly be promoted. This practice may not have been ideal for the Navy. Herman Melville, the novelist who served on a pre-war US Navy man-of-war for several years as a seaman, later wrote:

'A very general modern impression seems to be, that, in order to learn the profession of a sea-officer, a boy can hardly be sent to sea too early. To a certain extent, this may be a mistake. Midshipmen sent into the Navy at a very early age are exposed to the passive reception of all the prejudices of the quarter-deck in favour of ancient usages, however useless or pernicious; those prejudices grow up with them, and solidify with their very bones. As they rise in rank, they naturally carry them up, whence the inveterate repugnance of many Commodores and Captains to the slightest innovations in the service, however salutary they may appear to landsmen.'[1]

Nonetheless, this was the way naval careers were traditionally begun. The other was by appointment to the new Naval Academy, which had just opened its doors in Annapolis, Maryland, in 1845. Either way, it was not easy to get a midshipman's appointment. Generally it took some family influence: a senior naval officer would persuade a long-time naval officer acquaintance to take his son or nephew on board as a midshipman. William somehow managed to get his appointment in 1848, the last year of the Mexican War. He was posted to the *Raritan*, which served during the war in the Gulf of Mexico and later in the South Pacific.

William would not be in for a pleasant or soft life as a midshipman. Melville recalled:

'The middies live by themselves in the steerage, where, nowadays, they dine off a table, spread with a cloth. Indeed, they are something like collegiate freshmen and sophomores, living in the college buildings, especially so far as the noise they make in their quarters is concerned. The steerage buzzes, hums, and swarms like a hive; or like an infant-school of a hot day, when the school-mistress falls asleep with a fly on her nose.'

The midshipmen varied considerably in age, older boys quite often picking on younger ones and generally making their lives miserable. A period description of naval life commented:

'Delicate boys, transferred, at a tender age, from the school-room, or luxurious parlor, to the steerage of a man-of-war, with its coarse fare and hard accommodations, its noise and riot, its loss of rest and fatiguing duty on deck, are full apt to wilt and wither, like the tender plant torn from its native earth and placed in a harder and more ungenial soil.' 2

As to their time on duty, continued Melville:

'These boys are sent to sea, for the purpose of making commodores; and in order to become commodores, many of them deem it indispensable forthwith to commence chewing tobacco, drinking brandy and water, and swearing at the sailors. As they are only placed on board a sea-going ship to go to school and learn the duty of a Lieutenant; and until qualified to act as such, have few or no special functions to attend to; they are little more, while midshipmen, then supernumeraries on board... As the only way to learn to command, is to learn to obey, the usage of a ship of war is such that the midshipmen are constantly being ordered about by the Lieutenants; though, without having assigned them their particular destinations, they are always going somewhere, and never arriving. In some things, they almost have a harder time of it than the seamen themselves. They are messengers and errand-boys to their superiors.' 3

There was much to learn of the mysteries of sailing ships. Much care was needed, when handling the sails, to use the wind to best advantage. William had to familiarise himself with navigational equipment such as quadrants, maps and navigational manuals, compasses and sextants. Midshipmen also received basic schooling, including mathematics and writing. And they had to learn, mostly through observation, the delicate balances of relationships aboard ships – the captain in splendid isolation in his stateroom and quarter-deck, the officers in the wardroom, and the men in the berth deck. A sure but delicate touch was required to keep content, if not happy, a crew of some 400 stuffed into a 175-foot-long frigate like the *Raritan*.

Some men remained midshipmen many years into adulthood, since there was no retirement system in the Navy and promotions were slow at best. William's tour on the *Raritan* ended in 1854 and he was ordered to the Naval Academy. The Academy differed in many respects from the Army's West Point. According to the Secretary of the Navy at the time of its foundation in 1845:

'The laws of the United States do not sanction a preliminary school for the Navy; they only provide for the instruction of officers who already are in the Navy. The pupils of the Naval School being, therefore, officers in the public service, will be liable at all times to be called from their studies and sent on public duty. Midshipmen, too, on their return from sea, at whatever season of the year, will be sent to the school.'[4]

Because of this arrangement, midshipmen were given examinations upon entrance to the Academy, and then posted to a class on the basis of their scores. Examinations covered mathematics, nautical astronomy, the theory of morals, international law, gunnery, the use of steam, Spanish and French. If they scored high enough, they were considered to be the equal of a senior cadet and permitted to skip any schooling. William, as one of such high scorers, had only a nine-months' course of study at the Academy before being again sent to sea. When he left he was promoted to the rank of passed midshipman, which entitled him to take a lieutenant's examination, which he sat on 15 June 1854.

Like most midshipmen from the Academy, William probably wanted to be assigned to a small ship. One graduate recalled in 1859:

'We very young men had the impression that small vessels were better calculated to advance us professionally, because, having fewer officers, deck duty might be devolved on us, either to ease the regular watch officers or in case of a disability. This prepossession extended particularly to brigs, of which the navy then had several. This was a pretty wild imagining, for I can hardly conceive any one intrusting such a vessel to a raw midshipman.'[5]

Instead of this 'dream assignment', William was sent, in 1854, to the *Independence*, a 1,891-ton frigate which had been commissioned in 1815 and was now part of the Pacific Squadron. Just over a year later, on 16 September 1855, he was promoted to the rank of lieutenant. One of the largest ships of its class, the *Independence* had originally been commissioned as a ship-of-the-line but had been razed to a frigate's configuration in 1837. The year William was posted to her she carried sixty guns, more than most American frigates.

After three years on the *Independence*, he was posted to the *Sabine* – a frigate that had been laid down in 1823 but not commissioned until 23 August 1858 – to be part of that sailing ship's first crew. The *Sabine* was a 1,726-ton vessel over 200 feet long and armed with forty-four cannon.

The outbreak of the Civil War found William, making $1,875 a year as a lieutenant on active sea duty, still on the *Sabine*, then based in Pensacola, Florida, although recently returned, as part of a squadron, from an expedition to Vera Cruz, Mexico. In April 1861 the ship was ordered to the relief of Fort Pickins. On 19 April, only days after the firing on Fort Sumter in Charleston's harbour, President Abraham Lincoln declared that all the ports from Virginia to Texas were under a state of blockade.

Blockade duty was essential to the war effort, though exceptionally boring. Since the south had very few manufacturing facilities, indeed did not even produce many of its own foodstuffs despite being an agricultural society, virtually everything it required both for civilians and the military needed to be imported.

Any blockade followed international law. The nations of the world had agreed earlier that there were certain rules to a naval blockade. Thus the blockading force had to notify officials in the port that they were now under a state of blockade. Ships already in the port being blockaded were given a number of days to complete whatever they were doing and clear the port before being sealed in. This would be no problem, since the small pre-war navy would be hard-pressed to get enough ships together to impose little more than a paper blockade at the outset. However, it was required that a nation proclaiming a blockade establish an 'effective' blockade promptly. Therefore, the navy, instead of concentrating at one or two ports, made a show of ships at a number of ports, declaring a blockade as and when they arrived. Yet, although an initial proclamation was issued off Hampton Roads, Virginia, on 30 April, it was not until 9 May that a navy ship appeared to proclaim an official blockade of Charleston.

Once in position, the men-of-war would stop ships from entering and leaving the port. When the blockade was first declared, neutral ships arriving would be warned off and allowed to depart without sailing in. The fact of the warning would be entered on the neutral ship's registry. This requirement, however, fell into disuse as the war dragged on. There was no chance of trying to stop and warn any of the fast ships used as professional blockade runners that made the short run at night from such nearby ports as Bermuda, Nassau, Matamoros and Havana. Ships bearing the flag of the Confederacy were, of course, liable to be captured instantly.

Capturing vessels, even merchant ships, along a 3,500-mile coastline dotted with many small islands and inlets, was difficult. Initially, ships bound to southern ports, not afraid of the handful of US Navy vessels, made their run in broad daylight. A commander of a blockading vessel off Georgetown, South Carolina, noted such an example in his journal on 24 December 1861, when he ordered his ship to head towards the spot where a fellow blockader was reportedly chasing an unknown ship:

'The stranger and *Gem of the Sea* were not far apart ... and [we] soon ascertained that the latter was in chase of the former which proved in our sight a schooner. The latter seemed ahead and running for the northern entrance and we ran towards the lighthouse to prevent her getting through that passage. The *Gem of the Sea* opened fire upon her but the schooner succeeded in getting into North Inlet and grounded. Her crew abandoned her and in a boat succeeded in getting ashore not, however, before setting her on fire. A boat from the *Gem of the Sea* went around the Island to her and found no papers as the cabin was in flames. On her stern was "Prince of Wales, Nassau, N.P." and as far as could be ascertained was ladened with salt and oranges.'[6]

For the most part, however, blockading work, sailing up and down a short way just within sight of land or staying anchored in the same spot for long hours in hot sun and driving rain, was deadly dull. As one of the officers involved in the Charleston blockade recalled, there were always things to do at sea in keeping the ship in the best condition and the crew drilled for action, and when in port there were diversions in town:

'But the dead monotony of the blockade was neither sea nor port. It supplied nothing. The crew, once drilled, needed but a few moments each day to keep at the level of proficiency; and there was practically nothing to do, because nothing happened that required a doing or an undoing.'[7]

At times, when dense fogs covered the sea, the men felt peculiarly alone in the world. Other times they were relieved to have resupply vessels hail them, with relatively fresh newspapers, mail and food. Still, time weighed heavily. Only five days after the excitement about the *Prince of Wales*, the same officer noted in his journal that it had been:

'A very pleasant day and weather for which I feel thankful to the Great Disposer. It being the Sabbath Day I did not get the steamer underway but she lay at anchor all day. There was no excitement; three false alarms of strange sails gave a little change in the monotony of things. In the afternoon permitted the officers to take a boat to pull more seaward into deeper water to fish, but they returned unsuccessful.'[8]

When he reached Pensacola, on 13 May, Captain H. A. Adams of the *Sabine* issued notice that the port was officially blockaded. On the arrival of naval reinforcement, the *Sabine* was sent on to join a larger blockading force outside the much busier harbour of Charleston. It was more important to prevent cargoes reaching the South Carolina port, with its rail connections throughout the south, than to stop them reaching the smaller and less strategic city of Pensacola.

At the same time as it set up its blockade, the navy initiated plans for land/sea operations to capture, and hence close down, several small southern ports. These ports would also serve as good recoaling and provisioning stations for blockading ships that would not have to return north when supplies ran out. William would soon play a part in one such operation. While in Charleston, his ship was sent on to join a flotilla under sealed orders to attack and capture Port Royal, South Carolina. On 7 October, after driving off a small Confederate flotilla, the Federals crossed the bar into the harbour. One of the first southern strongholds had fallen into Union control – and with relative ease. William and the others of the *Sabine* were commended for having rescued the crew of the transport *Governor* during a fierce gale that had sprung up on 3 April. All but seven of some 650 officers and men from the sunken ship were saved.

By late 1861 it was obvious that pre-war naval ranking – midshipman, master, lieutenant, commander, captain and commodore – was inadequate to meet the needs of a suddenly enlarged fleet. Moreover, the ranks were not equivalent to those of the army. A midshipman was actually a cadet, although at sea he could serve in an officer's position, while a lieutenant rated much higher than an army second lieutenant. More ranks were needed. The navy created the rank of ensign, considered equal to an army second lieutenant, between midshipman and master. A lieutenant commander rank, equal to an army major, was inserted between the lieutenant and commander. And a rear admiral's rank, equal to a major general, was created as the top naval grade.

William was one of the first to benefit from these new ranks. On 16 July 1862 he was promoted to lieutenant commander, with an annual pay when at sea of $2,343. Sent to the Virginia coast as part of the naval build-up to support McClellan's Peninsula campaign, he was named executive officer of the *Maratanza*. She differed considerably from the ships on which he had served before. She was a side-wheel gunboat, called a 'double-ender', which had been especially built for use in narrow and shallow coastal waters and rivers. Her rudder at each end enabled her to reverse course quickly when coming under enemy fire. Although only 786 tons, she was heavily armed with a hundred-pound rifle, a nine-inch smooth bore, and four 24-pounders.

The ship's captain, Commander G. W. Scott, being called away from time to time, William gained experience during his absence in the practical realities of commanding a ship in action. Furthermore, he had to learn the differences between sailing a ship powered primarily by wind, as had been all his previous postings, and one powered by steam, as was his new assignment. The ship had a staff of four acting, i.e. not regular navy, engineer officers, and he had to work closely with them. It would be a learning experience for both the regular deep-water sailing ship officer and the newly minted engineers.

William would see a great deal of action patrolling on the James and Appomattox Rivers. Frequently the ship came under fire from guerrillas. On the James River, the *Maratanza* pounded southern defences at Yorktown during the siege of that city; took part in the engagement at West Point, 9 May; and fired into assaulting Confederate infantry during the successful defence of Malvern Hill. The ship also participated in the encounter at Point of Rocks, Virginia, between gunboats and Confederate infantry and artillery.

Sailing down the James on the afternoon of 4 July, William's ship rounded a bend and a crew member called out that an enemy ship lay dead ahead. Almost immediately the Confederate gunboat opened fire on the *Maratanza*, but did not move from her position near the bank where she had run aground. A Confederate shot passed through the *Maratanza*'s wheelhouse, but an answering Federal shot exploded in the enemy boat's boiler. As steam blew out of every porthole and gangway, the southern sailors leaped overboard and swam ashore. A party from the *Maratanza* boarded the vessel, which turned out to be the Confederate ship *Teaser*. William and his other crew members discovered a balloon that had been made in Richmond and filled with gas from the local gas works, which was to be launched from the deck of the *Teaser*. Later Confederate Lieutenant General James Longstreet wrote, 'This capture was the meanest trick of the war and one I have never yet forgiven.'[9] Even more importantly, boarders found details of a new Confederate ironclad, the CSS *Richmond*, and a vital plan of the defences of Richmond.

After the Peninsula campaign, the *Maratanza* was sent to patrol for blockade runners off the North Carolina coast. On 23 September 1862 she engaged the blockade runner *Kate* on the Cape Fear River.

William and the rest of the crew welcomed the capture of ships such as the *Teaser* not only for the glory, but for the award of prize money that would add to their bank accounts. Prize money was possibly the most important perk

of naval service, and the possibility of gaining some was always listed promi-
nently on recruiting posters. Essentially, prize money was the estimated value
of the ship divided among the whole crew. Originally, when there were no pen-
sions for naval service, it was intended that a prize money recipient would
invest this money to provide for himself and his family when his active career
drew to a close.

The possibility of winning a share of prize money was on everybody's
mind. The paymaster of the *Monitor*, a civilian until the war, wrote his wife in
July 1862:

'What my share of the prize money will be I am unable to say but I
think I shall have no difficulty in counting it. Did I tell you that in case we had
captured or destroyed the *Merrimac* our prize money would have been about
one million of dollars to divide among us? That was something worth while.'[10]

Nobody, not even a professional such as William, could actually tell how
much money he would make from any ships taken at sea. Although the process
of determining this was well regulated, there were a number of variables involved.

Essentially, what happened when a blockader arrested a ship at sea was
as described by John B. Marchand, who commanded a ship off Charleston harbour in March 1862 when he stopped a strange ship heading towards the
southern city:

'Her name was on the quarter: *Emily St Pierre*. She was amongst the list
of suspected vessels and upon her heaving to, I sent a boat on board with directions to take charge of her and anchor near Captain Goldsborough, the senior
officer, which was done. At Captain Goldsborough's request, I went on board
the *Florida* and consulted [with him]. I read her papers [and found that] she
was bound from Calcutta to St. John's New Brunswick, about 100 days out.
No ensign could be found on board. On her course she had no right to come
here and she had [once] belonged to Charleston [and] but recently changed to
English [registry] and had on her stern "Liverpool." We determined to send her
north to Philadelphia for adjudication and by night time a prize crew from all
the blockading vessels was sent on board and her crew taken on board the
James Adger.'[11]

The captured ship, now under command of a prize master, headed to
the nearest friendly port where the US attorney for the district filed a libel
against the property, obtaining a warrant from a federal court directing a federal marshal to take custody of it while trying to get the vessel condemned.
This would be done by a group of three prize commissioners, one of whom was
a retired naval officer, appointed by the local district court. They would weigh

the evidence, including bills of lading and testimony of the crew, to decide if the vessel should be released as innocent, or condemned and sold. If the latter, the US marshal was to sell the ship and its cargo through auction and send the gross proceeds to the Secretary of the Navy.

The system could be manipulated, too. For example, pleading damage to a captured ship, Admiral Farragut had it sent to Pensacola, Florida, rather than up north. There the local judge doubted his jurisdiction in such cases. Farragut wrote to the Secretary of the Navy begging

'that the Department will use its exertions to have the proper judicial power given to Judge Peabody, or to some other person, as the cargoes of these vessels will sell for twice or three times the amount here that they will bring at the North, besides the risk of sending them there. It being impossible to send many of the prizes North, they become total losses to both parties.'[12]

The defendants, including the ship owners, had rights as well. They were allowed their own lawyers and, if they lost in the prize commissioner's court, they could appeal all the way up to the US Supreme Court. Years could be spent before any of the capturing crew would see a dime of prize money. This led to a breed of businessman who bought the assignment to the prize money from those to whom it was due in exchange for a percentage of the total that would eventually be awarded. Given all the abuses of this system, whereby brokers, for example, took advantage of drunken seamen or those in desperate need, such transfers of authority required the signature of the ship's captain and paymaster. Moreover, according to regulations,

'the commanding officer of every vessel is required to discourage his crew from selling any part of their prize money or wages, and never to attest any power of attorney until he is satisfied that the same is not granted in consideration of money given for the purchase of prize money or wages.'[13]

When involved in any captured vessel that could qualify for prize money, William made sure that every 'i' was dotted and every 't' crossed – all the legal requirements exactly met. For example, in his official report on the his subsequent capture of the *Marshal J. Smith* on 10 December 1863, he took care to note:

I have preserved whatever papers or writings which were found on board for transmission to the judge of the district to which the vessel may be ordered. There was no other vessel in sight or signal distance at the time of this capture [and hence none to share the money with]. I herewith enclose a complete list of the officers and men of this vessel entitled to share in the prize money that may result from the capture of this vessel.'[14]

Crews shared prize money according to rank. William, as commander of a single ship such as the *Kennebec* when capturing the *Marshal J. Smith*, was entitled to one-tenth if he were acting independently and, if under a squadron or fleet commander, to three-twentieths of all the money. Everyone else on board, including William, received money in proportion to their individual ranks of pay.

The awarded sums could amount to a great deal of money, especially for those holding higher ranks. The steamer *Marshal J. Smith*, for example, carrying a cargo mainly of cotton, was sold for a total sum of $89,809.65. The court deducted $7,381.35 for costs, leaving $82,425.30 to be split up among the crew and squadron staff. William was therefore due three-twentieths of the money, or the very respectable amount of $12,363.79. For a man whose annual pay was $2,343, such a large sum would be a fine foundation for a retirement fund, which, as mentioned, was the original idea of prize money.

However, as local industry proved increasingly incapable of replacing the number of southern ships captured or destroyed, so the number of potential prizes declined. Between March and December 1863 William could only report two prizes taken.

In the fall of 1862 William finally received his own command, the *Hunchback*, a ship that had been built originally for civilian use as a ferry boat and that had been turned into a warship in 1861 in the rush to create a fleet. She was a 517-ton boat, with side wheels and a vertical beam engine capable of propelling her at 12 knots. Carrying a complement of ninety-nine officers and men, she was armed with three 9-inch smoothbores, and one 100-pound rifled gun. She had already seen service in the landings on Roanoke Island the previous February, as well as the capture of New Bern, North Carolina. Her crew had, therefore, been seasoned by action.

Now, William's life would change radically. He would no longer share the social life of the wardroom. Captains ate in their own staterooms, occasionally inviting other officers to join them. Of course, the captain could be invited to dine in the wardroom with his officers, but this would happen only from time to time. He would have his own clerk as well as a cook to prepare his food and serve him, and a servant to take care of his uniforms and equipment, and clean up his stateroom. At the same time, he would now be responsible for every aspect of life aboard his command, ranging from giving Sunday services if no chaplain were available, to punishing those brought up before 'captain's mast' on various charges. Anything that happened to his ship became his responsibility. He would now be a person apart, a man of splendid isolation.

On 11 October 1862 he took his ship close to shore to duel with enemy guns at Fort Casewlll and batteries off the Cape Fear River. He then commanded her in the attack on New Bern and Washington, North Carolina. On 14 March 1863 Confederate troops attacked Fort Anderson, outside New Bern, bombarding it all night. The next morning they stormed the fort, aided by cannon on their right. The *Hunchback* and another smaller schooner came up and added their guns to the fire against the enemy forces, soon silencing their artillery. In the counter-battery fire, the *Hunchback* was struck twice, but her crew suffered no serious casualties. The army commander wrote to William's squadron commander on 15 March 1863:

'Commodore – When, on the 14th of March, 1863, General Pettigrew, with eighteen pieces of artillery and over three thousand men, made his furious assault on Fort Anderson, an unfinished earth-work garrisoned by three hundred men of my command (the 92nd New York Volunteers), the capture or destruction of the brave little band seemed inevitable, but the gun-boats under your command, the pride of loyal men, and the terror of traitors, came promptly to the rescue.

'Your well-directed fire drove the enemy from the field, covered the landing of the 85th New York, sent to the relief of the garrison, and the repulse of the rebel army was complete.'[15]

The *Hunchback* was next part of the flotilla in early April dispatched by Commodore Davenport to the relief of Washington, North Carolina. Enemy batteries, as well as wrecks left in the water to block Union ships, halted the approach below Hill's Point. William's ship was forced to stop, but, despite enemy fire, he sent small boats to Washington with ammunition and dispatches. Named overall naval commander of the forces in the Pamlico River, he then set up a two-gunboat howitzer battery on shore overlooking the channel to check any sea-borne southern attacks on the ships. For days guns blazed both on both sides. On the 12th, Federal Navy cannon managed to silence one Confederate battery, protected by cotton bales, but remaining southern cannon continued their bombardment. Finally, the Confederates simply gave up the siege as not being winnable. 'Commander Renshaw, at Washington, and Lieutenant-Commander McCann, below on the river, conducted affairs with prudence and zeal,' wrote Rear Admiral David Porter later.[16]

April 1863 was a busy month for the *Hunchback*. William commanded his ship in three engagements, at Hill's Point, Swan's Point and Rodman's Quarter, with enemy batteries on the North Carolina shore. His aggressive nature was noted by naval top brass.

In November 1863 William was given an even better ship, the five-gun propeller-driven *Kennebec*, a screw gunboat commissioned in February 1862. She was a 691-ton vessel, equipped with two engines and a single screw that made her capable of ten knots. Her complement was 114 officers and men, and she was armed with an 11-inch smoothbore, a 20-pounder rifled gun and three 24-pounder howitzers. Since being commissioned, she had formed part of the Gulf Blockading Squadron.

When William joined her, the *Kennebec* was posted to the West Gulf Blockading Squadron. Thereafter he and his new crew would serve thirteen months stationed off the port of Mobile, Alabama, spending long, boring hours staring at the horizon, hoping to spot blockade runners trying to run into Mobile Bay. Patrolling was especially tiring since by that point in the war most enemy vessels waited until darkness to make their run, so that officers and men had to be especially wary during the darkest hours. Late at night on 9 December, for example, a lookout spotted the sails of an unknown ship to the southeast. Called up on deck, William ordered his ship to close with the stranger. When in range, he ordered a gun fired in her direction, yet the unidentified ship made no reply and, indeed, changed course. William continued to close and finally came close enough to board the stranger. The ship turned out to be the merchantman *Marshal J. Smith*, filled with some 260 bales of cotton and three packages of turpentine, that had lurked in one of the channels leading from Mobile Bay until dark when she tried a quick run to Havana, Cuba.

Again, on 30 December, a southern ship slipped out of Mobile Bay in the darkness. Although William's crew spotted her and gave chase, she disappeared into the inky blackness of night. Despite the angry, rough sea whipped up by a gale, William continued his pursuit, and next morning a crew member again spotted the enemy sails. William ordered a gun fired across her bow, and the southern ship hauled down her colours and hove to. She turned out to be the steamer *Grey Jacket* bound for Havana with a cargo of cotton, rosin and turpentine.

On 3 July 1864, in the course of attacking and eventually setting on fire the blockade-running Confederate ship *Ivanhoe*, William brought the *Kennebec* into action against the guns of Fort Morgan, located on the tip of a bar that overlooked the channel into Mobile Bay. The action earned him favourable notice from his squadron commander, the renowned Rear Admiral David Glasgow Farragut.

Farragut's plans involved more than just sitting outside Mobile Bay snapping up the odd merchantman. He aimed to lead his fleet into the bay, destroy the Confederate squadron there, and put an end to it once and for all as a southern base. The bay was well protected with forts on either side of the single channel that fed into it. Confederate engineers had placed a number of mines, then called torpedoes, along the channel, leaving a path through for blockade runners. A small Confederate Navy squadron, led by one of the South's bravest sailors, Rear Admiral Franklin Buchanan, defended the bay. The squadron included the dangerous, although weakly powered, ironclad *Tennessee*. Farragut called on William and the other captains to prepare well for the forthcoming battle with his detailed battle plan, General Orders No. 10:

'Strip your vessels and prepare for the conflict. Send down all your superfluous spars and rigging. Trice up or remove the whiskers. Put up the splinter nets on the starboard side and barricade the steersmen with sails and hammocks. Lay chains or sand-bags on the deck over the machinery to resist a plunging fire. Hang the sheet chains over the side, or make any other arrangement for security that your ingenuity may suggest. Land your starboard boats or lower them and tow them on the port side, and place the port boats down to the water's edge. Place a leadsman and the pilot in the port-quarter boat or the one most convenient to the commander.

'The vessels will run past the forts in couples, lashed side by side, as hereafter designated. The flag-ship will lead and steer from Sand Island N. by E. by compass until abreast of Fort Morgan, then N.W. half N., until past the Middle Ground; then N. by W; and the others, as designated in the drawing, will follow in due order, until directed to anchor; but the bow and quarter line must be preserved to give the chase-guns a fair range, and each vessel must be kept astern of the broadside of the next ahead. Each vessel will keep a very little on the starboard quarters of his next ahead, and when abreast of the fort will keep directly astern, and as we pass the fort will take the same distance on the port quarter of the next ahead, to enable the stern guns to fire clear of the next vessel astern.

'It will be the object of the Admiral to get as close to the fort as possible before opening fire: the ships, however, will open fire the moment the enemy opens upon us, with their chase and other guns, as fast as they can be brought to bear. Use short fuzes for the shell and shrapnel, and as soon as within three or four hundred yards, give the grape. It is understood that heretofore we have fired too high; but with grape-shot it is necessary to elevate a little above the object, as grape will dribble from the muzzle of the gun. If one or more of the vessels be disabled, their partners must carry them through, if possible; but if they cannot, then the next astern must render the required assistance; but as

116

the Admiral contemplates moving with the flood-tide it will only require sufficient power to keep the crippled vessels in the channel.

'Vessels that can, must place guns upon the poop and topgallant forecastle, and in the tops on the starboard side. Should the enemy fire grape, they will remove the men from the topgallant forecastle and poop to the guns below, until out of grape range.

'The howitzers must keep up a constant fire from the time they can reach with shrapnel until out of range.'[17]

Farragut finally ordered his fleet into Mobile Bay on 5 August 1864. Armoured *Monitor*-class vessels led the attack, passing along the right flank of the column. During the assault, the unarmoured *Kennebec* was lashed to the armoured *Monogahela*, protected from exposure to enemy shore-fire.

At the entrance to the harbour, one of the Monitors struck a mine and quickly sank. Admiral Farragut nevertheless pressed on with the attack. Soon the *Tennessee* steamed into view, aiming directly at the flag-ship, but veered away towards the rest of the fleet. At one point she lay abeam of the channel, exposing her side to the two Federal ships. The captain of the *Monogahela* gave the order to ram, but being slowed by the *Kennebec*, could only catch her a glancing blow. The *Tennessee* scraped across the *Kennebec's* bow, setting her on fire with a lucky shell burst. Later the *Monogahela* managed to strike the southern ship square amidships, but only sprang a small leak, while losing her own bow in the process. Eventually, however, the *Tennessee*, her feeble engines unable to stand the stress, came to a stop as the Union warships surrounded her, pounding her into submission. 'She was like a great buffalo of the plains, with a pack of wolves hanging to its flanks, finally compelled to succumb to superior numbers,' Admiral Porter later wrote. 'But the ram managed to inflict some dreadful wounds in her last efforts.'[18]

Mobile Bay was now in Union hands. It had not been a bloodless capture: William's crew reported one man killed and six wounded. In Farragut's book, however, no captain could do wrong in closing with an enemy, so the losses were justified by the victory.

It would be, however, the last battle in William's war. Afterwards, he was posted as an instructor to the Naval Academy, being promoted to the rank of commander on 25 July 1866. He stayed there only a year, serving on sea commands and in charge of navy yards. Shorebound, he finally leaped into the most dangerous of voyages. On 31 January 1867 he married Mary Elizabeth Vulte. He was made a full captain on 21 September 1876 and given command of the *Lackawanna*, then in the North Pacific.

On 26 January 1887 William was named a commodore and given command of naval forces off the coast of Chile in 1891. There he captured the *Itata*, a ship bringing arms from the United States to insurgents in that country's civil war. When the insurgents refused him use of the American cable, he had it cut several miles off-shore.

This was to be the last voyage for William. He retired in 1892 to a home in New Rochelle, New York. There he died on 15 January 1906. One of his country's leading naval officers, he was buried in Arlington National Cemetery, just outside Washington.

NOTES

1 Melville, Herman, *White Jacket, or the World in a Man-of-War*, New York, 1892, pp. 216–17
2 Howe, *Life and Death on the Ocean*, New York
3 Melville, op. cit., pp. 28–9
4 Crane, John, and James F. Kieley, *United States Naval Academy, The First Hundred Years*, New York, 1945, p. 24
5 Mahan, A. T., *From Sail To Steam*, New York, 1907, pp. 103–4
6 Symonds, Craig L., *Charleston Blockade*, Newport, Rhode Island, 1976, p. 67
7 Mahan, op. cit., p. 175
8 Symonds, op. cit., p. 72
9 Johnson, Robert Underwood, and Clarence Clough Buel, eds., *Battles and Leaders of the Civil War*, New York, 1956, Vol. 2, p. 513
10 Daly, Robert W., ed., *Aboard the USS Monitor: 1862*, Annapolis, Maryland, 1964, p. 185
11 Symonds, op. cit., p. 137
12 *ORN*, Series I, Vol. 19, pp. 498–9
13 Navy Department, *Laws Relating To The Navy And Marine Corps and the Navy Department*, Washington, 1865, p. 179
14 *ORN*, Series I, Vol. 20, p. 714
15 Porter, David D., *Naval History of the Civil War*, Secaucus, New Jersey, 1985, p. 417
16 ibid, p. 424
17 ibid, pp. 571-2
18 ibid, p. 576

10
William S. Muse
Second Lieutenant, US Marine Corps

A great many men in the border states where slavery was legal – Missouri, Kentucky, Delaware and Maryland – were torn between love of the United States as a whole and belief in the system of slavery and rights of states to regulate such a system themselves without Federal interference. Tension ran high throughout these states as men joined one side or the other, especially in Maryland – surrounding, to the north, the Federal capital District of Columbia and Washington City. Some of the first troops to march to Washington, the 6th Massachusetts, were met by a mob in Baltimore, the largest city in Maryland. In an exchange of bricks and gun shots on 19 April, one soldier was killed. Federal troops soon placed the city under martial law.

With an overwhelming Federal force opening the route through Maryland, the state legislature declared, on 28 April, that it was not constitutionally able to declare for secession. On 10 May it condemned the war as unconstitutional and unjust, urging the state's citizens to work for peace between north and south. It called for a recognition of the Confederacy as an independent nation by US authorities and protested against the US government for posting its troops on the soil of 'The Old Line State'.

In point of fact, Marylanders of military age did not work for peace. Instead, they joined the armed forces of either side. Generally, men from the Eastern Shore and around the Washington area went south, while those in western Maryland and the Pennsylvania border went north. Confederate Major General Isaac R. Trimble, after the war, figured that some 22,000 Marylanders joined the Confederate Army, while a number more – including Rear Admiral Franklin Buchanan who commanded the CSS *Virginia* in the first battle of ironclads – enlisted in the Confederate Navy. Officially, the US government credited the state with 50,316 white and 8,718 black men in its army. According to government figures, a further 3,925 Marylanders joined the Union Navy, according to government figures.[1]

One of these latter Marylanders was William S. Muse, who received a commission as a second lieutenant in the Corps of Marines on 18 March 1864.

According to an early history of the Corps, 'the Marines did continuous and efficient work in the four years of the Civil War'.[2] However, this service was not, for the most part, an independent organisation, but formed a part of ships' crews. The Marines had few chances for individual amphibious operations. As a rule, the 'leathernecks,' so called from the leather stocks worn by enlisted men to keep their heads upright, fought alongside sailors. Theirs was not a happy war.

Indeed, consideration was even given to disbanding the Corps, in large part due to its lacklustre performance. Reported Secretary of the Navy Gideon Welles in 1862:

'There has always been a divided opinion among naval officers in regard to maintaining a distinct organisation of marines for service on ships-of-war, even before the great change which the service has undergone by the introduction of steamers, with their corps of engineers, firemen, and attendants. An incongruity attaches to the system, for the marines are partly under the Army laws and regulations, and partly under the Naval code. On shore they are paid by a Marine paymaster, on shipboard by a Navy paymaster. They are subsisted on the Army ration on shore, while on shipboard they have the Navy ration. Consequently, the condition of the Marines varies from shore to ship, or ship to shore, as they may be employed.'[3]

At the beginning of the war the corps was authorised a colonel commandant with his staff officers, a lieutenant colonel, four majors, thirteen captains, twenty first lieutenants and twenty second lieutenants. They were divided into small parties assigned to guard naval installations and on ships where they served both as the ship's police force and infantry force. Herman Melville wrote that his frigate had a complement of something fewer than fifty Marines, 'two thirds of whom were Irishmen'. He went on:

'They were officered by a Lieutenant, an Orderly Sergeant, two Sergeants, and two Corporals, with a drummer and fifer. The custom, generally, is to have a marine to each gun; which rule usually furnishes the scale for distributing the soldiers in vessels of different force.

'Our marines had no other than martial duty to perform; excepting that, at sea, they stood watches like the sailors, and now and then lazily assisted in pulling the ropes. But they never put foot in the rigging or hand in tar-buckets.

'On the quarter-bills, these men were stationed at none of the great guns; on the station-bills they had no posts at the ropes. What, then, were they for? To serve their country in time of battle? Let us see. When a ship is running into action, her marines generally lie flat on their faces behind the bulwarks (the sailors are sometimes ordered to do the same), and when the vessel is fairly engaged, they are usually drawn up in the ship's waist – like a company reviewing in the Park. At close quarters, their muskets may pick off a seaman or two in the rigging, but at long-gun distance they must passively stand in their ranks and be decimated at the enemy's leisure. Only in one case in ten – that is, when their vessel is attempted to be boarded by a large party, are these marines of any essential service as fighting men; with their bayonets they are then called upon to "repel!"

'If comparatively so useless as soldiers, why have marines at all in the Navy? Know, then, that what standing armies are to nations, what turnkeys are to jails, these marines are to the seamen in all large men-of-war. Their muskets are their keys. With those muskets they stand guard over the fresh water; over the grog, when doled; over the provisions, when being served out by the Master's mate; over the "brig" or jail; at the Commodore's and Captain's cabin doors; and, in port, at both gangways and forecastle.'[4]

Obviously, sailors had little use for Marines; the feeling was, by and large, mutual. This animosity, however, did not extend to the officers' wardroom.

Despite often being confined to routine shipboard duties, Marines did train for amphibious operations. In January 1861, for example, an American squadron held a practice landing off the Mexican coast. According to Samuel Mercer, captain of the *Powhatan*, who commanded the landing force, the sailors manned boats with 12-pounder howitzers mounted on their bows. Then:

'The Marines of the Squadron and the small arm men [sailors trained in the use of small arms] took up their positions in Boats from their respective Ships immediately in the rear of their respective Howitzer Boats – after they were all arranged in the order here presented at a preconcerted Signal from me, the Boats having their Howitzers mounted upon them discharged their pieces twice – whereupon the Boats with the Marines and small arm men dashed in and landed formed in line immediately and delivered two discharges of musketry – when the Howitzer Boats pulled in and landed their Howitzers as fast as possible formed in line and fired each piece with a blank cartridge twice. After this the small arm men were exercised, and the Marines of the Squadron were maneuvered by their respective commanding officers.'[5]

With the rapidly growing navy, it was obvious that more Marines would be needed. In 1861 the corps was authorised 90 commissioned officers, 320 non-commissioned officers, 2,500 privates, thirty musicians for the famed Marine Corps Band in Washington, plus sixty drummers and sixty fifers. These numbers never mustered in at one time, and it soon became impossible to provide a Marine company for each commissioned ship worthy of such a complement. Virtually everyone not needed for barracks duty, therefore, was sure to get a sea assignment, and William was immediately assigned to the US sloop *St Mary's*, then in the Pacific Squadron.

Before his departure, however, he would need to spend much of the advance on his pay as a second lieutenant of $1,248 a year on new uniforms and equipment. Marine officers had several authorised uniforms, the standard one including a cap similar to that worn for fatigue in the army but braided black. The usual coat was dark blue, double-breasted with a standing collar and fringed gold epaulettes for dress and, for fatigue, a gold Russian knot bearing the rank insignia on each shoulder. The officer could also wear a similar white linen coat aboard ship in hot weather. The jacket authorised for fatigue had a single row of twelve small buttons down the front, scarlet lining, and gold-lace edging with gold pointed cuffs and a standing collar. Trousers were sky-blue with a scarlet welt down each leg, with plain white trousers authorised in hot weather. He would also need the unique sword worn by officers of Marines, along with a sword belt.

Aboard ship, most of the rest of his money would go into living expenses as he was a member of the officers' wardroom and contributed his share towards that. As with many other ship's officers, he would often have a servant to do his cleaning and keep his stateroom neat. Once at sea commanding a Marine detachment, however, William would receive another $10 a month for 'responsibility of' the detachment's clothing, weapons, and accoutrements.

William's new assignment, the *St Mary's*, was not a large vessel. Commissioned in 1844, she was a 958-ton ship carrying 20 guns with a complement of 195, all ranks. She had been in the Pacific Squadron, showing the American flag along the Pacific rim, since 1860. Most of William's days would be fairly routine. Another Marine lieutenant, Frank Church, recalled reporting on board his new ship where he would command the Marine detachment:

'Returned on board at 9 o'clock and inspected Guard. Found them very poorly disciplined. At 10 o'clock "Quarters" all the men accounted for. Overlooked the Sergeant's clothing account. Found it fairly correct but badly mixed up... At 3.30 p.m. took dinner with my new associates and found them a very agreeable set of young men. Some of them are regular officers and the rest Volunteers.' The following day: 'At 9 o'clock had inspection and ordered men in full dress in honour of Washington's Birthday. At 10.30 had "General Quarters." My command was posted on the Quarter Deck and I had the honor of being the first to report "ready for action." Quarters lasted 1 hour.'[6]

In October 1864 the Confederate cruiser *Shenandoah*, which had just been commissioned in Great Britain, received orders to head into the previously peaceful Pacific to destroy as many American whalers as possible. The ship reached Melbourne, Australia, in January 1865, having previously captured and destroyed several ships flying American colours. US government diplomats sent word to the Pacific fleet as the Confederate vessel loaded up with Cardiff coal. But no Federal ships could arrive off Melbourne before the *Shenandoah* set sail again, this time towards the North Pacific. While the US Pacific Squadron hunted the single Confederate cruiser, the *Shenandoah* captured thirty-eight American-flagged ships, destroying all but four of them.

Frustration must have run high among crews of the Pacific Squadron, including those on William's ship. Yet they could not find the Confederate cruiser. 'We felt no anxiety about Federal cruisers,' the *Shenandoah's* captain recalled, 'for we foresaw that they would in all probability be as unsuccessful in finding the *Shenandoah* as they had been in their search for the *Alabama*.'[7] On 23 June the raider captured California newspapers that told of Lee's surrender and Jefferson Davis's proclamation saying that the south would fight on. The Confederates continued their destructive spree. Finally, off the northern California coast, they met a British bark and learned that the war was indeed over. Rather than surrender his ship to Union authorities, the Confederate captain decided to take her back into the Atlantic, to hand her over to the British. Although the Pacific Squadron still hunted her, the *Shenandoah* finally reached England and surrendered without seeing an American naval sail. The Civil War was over.

William would stay in the corps, which survived the war despite talk of its being disbanded. He would spend the time on board the *St Mary's* until she was taken out of that squadron in 1866. He would remain in the corps, being promoted to first lieutenant on 27 April 1867; to captain, 21 December 1888; major, 11 July 1898; lieutenant colonel, 3 March 1899; and colonel, 31 January 1900. He retired from the corps on 14 August 1900.

NOTES
1 Manakee, Harold R., *Maryland in the Civil War*, Baltimore, 1961, p. 108
2 Leonard, John W. and Frederick F. Chitty, *The Story of the United States' Marines*, New York, 1920, p. 50
3 Lord, Francis A., *They Fought For The Union*, New York, 1960, p. 299
4 Melville, Herman, *White Jacket, or the World in a Man-of-War*, New York, 1892, pp. 349–50
5 No author given, 'Amphibious Exercise 1861,' *Fortitude*, Quantico, Virginia, Vol. II, Number 4, p. 14
6 Jones, James P. and Edward F. Keuchel, eds., *Civil War Marine*, Washington, 1975, p. 29
7 Horan, James D., ed., *C.S.S. Shenandoah, The Memoirs of Lieutenant Commander James I. Waddell*, New York, 1960, p. 139

11

Eli Nichols

Private, 114th New York Volunteer Infantry Regiment / Veteran Reserve Corps

In the end, it is the infantry private who wins or loses battles. He is the main-stay of the army, the man up the sharp end. He is also the most common individual in any army, even more in the nineteenth than in the late twentieth century. 'In the infantry is the main strength of an army,' wrote a period pro-fessional soldier in a handbook designed for new recruits. 'Cavalry and artillery are the auxiliaries. The final results of a war or campaign are achieved by this arm of the service; and the foot soldier should bear in mind the importance of his position, and seek to achieve the highest perfection of his arm.'[1]

Eli Nichols was a nineteen-year-old farmer from Delaware County, New York, when he enlisted on 14 August 1862, as an infantry private. He stood five feet eight inches tall, with black eyes and hair. He had gone to a recruiting office in Norwich where Platt Titus had sworn him into Company C, 114th New York Volunteer Infantry Regiment of the Army of the United States for a term of three years or the duration of the war, whichever would be shorter. His pay as an infantry private would be $11 a month, supplemented by his initial bounty.

Another New York farm-boy, Rice Bull, of the same age, joined an infantry regiment the day before Eli was sworn into service. He later explained why he joined:

'The war had started a year before and the period had been one of excitement and anxious waiting. We who lived on farms had no daily papers, only the weekly editions, so everyone who passed our house was questioned as to war news. At times we heard the distant sound of cannon at Whitehall or Glens Falls but the news, when details came, told either of a drawn battle or a defeat. Victories were few. We had met with so many military reverses that many feared that it would be impossible to reunite the country by force of arms. Thousands of boys like me felt a sense of duty to aid the Union cause for service in the Army.'[2]

The 114th was a new regiment. Although the country had been fight-ing for over a year, governors preferred, rather than send recruits to veteran reg-iments already in the field, to create new regiments, for which they could award new commissions. Established regiments sent veterans back home to drum up recruits, but they had to compete with newly formed recruiting organisations. As a result, new regiments, containing unseasoned recruits, were markedly inferior to Confederate infantry regiments which did not use this system. Furthermore, many good junior officers left their companies, who could ill spare them, to take higher rank in these new regiments.

The 114th was organised in Norwich where recruits drifted in slowly. It was officially mustered in and accepted into Federal service on 3 September. Then three days later, before Eli even had a chance to get uniformed, equipped or drilled, the men were all loaded on railroad cars and sent off to Baltimore. There they learned basic soldiering skills while assigned to the defences of the city in VIII Corps. Rice Bull described a scene much as Eli must have witnessed as his regiment boarded the train to ride off to war:

'The soldiers' relations, neighbors and friends were there to give the boys their farewell word, their good-by, their well wishes and to see them off on their long journey. For many it was to be the last farewell. It was not a happy day, it was a day of sadness. Finally, late in the afternoon, we shouldered our knapsacks and marched to the train, the great crowd following us. Then there was the last handshake and kiss. The train slowly started. The people lining the track were so wrought with emotions that they found no voice to cheer. They silently waved their hands while we could see their faces filled with tears.

'When we moved away from the station and were out of sight of our people, a feeling of relief came for most of us were only boys and the love of home and friends was strong.'[3]

Once they arrived in Baltimore and set up camp there was much for the new soldiers to wonder at in a city larger than most had ever seen. There were also a number of military lessons to be mastered. Eli would first learn to care for his uniforms. One private wrote home on the day Eli volunteered that he drew his uniform with his other equipment, which consisted of, 'Sky blue pants dark blue dress coat and blouse, fatigue cap, 2 pair drawers 2 shirts 2 pair socks one pair shoes, 1 overcoat, knapsack, gun, canteen, blanket, tin plate, tin cup, knife, fork.'[4]

For dress, the infantry private had a dark blue single-breasted frock coat with sky-blue edging to the standing collar and forming a pointed cuff. He wore a stiff, black, broad-brimmed hat, pinned up on the right, with a brass bugle horn, the infantry insignia and company letter on the front. The worsted hat cord was sky-blue, and a black ostrich feather was tucked into the side. Another brass insignia, bearing the US coat of arms, held the pinned side in place. (By 1862, volunteer regiments were often not issued with such hats.) His trousers were plain sky-blue both for dress and fatigue. For fatigue, too, he had a dark blue blouse fastened in front with four buttons and a lay-down collar. His cap was also dark blue wool, with a painted black leather peak, brass side buttons and a painted black leather chinstrap. Shirts came both in grey flannel and white cotton. Socks were white, usually made of cotton. Drawers were also white cotton and many rural boys, perhaps including young Eli, had never seen such elaborate undergarments before.

The next lesson was recognition of different ranks. Non-commissioned officers wore dark blue stripes down their trouser legs and sky-blue chevrons on both sleeves. NCOs had to be obeyed but not saluted. Officers, on the other hand, insisted on receiving a salute, given then in modern British Army fashion with the palm outward. When Eli entered a room in which there was an officer, he had to remove his cap, unless carrying a weapon (in which case he saluted with that) and stand stiffly at attention until invited to relax.

Eli's issued weapon was the muzzle-loading, 0.58 calibre Springfield rifled musket. He would learn how to keep the weapon clean, and how to load and fire it. He began by reaching behind into his leather cartridge box to remove a single, paper-wrapped cartridge. Dropping the musket butt to the ground in front of him, so that the muzzle was up and slightly away, tore the paper from the powder with his teeth and then poured the contents down the barrel. He next placed the conical bullet, called a 'minie ball' (after its inventor, French Army Captain Claud Minié) into the muzzle, the paper keeping it tight. Then he withdrew the slender iron ramrod. In a swift motion – less than swift if rounds had been fired earlier and left black powder fouling in the barrel – he rammed the round home. Then he returned the ramrod to the groove under the musket barrel, and swung the musket up so that the lock was roughly parallel to his belt. He snapped the hammer half-way back, brushed off the pieces of the last-fired copper percussion cap (left on to keep air from getting into the barrel while loading and prematurely firing the powder), and drew a new cap from his leather cap pouch worn on the right front hip. He placed the cap on the cone, or nipple, and pulled the hammer all the way back. Then he brought the butt to his shoulder, aimed down the barrel through the V-shaped iron sight, and pulled the trigger.

He also learned to take care of his equipment. Food went into a black, tarred haversack worn slung from the right shoulder over the left hip. Over that hung his wool-covered tin canteen. Spare clothing went into his black, tarred knapsack, along with his grey wool blanket, rubberised ground-cloth and white canvas shelter tent half rolled up on top of that. Most new infantrymen at first overloaded their knapsacks. One recruit recalled what his knapsack contained when he started on his first march:

'There were in it a pair of trousers, two pairs of drawers, a pair of thick boots, four pairs of stockings, four flannel shirts, a blouse, a looking-glass, a can of peaches, a bottle of cough-mixture, a button-stick, chalk, razor and strop, the "tailor's shop" spoken of above, a Bible, a small volume of Shakspere [sic] and writing utensils. To its top was strapped a double woolen blanket and a rubber one. It was boiling over, like a ripe cotton-pod. I remember, too, many other things left behind because of a lack of room in or about the knapsack. We would have packed in a portable cooking-stove each had there been room.'[5]

It did not take long to realise that this was far more than was necessary to carry. The same recruit later recalled:

'On the first long march the reaction sets in, and the recruit goes to the opposite extreme, not carrying enough of the absolutely necessary baggage and thereby becoming dependent upon his obliging comrades when a camp is reached. Old soldiers preserve a happy medium. I have seen a new regiment start out with all the indescribable material carried by raw troops, sometimes including sheet-iron stoves, and come back after a long march covered with more mud than baggage, stripped of everything except their blankets, haver-sacks, canteens, muskets, and cartridge-boxes.'[6]

It was not only recruits who tossed away things brought from home and even equipment issued by the roadside during a long march. Veterans in the Army of the Potomac, on the first march of a spring campaign, usually did like-wise. Ulysses S. Grant, just arrived with the army for the opening of the 1864 campaign, was shocked to see, when his troops headed south for the first time, 'scattered along the road from Culpeper to Germania Ford wagon-loads of new blankets and overcoats, thrown away by the troops to lighten their knapsacks; an improvidence I had never witnessed before.'[7] Civilians, quartermaster offi-cials and mounted soldiers towards the end of the column picked up many of the discarded items for reissue, or in many cases, private sale. A cannoneer with the 9th Massachusetts Battery, who supplemented his income in winter quar-ters selling scrap to junk dealers, wrote home on 21 June 1863: 'There is no knowing the amount of goods the army throws away on a march Coats pants blankets I got 2 new blankets and sold them for $1.00 [and] 50 cents each.'[8]

On 12 October the 114th was called away from its training to head into Pennsylvania where Confederate cavalry had burst loose on a raid. This was the first taste of life in the field for Eli and his friends. The heavily equipped, slow-moving Federal infantrymen would be on the road for two days, serving to block some avenues to the Southern horsemen, but not actually seeing action. Still, the march served to season Eli and his comrades. They began to look like actual infantrymen. One New York infantryman described a column on the march:

'The impression among those who have never seen an army on the march is that soldiers march in exact line and in step as when on parade. Not at all – At the route step every man bobs along to suit himself, straddling or mincing, as seems best to him, but he is not to lose his relative position and must be able to spring into place and maneuver at a moment's warning. We generally travel four abreast with rifles at a right-shoulder shift [i.e. on the right shoulder, lock facing upwards, muzzle up and to the left rear and butt in the right hand about chest high]...'9

After only a short time in the field, all infantrymen tended to look alike. Everyone was soon covered with dust from the dirt roads in dry weather and mud when it turned wet. Uniforms got dirty, turning sky-blue trousers into a shade of muddy brownish blue. They got snagged on bushes and tree limbs and tore. Faces and hands were tanned by the sun's rays. Major Abner Small of a Maine Infantry regiment wrote after the war:

'The ideal picture of a soldier makes a veteran smile. Be a man never so much a man, his importance and conceit dwindle when he crawls into an unteaseled [roughly finished] shirt, trousers too short and very baggy behind, coat too long at both ends, shoes with soles like firkin covers, and a cap as shapeless as a feed bag. Let me recall how our private looked to me in the army, in the ranks, a position he chose from pure patriotism. I can see him exactly as I saw him then. He is just in front of me trying to keep his balance and his temper, as he spews from a dry mouth the infernally fine soil of Virginia, and with his hands – he hasn't a handkerchief – wipes the streaks of dirty sweat that make furrows down his unshaven face. No friend of civilian days would recognise him in this most unattractive and disreputable-looking fellow, bowed under fifty-eight pounds of army essentials...

'His suit is a model one, cut after the regulation pattern, fifty thousand at a time, and of just two [actually four] sizes. If he is a small man, God pity him; and if he is a big man, God pity him still more; for his is an object of ridicule. His forage cap, with its leather visor, when dry curls up, when wet hangs down, and usually covers one or both ears. His army brogans, nothing can ever make shine, or even black. Perhaps the coat of muddy blue can be buttoned in front, and it might be lapped and buttoned behind. The army never bushels [tailors] army suits, and he doesn't crease trousers, although he is always generous in reinforcing them with the regulation patch.

'The knapsack (which is cut to fit, in the engraving) is an unwieldy burden with its rough, coarse contents of flannel and sole leather and sometimes twenty rounds of ammunition extra. Mixed in with these regulation essentials, like beatitudes, are photographs, cards, huswife [a sewing kit containing thread, needles, and a few buttons was called a housewife], Testament, pens, ink, paper, and oftentimes stolen truck enough to load a mule. All this is crowned with a double wool blanket and half a shelter tent rolled in a rubber blanket. One shoulder and the hips support the "commissary department"— an odorous haversack, which often stinks with its mixture of bacon, pork, salt junk, sugar, coffee, tea, desiccated [dried] vegetables, rice, bits of yesterday's dinner, and old scraps husbanded with miserly care against a day of want sure to come.

'Loaded down, in addition, with a canteen, full cartridge-box, belt, cross belt, and musket, and tramping twenty miles in a hurry on a hot day, our private was a soldier, but not just then a praiser of the soldier's life. I saw him multiplied by thousands. A photograph of any one of them, covered with yellow dust or mosaics of mud, would have served any relation, North or South, and ornamented a mantel, as a true picture of "Our Boy."'[10]

A British Guards officer, observing the infantry of the Army of the Potomac during the Mine Run Campaign of late 1863, reported home:

'The arms are kept particularly clean. The infantry appear overweighted: each man, besides his greatcoat, knapsack, arms, and accoutrements, carries his share of a shelter tent (the only tent used), a blanket, forty rounds of ammunition, three days' whole and five days' dry rations; and an endless quantity of pots and pans, waterproof coats, and other extras.'[11]

The 114th returned to Baltimore. But they were not to stay there long. On 6 November they marched down to the docks where they boarded a transport bound for Fortress Monroe, Virginia. Arriving there, they boarded yet another transport, this time heading for Ship Island, Mississippi. The two transports bearing the regiment arrived at Carrollton on 26 December and 4 January. The men spent only a few days there before marching inland to Algiers on 7 January, 1863. From there they marched off in companies and smaller detachments to perform guard duty along the Opelousas and Great Western Railroad. Relieved of this duty in February, the regiment was reunited at Brashear City.

A Federal officer later described Brashear City:

'Brashear City is at the head of Berwick Bay, forty or fifty miles west of New Orleans. As it is the terminus of a railroad, it has a depot and storehouses;

and as it is a port of entry with a respectable harbour, it has wharves and a few small craft; but all the same it is what we at the North would call a village. Two or three of our gunboats are anchored off the landing; on shore are the tents of four regiments of infantry, two batteries of artillery, and a troop of cavalry; and there you have about the whole population.'[12]

The 114th was only to stay there until 20 March when they marched off to Bayou Bœuff and Pattersonville. While there, they learned that a new system of infantry drill, known as Casey's, had replaced the older system written by William Hardee. The regiment spent long hours on the drill field changing old habits to fit the new requirements. One Illinois officer noted in his diary of 16 March, 'Casey's tactics had now been substituted for Hardee's and we had not yet got accustomed to the change.'[13] On 2 April the men returned to Brashear City and a week later marched off to Berwick City.

Life in Berwick City was mentally as well as physically exhausting since this was an area in which the war was fought without front lines. Confederate guerrillas darted out of swamps along railroad lines and roads to snap up Federal pickets. And, as a soldier in another regiment stationed in the area, wrote, 'The fate of Union prisoners captured by the Confederates was usually hard, and often pitiful in the extreme.'[14] The 114th was engaged in a war of marches to different points in search of reported Confederate forces - often pointless exercises that ended with neither pitched battles fought nor prisoners taken.

Between 9 April and 14 May the 114th was involved in operations in Western Louisiana. There was some real fighting in these operations, although most shots were fired in small skirmishes in which an elusive enemy fled when confronted. Finally the Confederates dug in at Fort Bisland which the brigade reached on 12 April. The Union commanding general ordered his infantry to lie down in line of battle, while Union artillery pounded the Confederate works. The next day, the Federal general ordered the 75th New York, with the 114th following as support, around the Confederate right flank. Confederates hidden in thick woods that broke up Federal formations drove the two regiments back and eleven enlisted men of the 114th were wounded. The next day the Federals found the Southern works deserted. The brigade pressed onward on its raid, moving through St Martinville, Opelousas, Vermillionville, and returning to a spot near Opelousas on 20 April when the raid was declared finished.

The regiment was assigned to guard livestock on its march, from 20 to 28 April, to Brashear City. The cattle delivered, they camped there until 4 May when they were sent to Newtown and on to Opelousas on 9 May. The regiment took part in the expedition from Berne's Landing to Brashear City that lasted from 21 to 26 May, being assigned to Franklin on 25 May. They moved to Algiers on 29 May and on to Port Hudson the next day.

There they joined Federals attempting to capture that city, a formidable bastion on the Mississippi River, the only one apart from Vicksburg still in southern hands. A political, rather than professional, general, Nathaniel P. Banks, gathered the force to capture the city, largely to avoid serving with Grant in his campaign against Vicksburg. While the 114th avoided being sent in to join the useless attack on the city's works on 27 May, it took part in the abortive assault on the Confederate works on 14 June. That attack began in the early morning hours when an entire division assaulted a part of the works known as the Priest Cap. Although some of the Federals actually penetrated into the southern works, heavy fire kept reinforcements in the rear. Banks continued to order units forward, but each attack that met with heavy fire was conducted with less enthusiasm. In all, 1,805 men fell in the battle of that day. Although Banks wanted to renew the attack the next day, a threatened mutiny if the attack were renewed ended that plan. Banks dug in for a regular siege.

The siege turned into an affair of digging saps closer and closer to southern lines. Meanwhile within the town, food fell into short supply. A tunnel dug towards the Confederate lines was destroyed by an explosion in a Confederate countershaft. Even though morale was low in his besieging forces, Banks decided to try another assault on 7 July. The men, having seen the mismanaging of the assaults of 27 May and 14 June, weren't at all happy when they learned of this decision. Luckily, up the Mississippi River, Vicksburg fell on 3 July. One Federal officer recalled:

'Finally came the news that Vicksburg had surrendered, and then a mighty hurrah ran around Port Hudson, like the prophetic uproar of ramshorns around Jericho.

"What are you yelling about?" an Alabamian called to us from across the ravine.

"Vicksburg has gone up!" a score of voices shouted.

"Hell!" was the compendious reply, reminding one of Cambronne at Waterloo, as told by Victor Hugo.'[15]

Disbelieving their reports at first, the Confederates asked for and received, through flags of truce, proof of Vicksburg's surrender. Figuring that they had then done their duty, the Confederates surrendered. Eli and his friends of the 114th were present at the handing over of the city on 9 July.

But Eli and his friends would have no rest as part of the city's new garrison. The next day they were sent on to Donaldsonville, part of an expedition that lasted until the end of the month. During the raid they took part in a minor action just outside Donaldsonville at Kock's Plantation on 13 July.

The 114th was camped near Thibodeaux until 19 August, then moved back to Brashear City where it remained until 2 September.

Banks, the capture of Port Hudson to his credit, now turned his attention west. He decided to invade southern Texas. The 114th was one of the regiments loaded onto seven transports that followed four federal gunboats out into the Gulf of Mexico towards Texas. On 8 September the men watched as the lead gunboats headed up the Sabine River. Waiting was a single artillery battery in earthworks called Fort Griffin. Unluckily for the Federals, the Texans had spent much time getting the range of the river channel before the US Navy arrived. As the gunboats headed towards Sabine Pass, the Confederate cannoneers opened fire just as the boats reached the range-markers the Texans had previously planted in the river. Within moments accurate, well-practised cannon fire disabled or repelled all the Union craft, forcing the surrender of one of the gunboats. The invasion had been foiled. After that expedition the regiment was sent back to Algiers, then to Berwick on 17 September.

The brigade commanded by Brigadier General Godfrey Weitzel, to which the 114th was assigned, was ordered on 24 October to move back by boat to Donaldsonville, some 100 miles up the Mississippi, as part of a force designed to capture a Confederate force that had been assembled at Thibodeaux. But the enemy fled before the brigade arrived, firing the town as they left. According to an officer in the brigade, John De Forest, the Federals found the town, the next day, 'a desert of smoke-blackened ruins'.[16] From there they marched south a dozen miles. 'The men, weak as yet from the summer's heat and quite unaccustomed to field service,' De Forest wrote, 'complained of the weight of their knapsacks and straggled woefully.' This was evidently a common fault. The Guards officer who spent time with the Army of the Potomac in late 1863 complained of the lack of discipline among Federal infantrymen:

'The want of it is most apparent when the army is on the move, and shows itself particularly in the shape of straggling. On the retreat I saw thousands of men – neither sick nor tired, but who apparently had merely "concluded" that night marching was a bore – straggling all over the country. They simply fell out and bivouacked for the night; lighting fires and cooking their suppers all along the road, and with an evident determination not to "move on" till morning. No attempt was made to urge them to rejoin their regiments, and they dropped in by twos and threes the following day...'[17]

The next day the head of the column ran into Confederate skirmishers whom they drove off easily. Then the force hit the main Confederate line, which held for several volleys before disappearing into the bushes. The Confederate commander, seeing that the Federals had greater numbers and knowing that his line of retreat was a narrow road through a swamp, decided discretion was indeed the better part of valour, and ordered an immediate retreat. He himself, staying on the field until his troops had successfully escaped, was mortally wounded.

The 114th was stationed at New Iberia from 17 November to 8 January 1864. It then moved to Franklin and went into camp.

The unhealthy area took its toll. In all, 192 enlisted men and two officers in the regiment died from disease. In February Eli took sick and was assigned to quarters. He eventually recovered but was so weakened by a complaint that was diagnosed as a liver disease that the regimental surgeon decided he was no longer fit for active service. In the first years of the war this would have led to a discharge. By this time, however, there was another option – the Veteran Reserve Corps.

The idea for such a unit had originated on 7 April 1862 when the War Department authorised the chief medical officer of each city to put to work men convalescing from wounds or illness who were nevertheless capable of assuming the duties of nurses, cooks and hospital attendants, in order to free able-bodied men now doing those jobs for combat roles. Although the plan was only partially successful, since many soldiers merely became hangers-on in the hospitals long after they were cured, the basic idea seemed sound. Therefore, on 28 April 1863, the army authorised an Invalid Corps of men permanently assigned to its duty. According to the acting adjutant general of the corps, J. W. De Forest:

'It was directed that the feeble and wounded men in hospitals who were unfit for field duty, but still not entirely disabled, should be organised into detachments under the charge of officers acting as military commanders. From these invalid detachments were detailed provost, hospital, and other guards, clerks, nurses, cooks, and other extra-duty men.'[18]

Needing as many able-bodied men as possible sent to the front, the army began to recruit for this new organisation, henceforth detailed to guard prisoners of war, equipment depots and other military sites, in addition to staffing hospitals. Officers who had previously been discharged because of wounds were recruited to serve as company commanders. According to the Army official report on the VRC:

'One of the first steps of the War Department with regard to the corps had been to devise a special uniform for it. For enlisted men it consisted of a dark blue forage cap and sky-blue trousers, according to the present regulation, and of a sky-blue kersey jacket, trimmed with dark blue and cut long in the waist, like that of the US cavalry. Officers were directed to wear a sky-blue frock coat, with collar, cuffs and shoulder-strap grounds of dark blue velvet, and sky-blue trousers, with a double stripe of dark blue down the outer seam, the stripes half an inch wide and three-quarters of an inch apart.'[19]

The uniforms were unpopular with the officers and men as, in their minds, they denoted something less than the ideal image of manly strength – especially in comparison with that of combat soldiers. Moreover, the very name 'Invalid Corps' reinforced that opinion. And because of the army practice of marking *matériel* no longer fit for use 'IC' – 'Inspected Condemned' – line soldiers called the sky-blue-clad troops 'Condemned Yanks'. According to the adjutant's report, 'Men frequently begged to be sent back to their old regiments in the field rather than remain in garrison at the price of being called Invalids.'[20]

The army was not prepared to let go these valuable men, nor could they afford to send them back to their original line units. Therefore, they changed the organisation's name to the Veteran Reserve Corps. Moreover, they attempted to build morale by ensuring that only men who had excellent military records got into the corps. Each man had to produce a surgeon's certificate of partial disability, accompanied by recommendations from at least three former commanders, and his complete military history. He had then to appear before a board of examination that would pass on the transfer. Recalled Private Alfred Bellard, disabled by a battlefield wound:

'There were two boards of surgeons, whose duty it was to examine all the men as to their fitness for the service, w[h]ether for active service with their regts. in the field, and if not, but still able to do duty round hospitals or cities, to determine w[h]ether they should go into the first or second batalion of invalids, [and] if not fit for either to grant their discharges. After being examined by the first board, I was sent back to my quarters as not being fit for active service, and on going before the second board, they had quite a discussion, w[h]ether to discharge me or not. They finally came to the conclusion to put me in the first batalion of invalids.'[21]

First Battalion VRC soldiers had all their limbs intact and were able to use rifled muskets. Second Battalion VRC soldiers, according to an article in New York's *The Evening Post* dated 30 October 1863, 'are all permanently disabled – men who have lost an arm or a leg – and are now necessarily kept actively at work... The men of the second battalion are not generally expected to carry guns, but are given side-arms.' Eli, not having been wounded, was assigned to a First Battalion unit.

On 1 March, after being examined, Eli was assigned to the Veteran Reserve Corps. He was returned east, to Washington, where he was assigned to Company K, 3rd Veteran Reserve Corps. In Washington, he was photographed by Baum & Burdine, a photographic company located near the Capitol Building. At the war's end, the VRC adjutant noted a brief outline history of the 3rd:

'During the part of the year has been stationed at Washington, performing the ordinary duties of the garrison of Washington, in course with conjunction with other troops. While at the Soldiers' Rest an immense number of troops, from 300 to 5,000 per day, passed through to the front. At Alexandria, Va., an average of 600 per day forwarded. At Eastern Branch corral many thousands of Government cattle guarded without loss... Duty of regiment severe; for weeks together on guard every other day; men known to fall asleep with exhaustion while walking their beats. Discipline excellent, notwithstanding that 608 men were received and 863 discharged, &c., during the year.'[22]

VRC duties in Washington, now virtually an enormous army base, were varied. Vast storehouses of supplies had to be protected; a large network of hospitals needed to be staffed; and the city prisons had to be guarded, which entailed escorting the prisoners – ranging from deserters to Confederate spies – to and fro. VRC troops also patrolled the streets, sending details to each theatre in the city, as Private Bellard reported, to 'examine the passes of all soldiers and arrest all of those who had none'.

Other squads were sent to 'houses of ill fame', looking for soldiers who lacked passes. That alone was almost a full-time job. The city was full of such places, with seventy-three 'bawdy houses' and another twelve 'coloured bawdy houses' registered with the Provost Marshal.

According to Bellard, the army was concerned about the health of the soldiers who visited such houses. 'Twice a week an army surgeon went with us, and while he and the officer in command went through the houses, we *the guard* had to wait on the sidewalk until they came out. When snow was on the ground or [it was] raining fast, we did not have a very pleasant wait.'[23] Patrols generally started out at 2 p.m. the men breaking a couple of hours later for rest and supper before getting back on the streets at seven. They would remain out, checking passes, until around 11 p.m. when they returned to barracks.

Many of these establishments were in such rough neighbourhoods that the soldiers would only enter them in large groups. One such group, the so-called 'Island Squad', visited buildings between Pennsylvania Avenue and the Potomac River given such picturesque names as 'Castle Thunder' (after the prison), 'Tin Cup Alley' and 'The Hospital'. The last, Bellard recalled, was the worst of the lot:

'The building was occupied by the worst cases in town, and the stench that came from it was enough to turn our stomachs, whenever we halted in front of the door. We were always glad to get away as soon as possible. Bad as the place was, we once found a soldier there in bed with one of the women. (He must have had a cast iron stomach.)'[24]

As the city's main garrison, the VRC served in ceremonies and parades. Its bands were attired in gaudy, non-regulation dress, and often were the highlight of such activities. For example, Eli and others of the three VRC regiments in Washington held a special parade on 17 March 1864, ending up in the grounds of the White House where they were reviewed by the President himself.

Little did any of them expect that before long the three VRC regiments in Washington would again see combat. In the spring of 1864 the war was going badly for the Confederate Army of Northern Virginia, pinned to its trenches below Petersburg, Virginia. Robert E. Lee decided to try what had worked often before, to send an army up north through the valley of Virginia. It would cross the Potomac into Maryland and then threaten both Washington and Baltimore. In past summers, such moves scared government officials who called on the Army of the Potomac to reinforce the city's garrison. If this were to happen again, Grant would have to weaken his siege lines around Petersburg, relieving Lee's army in the process.

The first part of the campaign went well for southern hopes. The Confederate troops under Jubal Early quickly cleared the valley and made it into Maryland. Grant, forward with the Army of the Potomac facing Lee, failed to realise the actual threat that this raid posed. Not until almost too late did he detach the veteran VI Corps and send it to the relief of Washington. Meanwhile, the ring of forts that had been built to defend the capital city had been virtually denuded to meet Grant's desperate need for infantry. By then the three regiments of VRC troops made up the bulk of Washington's garrison, They were, moreover, the most seasoned troops around, the rest being in organisations such as the Ohio National Guard in Baltimore, which had been mustered in for only a short time to perform garrison duties.

On 8 June the regiments were mustered, the men falling in with packed knapsacks and thirty-five rounds of ammunition. Those who had served in the artillery before being transferred were detached and sent to brigade headquarters and thence to man the guns standing silent in the city's forts. The men were then dismissed with the warning that they were to sleep in their clothes, not leave the barracks, and be ready to march at five minutes' notice.

That notice came two days later when they marched off, bands playing and colours flying, westward to Georgetown along Pennsylvania Avenue, and then up the Rockville Pike, through Tennallytown, and into the forts facing north. There the men went into lines, listening to sounds of gunfire and watching as clouds of dust indicated that a large body of enemy moving along their front. That night they slept uneasily on their arms. The next day, the 11th, was clear and hot. Finally, the Confederate line all around the city drew into view and halted. Southern skirmishers approached the Federal lines and opened fire. A brisk exchange between the two skirmish lines developed. One veteran Confederate infantryman recalled seeing the Federal defences:

'As far as my eye could reach to the right and left were fortifications, and the most formidable looking I ever saw! The trees in their front had been cut down, and the sharpened limbs pointed towards us. About midway of the clearing was a creek that seemed to run near the fortifications and parallel to them. The enemy had a full sweep of the ground for at least a mile in their front. If there works were well manned, our force would not be able to take them – since, as I suppose, General Early's entire command did not number 10,000.'[25]

Early agreed with his veteran private's opinion. Moreover, his orders had been simply to threaten Washington; he understood that he was not expected to take the city. Both sides skirmished at long range that day and then slept on their arms that night. The next day the Confederates quietly withdrew, just as the VI Corps filed into the forts to relieve the weary VRC troops. As Bellard recalled:

'The morning of the 14th every thing was quiet along the line, and scouting parties were sent out. They were soon marching over the ground lately held by the rebs, but not one could be seen, with the exception of two dead ones, who had been left unburied. The enemy had fled. In the afternoon the 6th corps were sent off in pursuit.'[26]

The VRC returned to its Washington barracks, many slowly, since the campaign had exhausted them. Although he did not know it, Eli's fighting days were over. The 114th, oddly enough, was part of the relieving force sent to Washington during Early's raid. It served in Sheridan's Valley Campaign that finally cleared the valley of Confederate troops, and then returned to Washington in January 1865. Eli must have renewed old friendships there. Indeed, he would spend the rest of his three-year enlistment doing duty in the city with the 3rd VRC; but in accordance with practice, as a man due for discharge, Eli accompanied his old unit back home for muster out on 3 July 1865. On 29 October 1878 he married Mary Daniels. He died 26 December 1898.

NOTES
1   Kautz, August V., *Customs of the Service*, Philadelphia, 1864, p. 52
2   Bauer, K. Jack, *Soldiering, The Civil War Diary of Rice C. Bull*, New York, 1988, p. 1
3   ibid, p. 5
4   Schilling, Edward, *My Three Years in the Volunteer Army of the United States of America*, Baltimore, 1985, p. 2
5   Gross, Warren Lee, *Recollections of a Private*, New York, 1890, p. 6
6   ibid, p. 7
7   Grant, U. S., *Personal Memoirs*, New York, 1952, p. 401
8   Deane, Frank Putnam, 2nd ed., *'My Dear Wife "*, Richmond, Virginia, 1964, p. 57
9   Longacre, Edward G., *From Antietam to Fort Fisher*, Rutherford, New Jersey, 1985, p. 58
10 Small, Abner R., *The Road to Richmond*, Berkeley, California, 1957, pp. 192–3
11 'C.L.P.', 'A Short Campaign with the Federal Army of the Potomac', *The Journal of the Household Brigade for the year 1863*, London.
12 De Forest, John William, *A Volunteer's Adventures*, New Haven, Connecticut, 1946, p 78
13 Barber, Lucius W., *Army Memoirs*, Chicago, 1894, p. 104
14 Carpenter, George N., *History of the Eighth Regiment Vermont Volunteers*, Boston, 1886, p. 61
15 DeForest, op. cit, p. 145
16 ibid., p. 55
17 'C.L.P.', op cit.
18 *ORs*, Series III, Vol. V, p. 543
19 ibid., p. 549
20 ibid, p. 552
21 Donald, David H., ed., *Gone for a Soldier*, Boston, 1975, p. 235
22 *ORs*, op. cit., p. 561
23 Donald, op. cit., p. 254
24 ibid, p. 257
25 Worsham, John H., *One of Jackson's Foot Cavalry*, Jackson, Tennessee, 1964, p. 156
26 Donald, op. cit., p. 273

12

Marshall Frederick Price
Surgeon, 1st Pennsylvania Light Artillery Regiment

Medicine is similar to religion: people only believe in it when it works. And frankly, the mainstream of medical science, which developed into the practice of medicine as known today, largely did not work in the 1860s. Many of the basic causes of illness, especially those involving microbes and viruses, were simply unknown. The cause of infection following surgery was not understood, and hence surgery itself was extremely dangerous and, if possible, to be avoided. In the face of serious illness, such as heart disease, cancers, polio, yellow fever and even childhood ailments such as whooping cough or measles, there was little that could be done for a patient. Since surgery was of little avail for most of these diseases, medicine of the period consisted mainly of prescribing a variety of drugs. Few of these drugs did little actual good, and some often did harm.

Since this was obvious to most intelligent individuals, it was also clear that visiting a doctor was basically a last resort. One soldier wrote in his diary in April 1863 that he was in poor health but, 'I dread any thought of applying to our [regimental] Doctor – and risking Army Treatment.' Indeed, he noted in his diary a short time later, 'I am really very weak. If only I were with Darling. She would soon doctor me up rationally – no medicene [*sic*] – no powders – no stuff –'[1]

When there is no clear path of knowledge in any field, be it theology or medicine, a wide variety of ways to the final goal appear. When people lack positive proof of one method working over all others they follow those that make the most sense to them or boast the most plausible practitioners. So it was that during the 1860s there were a number of medical theories and men to practise them.

There were, first of all, doctors who had graduated from a medical college. They had passed courses in anatomy and chemistry and were the best qualified doctors of their period, although even the better schools were not as well equipped as they would later be. Harvard's medical school lacked stethoscopes until 1868 and microscopes until 1869. Among medical practitioners, however, graduates were in the minority. Some men who called themselves doctors attended lectures for two years and then served an apprenticeship under an established doctor to earn a medical degree. Then there were those who had attended a number of such courses and, without graduating, went into practice. Others simply apprenticed themselves to a practising doctor and learnt from him on the job before going into practice for themselves.

Whatever his background, each practising doctor subscribed to a specific theory of medicine out of a variety then in vogue. In what might be called the mainstream, even the medical college graduate doctor adhered to no single overall theory as to the cause and likely cure of a particular disease, and therefore prescribed medicines that he had been taught to believe worked best for various illnesses over generations. Many of his cures dated back to the times of ancient Greece; others were based on general theories whereby all illnesses were treated by a single approach.

The largest group of individuals who called themselves physicians but were not in the mainstream practised homeopathic medicine. They followed the teachings of Samuel Hahnemann who believed that diseases were cured by medicines that mimicked the symptoms of the disease itself. Quinine, for example, produced similar reactions in a patient as did malaria, and therefore was best in treating that disease. Doses for each illness, however, were relatively small. Hahnemann felt that ordinary physicians, who prescribed ever increasing amounts of drugs in an attempt to fight illness, were wrong, and he termed these doctors 'allopaths'.

Many people took treatments in hydropathic medicine that stressed natural forces, self-help and a good diet, which included drinking plenty of water as well as frequent bathing. On the whole, such advice would have done more good to a patient than doses of mercury, a much prescribed drug, or bleeding, although by the 1860s this was finally going out of favour among practitioners.

City directories of the period also list 'physicians, eclectic', doctors who borrowed those treatments which appeared to work from various systems. Indeed, a practising Czech physician, argued that the ablest doctors should not use treatments that did not work but spend the bulk of their time in diagnosis. In so doing, he became the leading exponent of a school in Vienna, the so-called 'nihilists'.

Since there were no state licensing boards for the practice of medicine in 1861, virtually anybody could claim to follow one or another of these schools and set up in business. At the outbreak of war, the army, under whose organisational plans each infantry regiment would be assigned a surgeon and an assistant surgeon, was hard pressed to come up with as many educated physicians as it needed. At first, regimental colonels selected their own surgeons, usually men from their own communities who may or may not have had the ability to serve ill and wounded soldiers in the field. Each state was allowed to screen the surgeons for its regiments as it best saw fit. As late as 1862 Indiana's governor proposed one man for a surgeon's commission whose sole qualifications were that he had served a year as an enlisted hospital steward and had read medicine in a doctor's office for a year. Wisconsin even gave the colonel the right to choose his own surgeon without the candidate even having to be examined by a board of professional medical practitioners.

There was some outrage about the abilities of many of these newly commissioned surgeons, who rated as majors, and assistant surgeons, who rated as captains. Boards were created to weed out incompetents, but even these were not enough to do a thorough job. 'We may estimate by hundreds the number of unqualified persons who have received the endorsement of these bodies [the medical examining boards] as capable surgeons and assistant surgeons of regiments. Indeed these examinations have in some cases been so conducted to prove the merest farce,' wrote the editor of a leading medical journal in June 1861. 'Whoever has examined the list of surgeons, passed by the different State examining committees, must have regretted to find so few names of eminent surgeons.'[2]

All too often, too, the soldiers were aware of the inability of their assigned surgeons and dismissed them as worthless. One soldier later wrote:

'We had one of those ignoramuses for a doctor that was a disgrace to the profession. He used quinine in powder or pills for all diseases from a fever down to a sore finger – in fact, he considered it a panacea for all the ills that flesh is heir to. I believe he did have a little blue mass and calomel which he gave to persons in a dying condition to make them die easier.'[3]

In early 1862 Marshall F. Price, a twenty-eight-year-old native of Brimfield, Ohio, and a graduate of common school and the Abingdon Academy, applied for an assistant surgeon's commission from the governor of Pennsylvania. Marshall, although not a medical college graduate, was a practitioner of what the homeopathic practitioners disparagingly called 'allopathy.' Another physician, Daniel Holt, who applied for a commission at the same time wrote about his experience:

'Being desirous of entering the army and feeling that I could do more good to my country in the capacity of Surgeon, than in any other, I made application to the proper authorities at Albany [capital of New York] for such a position, and upon the suggestion of [New York State] Surgeon General S. Oakley Vanderpoel, went to Albany on, or about the 20th of July, 1862, where I underwent an examination before a medical board then in session for that purpose and in a day or two afterwards, received a note from the Surgeon General informing me that my examination had been satisfactory, and that my name had been sent into the Executive Department as a proper person to control the Surgical Department of any regiments of volunteers at that time formed or then in proccess [*sic*] of formation in the State.'[4]

On 31 July 1862 Marshall was appointed an assistant surgeon in the 1st Regiment of Pennsylvania Light Artillery, also officially designated the 43rd Pennsylvania Volunteer Regiment. He replaced an original vacancy in that position. As an assistant surgeon with under five years' worth of service, he would receive $53.33 a month in pay with four rations a day and forage for a horse. He would wear the single-breasted dark blue frock coat of a captain, with dark blue trousers and a gold stripe down each leg and a gold wreath surrounding the Old English letters US on his hat or cap front.

The regiment consisted of eight batteries assigned to the Army of the Potomac. However, unlike an infantry regiment which would serve as a single unit, the batteries of the 1st were split up among different infantry brigades and divisions, as well as some of them that went into the army's artillery reserve. Marshall would serve at the reserve artillery hospital.

Marshall had come into the Army of the Potomac at a turning point for its medical operations. Its previous chief surgeon had not proved a success. An old pre-war army officer, he could not get used to the enormous size and needs of the war-time army. Under him, it was the practice to have bandsmen act as stretcher bearers during battle. Untrained in medical skills and often unwilling to go under fire to rescue the wounded, bandsmen made terrible stretcher bearers. Moreover, the army used the old system of a small hospital for each regiment, manned by the regiment's surgeon and, if available, an assistant surgeon. In action, some of these hospitals were swamped with the wounded, while others lay empty.

Finally, Jonathan Letterman, a younger doctor who came to the post filled with ideas, was named the army's medical director. First of all, he did away with bandsmen as stretcher bearers. Instead, he had two men and a driver assigned to each ambulance, which would also have two stretchers. Two of these two-horse ambulances would be assigned to each regiment, while corps head-quarters would have another two. While a sergeant would be in charge of each pair of regimental ambulances, a lieutenant would command all the ambulances in the division, and a captain in the corps. All would be trained and under medical corps supervision. This would improve the old system where most wounded had to find their way to a hospital on their own or helped by capable soldiers since the musicians who were officially to help them rarely did.

Moreover, on 30 October 1862 Letterman ordered a system of division hospitals. The division, or in Marshall's case the artillery reserve, hospital would be set up just out of the range of enemy fire, usually in some building such as a barn, tavern, church, hotel, or private home. Straw for bedding would be laid around, while cooks prepared hot food to serve such of the wounded as could eat after being treated. Black rubber-coated cloths were stretched on operating tables made from such objects as boards on sawhorses. The water-proofs could be splashed off between operations.

Assistant surgeons headed towards the front to set up first aid stations just behind the battle line. There they would do rudimentary first aid before sending the wounded back to the reserve hospitals.

Back at the reserve hospitals, usually the chief surgeon of the hospital would assign the three most proficient surgeons to operate while others would diagnose injuries and perform what essentially amounted to first aid, especially if the wounded soldier had not had any emergency treatment before arriving at the hospital. The least proficient surgeons would find themselves in charge of administering drugs and doing the mountains of paper work required by the Army Medical Corps. They would be assisted by regimental hospital stewards, who were senior non-commissioned officers with some knowledge of drugs. These men, however, did not do medical procedures.

Even when not in battle a surgeon's day was a busy one. Daniel Holt described a typical one to his wife in October 1862: 'At early dawn, while you were, I hope, quietly sleeping, I was up at Surgeon's Call and before breakfast prescribed for eighty-six patients at the door of my tent.'

Buglers in the artillery, and drummers in the infantry, sounded surgeon's call at 6:30 in the morning. According to period Army Regulations, 'At surgeon's call the sick then in the companies will be conducted to the hospital by the first sergeants, who will each hand to the surgeon, in his company book, a list of all the sick of the company, on which the surgeon shall state who are to remain or go into hospital; who are to return to quarters as sick or convalescent; what duties the convalescents in quarters are capable of; what cases are feigned; and any other information in regard to the sick of the company he may have to communicate to the company commander.'[5]

At first soldiers made every effort to go to surgeon's call whenever they felt ill at all. 'There are two Surgeons to each Regt,' wrote one Pennsylvania recruit home in July 1861, 'all very good and kind men to be a bout [sic] and skillful physicians.'[6] Later, however, when it became obvious that the surgeons could not cure most of the common camp illnesses, especially the most common, diarrhoea and dysentery, surgeon's call became something to avoid if sincerely sick. 'At first "Surgeon's Call" suggested care for the sick, and certain remedies for nostalgia; but our soldiers became disinclined to heed the call, and shrank from the mysteries of that long, white tent, with its rows of cots so close together that a patient could reach over and clasp the feverish hand of his neighbor,' wrote Abner Small who rose from the grade of private to major during the war. Small went on to describe a typical surgeon's call:

"The regular prescriptions were numbered six, nine, and eleven, which were blue pill [mercury], quinine, and vinum. We soon learned that "vinum" meant either wine or brandy. I have seen men count from right to left, "six, nine, eleven – six, nine, eleven – six, nine, eleven," and step into the line just where "eleven" would strike. It was a sure thing, since the surgeon gave in regular order, as the men filed past him, something as follows:

"Well, what's the matter with you?"

"I don't know, Doctor. I've got an awful pain in my bowels; guess I've got the chronic diarrhea."

"Let's see your tongue! Give him number six! Next, what's the matter with you?"

"I was took with an awful griping pain in my bowels – guess I've got the chronic diarrhea."

"Give him number nine! Next, what ails you?"

"I've g-g-got an almighty b-b-bellyache, g-g-guess I've got the chronic d-d-diarrhea."

"Run out your tongue! Give him number eleven!"'[7]

After the last man was seen at surgeon's call Holt ate breakfast, he wrote. Then, for the rest of the day: 'After meal I visited the hospitals and a barn where our sick are lying; in all visited and prescribed for, one hundred and eighty-six men. I had no dinner.' Then, after a full day including visiting a medical purveyor four miles away to get more medical stores, he returned only to be awakened at three in the morning to attend an officer dying of typhoid.[8]

Marshall would not have much time for daily garrison routine for the Army of the Potomac was on the move when he joined it. As it turned out, from July to December 1862 there would be much action, although the ranks of the artillery reserve would not be as sadly depleted as would infantry regiments. But cannon would roar at the Second Manassas, Antietam, Fredericksburg, and the artillery reserve hospital would receive wounded cannoneers, as well as others who got hurt fairly near the hospital. Most artillery wounds would come from small arms (as cannon operated generally within musket range) and shell, as batteries exchanged fire in an effort to silence each other.

Slowly, through 1862 and well into 1863, Letterman's changes began to prove themselves. 'Never had wounded men been so quickly or so well cared for,' recalled George Stevens, a VI Corps surgeon, after Fredericksburg in December 1862. 'It was the beginning of an era of *organized* labor in that department.'[9] Even with these changes, however, the hospitals were no more attractive than before. Stevens described the hospitals after Antietam:

'Sickening as is the sight of the battle-field, the scenes about the hospitals are worse, except to those who are actually engaged in ministering to the relief of the wounded. To these the excitement and labor incident to their duties, crowd out the thoughts of the ghastly surroundings. They see only so many demands upon them for assistance, and have no time to indulge in sentimental emotions.

'Here in the rear of the army for miles, was a succession of hospitals. Every house, and barn, and haystack, formed the nucleus of a hospital, where men, shot through the head, through the limbs, through the body; with every conceivable variety of wounds, lay groaning in anguish. Surgeons toiled day and night with never lagging zeal to relieve these sufferings, but all their labor could only afford slight relief. The labors of medical officers after a great battle are immense, and there is no respite from their toils so long as a wounded man remains uncared for.'[10]

There was no scrubbing up for operations, no covering the area with germ-killing sprays. Lacking any knowledge of infection, surgeons operated on while wearing the same dirty, wool coats, trousers, and vests they'd worn all day. At best, they'd replace their coats with a white linen vest, soon to be splashed red with blood. They probed wounds with the same dirty fingers that had minutes before probed another wound. They dipped off their knives and saws in bowls of bloody, filthy water between operations. They peered into cavities, breathing germ-laden air into body cavities. General Carl Schurz described such a scene after Gettysburg, where Marshall and his compatriots would work for dozens of hours without even a break:

'Most of the operating tables were placed in the open where the light was best, some of them partially protected against the rain by tarpaulins or blankets stretched upon poles. There stood the surgeons, their sleeves rolled up to their elbows, their bare arms as well as their linen aprons smeared with blood, their knives not seldom held between their teeth, while they were helping a patient on or off the table or had their hands otherwise occupied... As a wounded man was lifted on the table, often shrieking with pain as the attendants handled him, the surgeon quickly examined the wound and resolved upon cutting off the injured limb. Some ether was administered and the body put in position in a moment. The surgeon snatched his knife from between his teeth..., wiped it rapidly once or twice across his bloodstained apron, and the cutting began. The operation accomplished, the surgeon would look around with a deep sigh, and then – "Next!"[11]

With the large number of patients arriving within seconds of each other, there was little time for elaborate reconstructive surgery. Indeed, operating surgeons had little time for anything other than straight amputations. Men with wounds in places such as the body cavity or head which did not lend themselves to amputation often had little done to them. There was, in fact, little that period physicians could do for them, but leave them to rest and recover as best they could. Still, this apparent neglect brought scorn from those so wounded and their friends. Rice Bull, a New York infantry private, was shot in the head at Antietam. Later, he recalled:

'After the rain had ceased the Surgeons continued their work of amputation and during the whole of our stay did nothing as far as I could see to treat any of the wounded except those requiring amputation. I presume they did what they thought was the best but we wounded men through that they should have given some attention to all the seriously wounded.'[12]

For wounds to the extremities caused by pieces of cast iron shot or slow-moving lead bullets that shattered bones and tore blood vessels and muscles, amputation was the treatment of choice. Most amputations were performed quickly, the limbs tossed out to an ever-growing pile of limbs outside the hospital. Luckily, several decades earlier American surgeons had began using chloroform, for the most part, to put patients asleep during operations, so most patients were unaware of the hacking and sawing.

After such treatments, patients were returned to rest, usually on straw, for a time, usually a day or so, until they could be transported back to a main hospital in a place such as Philadelphia or Washington. Surgeons lost track of their patients, unless the man was someone they knew from their own regiment, thereafter.

In early September 1862 the 1st Pennsylvania Light Artillery's surgeon, Edward Shippin, resigned to accept a position as a surgeon of volunteers within the army's hospital system, and Marshall was breveted to take his place. A commission as a full surgeon followed, arriving 3 April 1863. Marshall now wore the double-breasted coat of a field grade officer and received $80 a month.

But life in the field was proving too much for Marshall. He had put in long hours after fighting at Antietam, Fredericksburg, Chancellorsville and Gettysburg. One surgeon wrote home after equally heavy fighting in the Wilderness, 'I've had no sleep on any account for three days now, only little snatches caught by the woodside. I am tired out.'[13] Marshall had also suffered from the cold at Fredericksburg and long exposures to rain after Gettysburg. A heart that appears to have been none too healthy when he joined was further weakened by these long hours and constant exposure. On 12 September 1863 he wrote the Army of the Potomac's adjutant general:

'I have the honor hereby to offer my resignation as an officer in the Military Service of the United States for the reason that my health is such that I cannot endure the exposures of Camp life.'[14]

Along with his resignation, Marshall submitted a certificate signed by Assistant Surgeon Franklin Grube that outlines his ailments:

'1st. That his pulse is *fluctuating* – beating more rapidly at times, and slower on expiration than on inspiration. These irregularities are very marked after the slightest fatigue.

'2nd. After fatigue, there is a blowing murmur indicating imperfect closure of the *mitral* valves.

'3rd. The 1st sound on impulse of the heart is double – indicating that the closure of the valves is not synchronised with the heart's contraction.

'4th. Frequent and varying degrees of pallor and general debility.

'In my opinion, the disease of this Officer is *organic* and of Rheumatic origin – resulting from the unavoidable exposures of camp life, and having existed to my personal knowledge for four months. I believe a removal from the exposures of camp is necessary to prevent permanent disability and perhaps to save his life.'[15]

The army acted quite quickly, and on 18 September 1863 Marshall was discharged because of his physical disability. However, he still wanted to contribute to the war effort, and on 1 October 1863 he was hired as a 'contract surgeon.' Contract surgeons were civilians who were hired, for the most part to staff army hospitals, for a short time, usually between three to six months. During the war, the army hired some 5,500 contract surgeons, although at any given time there would be generally no more than 1,500 at work at any given time. Pay was the same as for commissioned surgeons, at some $80 to $100 a month, and no uniforms were required.

'I am a contract surgeon with one hundred per month & without the stripes or other uniform, which I like better,' one such doctor wrote home, adding later that he did wear a 'military cap'.[16] Many other such surgeons wore types of uniforms, often plain dark blue trousers and frock coat, and Marshall probably wore his old army uniform. The duties he now performed were inside reasonably comfortable, heated hospitals, with shorter hours. It would be a much easier life than that of a regimental surgeon. Marshall would do a number of stints as an army contract surgeon, from 1 April 1865 to 22 September 1865; from 22 July 1878 to 3 October 1881; and from 27 December 1881 to 27 December 1882.

While working in this capacity, on 15 June 1865, he married a Washington woman, Olivia A. Tingle. It was one of thousands of war-time marriages, propelled by loneliness and distance from home, as well as a need for some sort of feeling of permanence in what the war proved to be a very impermanent world. Most of these war-time marriages were with women from back home (as in the case of Franklin Case and Charles Trotter): but men away from home frequently found local women to marry. The couple had two children who died in infancy.

As it turned out, however, his heart condition, dangerous as it sounded, was not to kill him quickly. Indeed, he went on to attend medical school at the Chicago Medical College, the medical department of Northwestern University, being graduated as an MD from there in 1875. Then in 1884, his marriage apparently going sour, he went west. He left behind his wife Mary – a war-time marriage that failed – as so many did. In many ways the problems created by these marriages contributed to the loosening of divorce laws in the years after the war. Eventually he reached California where he settled in Colton, San Bernardino County. On 30 June 1886 she was granted a divorce from him, something fairly rare, for having been abandoned two years.

One of five doctors in Colton, he became the first president of the Southern California Medical Society. He also eventually was remarried, when fifty-two years old, to a thirty-nine-year-old woman, Martha Moad, a widow from Illinois, on 3 February 1887. And he would live a fruitful life until his peaceful death on 18 October 1919, in his home.

NOTES

1 Mohr, James C., ed., *The Cormany Diaries*, Pittsburgh, Pennsylvania, 1982, pp. 307, 312
2 Adams, George Washington, *Doctors in Blue*, New York, 1961, p. 17
3 Barber, Lucius W., *Army Memoirs of*, Chicago, 1894, p. 64
4 Greiner, James M., Janet L. Coryell and James R. Smither, eds., *A Surgeon's Civil War*, Kent, Ohio, 1994, p. 5
5 Official, *Revised Army Regulations 1861*, Philadelphia, 1863, p. 283
6 Flower, Milton E., *Dear Folks at Home*, Carlisle, Pennsylvania, 1963, p. 15
7 Small, Abner R., *The Road to Richmond*, Berkeley, California, 1957, pp. 187–8
8 Greiner, op. cit.,, pp 34–6.
9 Stevens, George T., *Three Years in the Sixth Corps*, Albany, New York, 1866, p. 171
10 ibid, p. 154
11 Adams, op. cit., p. 106
12 Bauer, K. Jack, ed., *Soldiering: The Civil War Diary of Rice C. Bull*, New York, 1988, p. 80
13 Heslin, James J., 'From the Wilderness to Petersburg: The Diary of Surgeon Frank Ridgway', *The New York Historical Society Quarterly*, April 1961, p. 130
14 Price, Marshall F., personal file, National Archives, Washington, D.C.
15 ibid
16 Joseph, Peter, ed., *The Wounded River, The Civil War Letters of John Vance Lauderdale, M.D.*, East Lansing, Michigan, 1993, p. 64, p. 152

13

Charles Borromer Rohan,
Second Lieutenant, 12th Infantry,
Corps d'Afrique / Staff Officer

It is an odd twist of fate that those whose fates were most linked to the Union cause – the African-Americans living in the country – were at the beginning of the war the least able to contribute directly to that cause. The great Army of the Union was to be an all-white force, while black citizens, free or slave, were required to watch from the sidelines as operations continued.

As the war dragged on, however, and casualties mounted, Congress responded to the growing demand for black military participation with its Second Confiscation Act, passed 17 July 1862, which 'authorised the President to receive into the service of the United States, for the purpose of constructing entrenchments or performing camp duty, or any labor, or other military or naval service for which they found to be competent, persons of African descent, and provided that such persons should be enrolled and organised, under such regulations not inconsistent with the Constitution and laws as the President may prescribe'. This was followed up with the Militia Act of the same date that allowed that 'persons of African descent who under this law shall be employed, shall receive $10.00 a month, one ration, $3.00 of which monthly pay may be in clothes'.[1]

The Union commander of New Orleans, Massachusetts, politician turned soldier Major General Benjamin Butler, was one of the first to take advantage of Congress's orders. His own General Orders No. 63 called for free African-Americans in the city to join the Federal forces where they would be armed, uniformed and organised into companies with proper officers appointed over them. What was not said was that these proper officers would be, for the most part, although not altogether, white. By early 1863 Butler had organised four infantry regiments of Native Guards. On the 6th of that month the regiments were transferred into a newly organised 'Corps d'Afrique', which fell under command of the Department of the Gulf.

'The Major General commanding the Department proposes the organisation of a corps d'armée of colored troops,' read General Orders No. 40, 1 May 1863, 'to be designated as the "Corps d'Afrique". It will consist ultimately of eighteen regiments representing all arms – Infantry, Artillery and Cavalry, organised in three Divisions of three Brigades, each with appropriate corps of Engineers and flying Hospitals for each Division. Appropriate uniforms, and the graduation of pay to correspond with value of service, will be hereafter awarded.'[2]

Command of the Corps d'Afrique fell to Brigadier General Daniel Ullmann, who before the war had been a New York lawyer and once ran for governor of New York on the Know-Nothing party – based essentially on being against immigration. He began his military career as colonel of the 78th New York Infantry in the eastern theatre where he was captured after Cedar Mountain. On his exchange he was awarded a general's star and sent to Louisiana with the specific assignment of raising units from among the state's African-Americans.

The problem from the start was, where to get the 'proper officers' to command these new African-American formations? 'With a race unaccustomed to military service, much more depends on the immediate influence of officers upon individual members, than with those that have acquired more or less of warlike habits and spirit by centuries of contest,' read the orders that created the Corps d'Afrique. 'The Commanding General desires to detail for temporary or permanent duty the best officers of the army, for the organisation, instruction and discipline of this corps.'[3]

Where to get such officers? Major General David Hunter wanted 'the most intelligent and energetic of our non-commissioned officers: men who will go into it with all their hearts' for his 1st South Carolina, one of the first black regiments which had been organised from escaped slaves on that state's coast.[4] Ullmann, however, felt that no previous military experience was actually needed even by field grade officers. Instead, a prospective officer needed to be intelligent enough to grasp quickly the fundamentals of the school of the soldier, company and battalion, along with the basics of Army Regulations. Moreover, he had to have a good character. This policy certainly opened the door to many applicants who might not have had a chance to get a commission, but it was bound to let in a few misfits as well.

On to this scene came Charles Borromer Rohan, who referred to himself as C. Borromer Rohan. Rohan, a twenty-year-old native Bostonian whose father came from Ireland, first appeared in New Orleans in the fall of 1863 looking for a meal ticket in the form of a commission with one of the new black units. Apparently witty, charming and intelligent in a clever sort of way, especially with words, he talked Ullmann into commissioning him a second lieutenant in the Corps d'Afrique, his commission being dated 14 November

1863. But the newly minted lieutenant did not seem in a hurry to join a field company and hung around the city drawing his $45 a month pay and spending it as quickly as he drew it. New Orleans was then, as now, famed as a free-living, high spirited city, filled with fine restaurants, theatres and luxurious houses of ill fame. There was plenty for a single young man to do.

The good life was not to last forever, and eventually the corps adjutant caught up with the young lieutenant and posted him to a line unit. On 19 December 1863 Borromer was assigned to Company A, 12th Regiment of Infantry, Corps d'Afrique. The 12th had been raised in Port Hudson in September 1863 and in December was part of the garrison there. Borromer had to leave the fleshpots of New Orleans and travel up-river to his new post at Port Hudson, one of the Confederacy's last positions on the Mississippi River to fall into Union hands. After the long siege that preceded its capture, the war-torn city presented a far cry from what Borromer was used to.

Nor does Borromer seem to have been keen on being a line infantry officer, with all the dangers and potential discomfort that involved. It is possible that Borromer's new commanding officer recognised immediately that the young, untried lieutenant was simply not cut out for line work. The question was, what to do with him?

At first the commander of the 12th, Colonel William H. Dickey, assigned Borromer to be the regimental adjutant, but he must have realised, almost as soon as he had appointed the lieutenant, that Borromer had no grasp of what was required. The post was a demanding one, one of the most important at the regimental level. Another Federal lieutenant, Charles Haydon, adjutant of the 2nd Michigan Infantry Regiment, described the job: 'The office has not a few advantages & is generally considered the most desirable of any below "Field". It gives more extended acquaintance at HdQrs, a larger knowledge of business in all its branches and is in fact a very useful school of instruction in almost every branch of military affairs. It is a most desirable position for anyone who expects to be Capt. & is regarded as the legitimate road to that office. He has good quarters & no nights on guard or days on fatigue. He is expected to dress well, be neat & punctual & polite & a sort of special pleader to all the nice points of drill & etiquette.'[5] Clearly, Borromer had no special knowledge of drill and military etiquette.

So the job of adjutant was too much of an order for someone with absolutely no military experience. Apparently the regiment's colonel went to his commander, Brigadier General George L. Andrews, to ask help in getting Borromer a new post. Andrews was one of the brighter lights in the army, graduating first in his class of 1851 at West Point and having served well in the eastern theatre as a colonel and brigadier before becoming Major General N. P. Banks's chief of staff for the siege of Port Hudson. After some thought, Andrews, on 20 December 1863, gave Borromer the job of commissary of musters on his staff.

This post was one of authority, but did not require a great deal of specialised knowledge. According to the 13th Article of War:

'At every muster, the commanding officer of each regiment, troop, or company there present, shall give certificates, signed by himself, signifying how long officers who do not appear at muster have been absent, and the reason of their absence. In like manner, the commanding officer of every troop or company shall give certificates, signifying the reasons of the absence of the non-commissioned officers and private soldiers, which reasons and time of absence shall be inserted in the muster-rolls, opposite the names of the respective absent officers and soldiers. The certificates shall, together with the muster-rolls, be remitted by the commissary of musters or other officer mustering, to the Department of War, as speedily as the distance of the place shall admit.'[6]

This was certainly not a demanding position. The forms Borromer had to have filled out were pre-printed; he had a clerk at hand actually to fill out the forms; the unit commanders had to give him the information and he would simply sign the completed forms. Moreover, musters were not required more often than every two months, the last days of February, April, June, August, October and December.

Indeed, Borromer seems to have fulfilled the minimal requirements of his office well enough, since the War Department issued him a commission in the volunteer army, to be carried on the rolls of the regiment he had not actually spent much time with, on 30 January 1864. Borromer seems to have appeared to grow in his job since, on 30 April of that same year he was named an acting inspector general on staff. Army Regulations required an Inspector-General, or someone of that department, to hold full bi-monthly musters as well as inspections to see what condition were all arms, uniforms, and equipment. His reports were to indicate:

'the discipline of the troops; their instruction in all military exercises and duties: the state of their arms, clothing, equipments, and accouterments of all kinds; of their kitchens and messes; of the barracks and quarters at the post; of the guard-house, prisons, hospital, bake-house, magazines, store-houses, and stores of every description; of the stables and horses; the condition of the post school; the management and application of the post and company funds; the state of the post, and regimental, and company books, papers, and files; the zeal and ability of the officers in command of the troops; the capacity of the officers conducting the administrative and staff services, the fidelity and economy of their disbursements; the condition of all public property, and the amount of money in the hands of each disbursing officer; the regularity of issues and payments; the mode of enforcing discipline by courts-martial, and by the authority of the officers; the propriety and legality of all punishments inflicted; and any information whatsoever concerning the service, in any matter or particular that may merit notice, or aid to correct defects or introduce improvements.

'Inspectors are required particularly to report if any officer is of intemperate habits, or unfit for active service by infirmity or any other cause.'[7]

It was while holding this post in April 1864 that Borromer had himself photographed in Port Hudson by the photographic company of Brooks & Blauvelt. He gave one print to General Andrews; the one seen here went to a fellow staff officer.

Yet by the summer General Andrews appears to have felt that Borromer was not up to the task of being an inspector general. Instead of returning him to his regiment, however, Andrews kept him on the staff and gave him the title of aide-de-camp on 6 August 1864. The job did not come with specific duties. According to Scott's *Military Dictionary*, aides-de-camp 'are confidential officers selected by general officers to assist them in their military duties'. Moreover:

'Attached to the person of the general, they receive orders only from him. Their functions are difficult and delicate. Often enjoying the full confidence of the general, they are employed in representing him, in writing orders, in carrying them in person if necessary, in communicating them verbally upon battle-fields and other fields of maneuver. It is important that Aides-de-Camp should know well the positions of troops, routes, posts, quarters of generals, composition of columns, and orders of corps; facility in the use of the pen should be joined with *exactness* of expression. Upon fields of battle they watch the movements of the enemy; not only grand maneuvers but special tactics should be familiar to them. It is necessary that their knowledge should be sufficiently comprehensive to understand the object and purpose of all orders, and also to judge in the varying circumstances of a battle-field, whether it is not necessary to modify an order when carried in person, or if there be time to return for new instructions.'[8]

Borromer's actual duties, therefore, were up to the general, and they naturally varied. His main duty, however, was being in charge of the headquarters officers' mess, arranging for purchases of food and having it cooked and served, since officers were not supplied rations as were enlisted men and had to fend for themselves. At the same time, he was given other odd jobs as the need arose. For example, on 28 December 1864, Borromer had the task of greeting a visiting dignitary at Port Hudson, Major General Quincy A. Gillmore, soon to be named commander of the Department of the South. Borromer alerted his boss of the visit, sending him a telegraph to advise him that, 'General Gillmore is here. Will make but a brief inspection and visit Baton Rouge to-night.'[9]

Eventually something went wrong in the relationship of Borromer and the general. This much would be clear from the fact that even with his time in service, Borromer never even received a promotion to the rank of first lieutenant, something that virtually every officer with a similar amount of time in grade received. Possibly it had to do with rumours of misspent mess funds. No matter what it was, on 13 February 1865 Andrews dropped him from the staff, ordering him to New Orleans to wait for new orders. There Borromer cooled his heels while the army decided what to do with him. Finally, seeing that he had served as a mustering officer before, the headquarters in New Orleans shipped him off to Brigadier General Thomas J. McKean, a fifty-four-year-old West Pointer who was considered too old for field service and so was assigned to command in western Florida. Orders shipping Borromer to this post were issued on 27 February, but Borromer never obeyed them. Instead he remained in the city, apparently talking his way out of such an assignment. The orders were revoked on 1 March, and new orders assigning him to the Board of Enrollment in New Orleans were cut the same day.

Boards of Enrollment were created by a Congressional act to oversee the Conscription Act. They also were to serve as a board of appeal for men who had been conscripted but claimed an exemption for reasons such as conscientious objection to military service, alien status, ill-health or the like. They were 'to employ the most diligent exertions in forwarding soldiers to the front, and arresting deserters, shirkers, and all fit for duty who are absent without proper authority'.[10] Since freed African-Americans fell under the law that created the draft, it is possible that Borromer's commission, which was still for the 12th Corps d'Afrique, now retitled the 84th US Colored Infantry Regiment, helped him gain this job. It is, however, ironic that Borromer, a man who had never seen a minute at the front since joining the army, was now one of those responsible for sending men into combat.

While duty on the Board of Enrollment was relatively light, mostly involving sitting on a panel in judgment of each draftee's case and signing papers, and New Orleans was as exciting a place to be as ever, a position on the Board essentially put Borromer in the backwater. There were definitely no promotions to be had on the Board of Enrollment. Therefore, he tried to get reassigned to a staff position where he could find someone who would help him get that gold bar for his shoulder straps. On 2 May 1865, the war virtually over, he got an assignment to the staff of Major General John Newton. Graduating second in his West Point class of 1842, Newton had had a brilliant combat career in both the east and west until the siege of Atlanta. After that city fell, the general was assigned as commander of the District of West Florida, headquartered in Key West.

Borromer reported to his new superior on 15 May. There Newton could find no specific task for the young officer. He kept him on his staff for only a month before forwarding him to another staff, that of Brigadier General Alexander S. Asboth, a Hungarian who had been badly wounded in the face earlier and had not yet recovered. Borromer was not long to remain at Asboth's Alabama headquarters, for he was sent to headquarters in Tallahassee on 3 August, and from there ordered back to New Orleans on 8 September.

Perhaps the generals had heard troubling stories about Borromer's prior service. Certainly there must have been such, and they were catching up with him by the time he got back to New Orleans. On 27 November 1865 a report from the Inspector General's Department of the Military Division of the Gulf was forwarded to Major General Philip H. Sheridan, commander of that division, that read:

'I have the honor to state for your information, that whilst I was at Key West Florida, I was informed and had papers (pay accounts and order assigning to duty) placed in my hands by Mr. E. B. Rawson showing an indebtedness on the part of Lieut. Charles B. Rohan 84th USCI of $510.37/100 to Mr Rawson. This amount was given to Lieut Rohan for said pay accounts as a personal favor because he, said Rohan, was in need of the money and about to leave Key West for some other post in Florida.

'The said pay accounts were sent by Mr Rawson to this city and presented to the Pay Department to be paid but the gentleman presenting the accounts was informed that Lieut Rohan was in New Orleans and had personally drawn his pay for the period named in said accounts. In fact he had got his pay for the months of June, July, and August from Mr Rawson and the Pay Department. I have had several interviews with this young man and tried to get him to pay this amount $510.37/100 to me to be sent to Mr Rawson, but have at last been obliged to give up the case as hopeless.

'Lieut Rohan was during the past war caterer to General Andrews's mess at Port Hudson. Monies received by said Rohan from General Andrews and other members of the mess for the purpose of liquidating the debts of the mess of which he was caterer were appropriated by him, Lieut Rohan, to his own personal use, and the said debts contracted by Lieut Rohan as Caterer for said mess and for which the aforesaid monies were paid him were never paid.

'This young man Rohan is in my opinion a cad and swindler and if nothing else can be done with him he should at least be dishonorably dismissed from the service.'[11]

Borromer must have learned that this report was going to be forwarded to higher authorities – a report that was certain to result in a court martial and quite possibly a prison term at such an unpleasant place as Dry Tortougas, a prison at the very end of the Florida peninsula. Therefore, he managed to strike first. On 12 November 1865 he wrote the following letter:

'I have the honor to tender my resignation as Second Lieutenant of "A" Company, 84th United States Colored Infantry.

'I certify on honor that I am not responsible for any public property and that I am not indebted to the United States any amount on any account or material.'[12]

He had not acted in time. Borromer was called before a general court martial to answer the charges of embezzlement. In these proceedings Borromer was called before a board of between five and thirteen officers, ranging in rank, with the senior officer serving as president of the court. None of the officers had legal backgrounds. One officer was assigned to be the prosecutor, while another was assigned as defence attorney. They, too, did not have legal backgrounds, although Borromer was free to hire a civilian attorney if he pleased. A judge advocate, whose job was to be the official prosecutor, could summon witnesses, and would sign a copy of the proceedings and send the proceedings on to the higher authority who could confirm the sentence. He also, however, had to make sure the defendant got a fair trial, without being forced to reply to leading questions or being forced to incriminate himself. The judge advocate was often an officer with a legal background – usually the only such individual in a court room.

Borromer's case was only one of several that a specific court martial board would try. And, while it was still in session, and the outcome of Borromer's case not yet announced, army headquarters accepted Borromer's resignation from the service on 22 November. At the end of the trial, however, the court martial board found Borromer guilty, but remitted the sentence. This was not acceptable to the headquarters of the Military Division of the Gulf. It issued orders on 26 November that the original sentence that called for the lieutenant 'to be dismissed from the service of the United States' was confirmed. Either way, Borromer was out on his ear.

But the waters were muddy. Someone who had been dismissed from the service could not receive a pension while someone who had resigned could. Possibly this distinction was in Borromer's mind when he returned to Boston after the war. He became a reporter, one hoping his newspaper stories were a bit more honest and successful than his military reports. There, too, he married Susan Harrington in June 1880, and they had three children before the failed soldier died on 12 December 1894.

Borromer's widow then applied for a pension. She claimed to the Pension Board that her husband had told her that he served as a lieutenant in the 55th Massachusetts Infantry Regiment from 2 August 1862 until that regiment was mustered out on 1 January 1863. In fact, however, the only 55th Massachusetts Regiment was not mustered in until 6 April 1864 and then was mustered out on 30 July 1865. And Borromer was not a member of such an organisation.

Then, she told the Pension Board, her husband had served on the staff of a 'General Burt' from 8 June 1863 until 1 August 1863. No such general is listed as a regularly appointed or breveted general in the US Army at that time – or indeed at any point in the war.

Even so, Borromer beat the army in the end. The Pension Office ruled on 25 April 1896 that his widow was entitled to a pension because his resignation was accepted and special orders were cut to that effect before the court martial had dismissed him.

NOTES

1 Gladstone, William A., *Men of Color*, Gettysburg, Pennsylvania, 1993, p. 1
2 ibid, p. 29
3 ibid, p. 29
4 Glatthaar, Joseph T., *Forged in Battle*, New York, 1990, p. 36
5 Stephen W. Sears, *For Country Cause & Leader*, New York, 1993, pp. 266–7
6 Scott, Col. H. L., *Military Dictionary*, New York, 1864, p. 427
7 War Department, *Revised Regulations for the Army of the United States, 1861*, Philadelphia, 1863, p. 71
8 Scott, op. cit., p. 21
9 *ORs*, Series I, Vol. XLI, Part IV, p. 948
10 *ORs*, Series III, Vol. IV, p. 999
11 Rohan, Charles B., Pension Record, National Archives, Washington, DC
12 ibid

14
Jacob Henry Sleeper
Brevet Major, 10th Massachusetts Light Artillery Battery

Jacob Henry Sleeper, known to all by his second name to avoid confusion with his father, turned twenty in 1861. Until then he had led a rather privileged life in Boston, the city locals called 'the hub of the Universe'. His father was the Hon. Jacob Sleeper, a member of the Governor's Council. But when the war broke out, the entire family threw themselves into the cause of the Union. Jacob Sleeper joined the Boston committee of the Christian Commission, a group of clergymen and mostly evangelical church laymen who raised money to send agents to the armed forces to aid the wounded and encourage the spiritual wellbeing of the men in the field. In all, the committee raised $348,581.41 in funds and provided another $526,980.10 worth of religious and other reading materials, kitchen supplies and the like to the Commission delegates.

Henry decided that he too should serve his country, as a serving soldier. He had an advantage, besides family connections, in that before the war he had been a member of the volunteer militia company, the Boston Light Artillery. Therefore, he looked for, and was soon awarded, an officer's commission. In April, only days after Fort Sumter was fired on, Henry accepted the commission of a first lieutenant of infantry in the 5th Massachusetts Infantry Regiment, which had been ordered to report for duty on 19 April 1861 for three months' Federal service.

Without much time for drill or preparation, the regiment was rushed to Washington, then threatened by Confederates just across the Potomac River. The 6th Massachusetts Regiment had passed through Baltimore on its way to Washington and had lost men to an angry pro-Southern mob; ensuing regiments took no chance of that being repeated. The 5th went via Annapolis, which they reached on 29 April, arriving in Washington a short time later. The city was not ready for the imminent influx of volunteers, and the regiment found itself quartered in the Treasury Building on Pennsylvania Avenue next door to the President's mansion, the White House.

Once the city was safe, the Union Army went on an offensive designed to clear the Virginia side of the Potomac from Confederates. Major General

Charles Sanford led a group across to Alexandria and, without serious incident, occupied the area. The 5th left its comfortable quarters and moved to a new tented camp located between a small creek known as Four Mile Run and the city of Alexandria, Virginia. On the way over, they were met by a group of men from Massachusetts then living in Washington, who presented the regiment with a US flag to accompany the state flag they were carrying. Once in Virginia, they set up Camp Massachusetts and played host to a stream of visitors who inspected their ranks. These VIP visitors included the President himself, the Secretaries of the Treasury and War, and the governor of Massachusetts.

Time passed as the men worked daily on the drill field while waiting to be led out to battle. Newspapers demanded a drive on the enemy's capital of Richmond. Lincoln pressed his commanding general, Irwin McDowell, for just such a drive. Finally, although he knew his men were poorly prepared, McDowell gave in to the pressure and drew up a plan for an overland march to Richmond. A Confederate force blocked his way near a crossroads, Manassas Junction.

With its three months of service almost over, the 5th was assigned to the First Brigade, Third Division of the army organised for McDowell's offensive. They would come under command of an old army professional, William B. Franklin. The brigade, which was part of the force that was to turn the enemy's flank along the Bull Run creek, reached Centerville about 4.30 in the afternoon of 20 July. Early next morning they started on their flank march, and soon ran into the enemy. The regiment followed the 8th New York State Militia Regiment on to the field, when the 8th ran into heavy enemy fire and was routed. The 5th and 11th Massachusetts Regiments, originally held in reserve on the left bank of the run, were ordered forward, to the right of Henry Hill where two Federal Artillery batteries were posted across a vale from a stock-still line of Confederate infantry. There they came under Confederate artillery fire, always a hard experience for raw troops, 'and were consequently thrown into some confusion. This was shown,' the brigade commander reported, 'by wild firing made by both regiments. They fired without command, and in one or two instances, while formed in column, closed in mass.'

Despite this, as a Confederate infantry regiment closed with and over-ran the cannon on the hill, the regiments were ordered to charge and recover the guns. Their charge was successful, and they quickly regained the guns. 'It was impossible, however, to get the men to draw off the guns, and when one or two attempts were made,' General Franklin wrote, 'we were driven off by the appearance of the enemy in large force with heavy and well-aimed volleys of musketry.'

The 1st Minnesota, another regiment in the brigade, now came up, but it, too, was beaten back. Although the 1st retired in good order, the brigade commander reported: 'The other two regiments of the brigade [including the 5th] retired in confusion, and no efforts of myself or staff were successful in rallying them.'[1] The 5th lost five men killed, twenty-six wounded, including Colonel Samuel Lawrence and two other officers, and had twenty-eight missing. The thoroughly beaten men headed back to Washington, frequently throwing away weapons and equipment so as not to be slowed down, and not stopping until they arrived at the city. There they gathered again and returned on the train to Boston, where they were met, perhaps somewhat undeservedly, 'with the most enthusiastic demonstrations of grateful regard' by local citizens.[2] The regiment was mustered out on 30 July 1861.

Henry, however, was not ready to give up the fight. He wanted to get back into the army to save the Union, and applied to the governor for a new commission. He would have to wait two months for his wishes to be granted.

On 27 August 1861 the Commonwealth authorised the organisation of a battery of light artillery. The First Massachusetts Light Battery was mustered in at Camp Cameron. According to Army General Orders, the battery was to consist of Captain Josiah Porter, First Lieutenant William McCartney, Second Lieutenant Jacob Federhen, a first sergeant, a company quartermaster-sergeant, four sergeants, eight corporals, two musicians, two artificers, a wagoner, and a minimum of fifty-eight privates. A maximum-strength battery would have comprised another first lieutenant and second lieutenant, two sergeants, four corporals, four artificers, and sixty-four privates. In fact, the First, when mustered in, consisted of 150, all ranks, mostly seamen from Marblehead, Lynn and other small ports on the seacoast. Recruiting was easy, since the artillery was a popular branch of the service. 'This is about the best branch of the service as there will be no picket duty nor carrying knapsacks,' wrote a New Jersey cannoneer home to his parents in Britain. 'I shall ride a horse and have very light work.'[3]

September was spent learning the basics of artillery drill – vital for general safety. Drill, drill and drill again was the order of the day. It was while the battery was undergoing this first drill, on 1 September 1861, that Henry was commissioned a first lieutenant and assigned to the new battery.

Henry would need a new uniform, consisting of a single-breasted dark blue frock coat with his red shoulder straps edged with gold embroidery, and a broad-brimmed dress hat with gold and black hat cords and gold-embroidered crossed cannon on its front. For field duty, most field artillery officers preferred a waist-length jacket, as was allowed them by Army Regulations, with a gold Russian knot on each shoulder instead of the shoulder straps used by officers in the rest of the army. For many, these uniforms would come out of a first lieutenant's pay of $50 a month. Henry, of course, had money of his own.

On 1 October the Commonwealth's governor notified the War Department, 'Massachusetts will send on Thursday, the 3rd instant, to Washington a full battery of light artillery, completely equipped for service, under the command of Captain Porter...'[4]

Arriving in Washington several days later, the battery, now designated Battery A, Massachusetts Light Artillery, went into defensive lines around the city. Then, all that winter, it was back to the drill field, practising on its three 10-pounder Parrott rifles and a 12-pounder howitzer. In the spring, McClellan's Peninsula Campaign got under way. The First accompanied the army, assigned to a division commanded by William B. Franklin, under a regular army artillery officer, Captain Richard Arnold of the 5th US, as chief of artillery. The battery landed near Yorktown on 6 May 1862, landing at ten in the morning, the last battery off the boat, and was assigned to give artillery support to Dana's brigade of Sedgwick's Division. Although fighting on the peninsula was largely between bodies of infantry, due to the heavily wooded terrain, broken up by marshy creeks and muddy roads, the battery did manage to see some action. 'The First Massachusetts Battery, under command of Captain Porter, is entitled to great credit for the accuracy of its fire,' reported Brigadier Henry Slocum.[5]

Henry would not remain long in the battery. He had already been noted as a man on the way up. On 4 August 1862 the commander of the artillery brigade of the 1st Division, VI Corps, Captain E. R. Platt, another regular of the 2nd US, wrote to the Massachusetts governor, 'Lieut. J. H. Sleeper of Porter's Battery "A," Mass. Vol. Art'y has been under my command some months. During that time I have observed him in the camp, on the march and on the battlefield, and it gives me pleasure to state that on all occasions and in all situations he has acquitted himself as a soldier should. He is an excellent officer and a good artillerist.'[6]

Marked for higher rank, Henry was recalled to Massachusetts and given a new assignment. He would become a captain, the battery commander – BC, as the men called the position – of the 10th Massachusetts Light Artillery. On 9 September Henry received word of his new appointment and was ordered to report to Camp Stanton, in Lynnfield, Massachusetts, to join his new command and begin its training. Technically, a battery commander was equal in all ways to a captain commanding a company of infantry or cavalry. In fact, though, this was not the case for the command was only very slightly larger than companies of other branches of service.

A battery commander, nevertheless, had a rather larger responsibility in his position than did other company commanders. He was given responsibility for very expensive equipment, more than the $13 muskets and assorted matériel available to an infantry company commander. In addition to the four to six cannon themselves, there was a limber for each gun, plus caissons that contained extra limber chests with ammunition packed in them. Each battery had a wagon in which was stored the tools, spare parts of carriages, spare harness and other stores required to keep a battery in the field. As well, there was a travelling forge, consisting of a body, a bellows house and coal box, used to shoe horses as well as to provide metalwork needed to repair carriages and wagons. Henry's battery also had three army wagons, in which the forage, rations and camp equipage, including the useless sabres issued to the men, were stored. Finally, the battery was also assigned an ambulance to carry sick and wounded.

It required almost as many horses to haul all these things as were used in a cavalry company. A six-gun battery would use twenty six-horse teams – six teams for guns and limbers, twelve for the caissons and limbers, and two for the battery wagon and forge – along with another ten spare horses. Each army wagon required four horses, while the ambulance took another two. All the officers, sergeants, buglers and the battery guidon bearer were also mounted, while the cannoneers either rode on the horse teams, on top of the limber chests, or walked. All in all, a battery represented some tens of thousands of taxpayers' money; much more, in fact, than was spent on any other type of company.

Moreover, while infantry and cavalry companies generally served jointly in battalions or regiments, artillery batteries were assigned to support infantry brigades at division levels, thus often serving quite independently in their parts of the field. It was uncommon to mass guns under artillery field-grade officers; hence, a battery commander was usually as independent in the field as was an infantry or cavalry colonel. Indeed, in terms of responsibility, a battery commander was virtually an equal to a colonel in any other branch of the service. This fact, however, was not reflected in pay, as infantry and artillery pay grades were identical, with a captain making $60 a month in both branches of the service.

The battery Henry was now to command had been authorised on 12 August 1821 under the temporary command of First Lieutenant Henry H. Granger, who understood that a captain would be appointed later as battery commander. By 14 August the *Boston Journal* reported: 'The 10th Massachusetts Battery recruiting by Lieut. H. H. Granger, is rapidly filling up, over 125 men having already enlisted.' These men reported to the battery's camp of instruction on 23 August, while Henry arrived there on 1 October. Two weeks later, the battery was off to war: 'Our march through Boston called forth quite enthusiastic demonstrations from the citizens,' a battery member recalled, 'which were continued until our arrival at the Old Colony Railway Station, where we were to take the cars.'[7]

From there they went to Fall River where they boarded a ship for Jersey City, then back on to railroad cars for Washington. Here they were assigned to Camp Berry, a mile east of the capitol building, setting up their tents on 17 October. They drew their 3-inch rifles and began artillery drill. 'The frequent and vigorous drills of our efficient Captain made us, on the authority of a no less competent judge than Gen. Barry himself, accomplished as artillerists, and of this education we were reasonably proud,' Cannoneer John D. Billings recalled.[8] When practising marching the battery as a column, Henry would take his post fourteen yards from the column and opposite its centre; when placing the battery in line, Henry would be posted four yards in front of its centre. He would, however, move about to where he was most needed when in action.

The officers and men also took advantage of being near Washington to do sightseeing and in November packages arrived from home for Thanksgiving dinners. According to Billings, 'Capt. Sleeper generously added to the occasion a contribution of six turkeys, which, with others already purchased, enabled us, so far as eatables affected the subject, to pass the day in a manner at least approximating its accustomed dignity and importance.'

Henry was making an excellent commanding officer. He drilled his men hard and long to make them proficient in their jobs, at the same time keeping up their morale with extra food and the like for special occasions. These efforts would pay off in the long run.

On the day after Christmas, the battery mounted up and headed west to Poolesville, Maryland, where it was assigned to guard fords along the Upper Potomac River. There, at a post named Camp Davis, they remained during the winter. Henry had his hands full with administration duties, both on and off the drill field. For example, one of his privates was caught stealing chickens from a local farmhouse. According to the Articles of War, Henry could have turned over the man to local civilian authorities for punishment or sent him to be court-martialled. Instead, however, Henry took the reasonable way out, ordering the man to return the birds and make a suitable apology to the offended civilian. Volunteer soldiers did not deserve to be treated the same way as regulars.

Henry organised an officers' mess, and allowed the men to use the mess tent for shows put on by the battery's minstrel troupe. During this winter, too, Henry was directed to inspect a detachment of cavalry, part of a regiment known as 'Scott's Nine Hundred'. His report indicated that it was in a poor state of discipline, so enraging its commander that he showed up at Henry's tent one night, revolver in hand, hell-bent on revenge. Fortunately, Henry was away that night.

On 18 April the battery moved a mile away to Camp Heintzelman, where Henry oversaw the building of a horse shelter awning with trees arranged over the tents to keep them cool. They remained there until 24 June when they were sent to Maryland Heights, where they remained until 30 June. On 1 July they were in Frederick, Maryland, and sent to guard the Monocacy River railroad bridge. The battery missed Gettysburg, joining the Army of the Potomac instead as it advanced into Virginia after Lee's army. Henry was given the responsibility for the entire III Corps wagon train. The battery was then posted to Warrenton, Virginia, until 15 September. Here battery members were ordered to wear the badge of the Artillery Brigade, III Corps on the sides of their caps, a lozenge divided into four smaller lozenges, two of which were blue, one red and one white. There, on 9 September, the anniversary of the battery's muster date, Henry allowed the men the day off to do as they chose. Seven days later, the battery rejoined the army, having its first engagement with Confederate cavalry near Auburn.

Henry's insistence on drill paid dividends. Wheeling into position, the battery halted the enemy cavalry in a twenty-minute action and soon drove them off. Its proficiency was noticed in General Orders No. 93, 18 October 1863: 'Especial credit is due the first brigade, Col. Collis, and to the Tenth Massachusetts Battery, Capt. Sleeper, for their gallantry in repulsing the enemy's attack on the head of the column at Auburn.'[9]

On 19 October the battery joined the army's advance in the Mine Run campaign, reaching Warrenton on 30 October. While there, Henry encountered trouble. One of his officers, Second Lieutenant Thomas R. Armitage, submitted a letter to Captain George E. Randolph, chief of artillery for III Corps, on 25 September: 'Having been grossly insulted by Captain J. Henry Sleeper, commanding the Tenth Mass. Battery, it is my desire that he be placed under arrest, in order that I may prefer charges against him.' He cannot have been pleased with the reply which advised him that, 'It is not proper that Capt. Sleeper be placed in arrest until his superior officer has decided whether the charge preferred be well founded or frivolous.' The details of the actual incident are unknown; the battery historian chose to ignore the matter.

Henry, however, faced bigger troubles than an irritated second lieutenant. Captain Randolph himself had requested that he be tried before a court martial on a charge of neglect of duty. The specification was 'that the said Captain J. Henry Sleeper commanding 10th Mass Battery did on or about the 15th day of September 1863 needlessly abandon at camp near White Sulphur Springs Virginia 3,000 lbs of mixed grain.'[10] Even if your army is suddenly pulling back, a commanding officer is supposed to be responsible for every item he is signed for: and that would even include 3,000 pounds of mixed grain.

Whether it was his father's political influence or the realisation at higher headquarters that the loss of 3,000 pounds of grain was not a major loss compared to other things thus far misplaced during the war is not clear. But there is no record that Henry was ever brought to trial and the entire matter of the missing grain seems to have been let slide. Nor was there ever a trial to satisfy the insulted Lieutenant Armitage. Indeed, on 27 October, Armitage was quietly transferred to Battery K, 4th US Artillery. He would be replaced by the battery's quartermaster sergeant, William G. Rollins.

While the wheels of justice were grinding on, or squeaking to a stop, as the case may have been, Henry had other things to do. Meade's Mine Run campaign was still in progress, and on 7 November the battery set off at the head of the column towards the Rappahannock. At Kelly's Ford, Henry deployed his men into line. There they spotted a Confederate battery protected by a redoubt. At two in the afternoon, they opened fire, soon driving the enemy away, and then switching their fire against sharpshooters hidden in brick houses at the ford on the other side of the river. Federal infantry now charged forward. Although David Barnett of the 99th Pennsylvania fell with his shattered knee, the 10th Massachusetts Battery came through without a loss, the only damage being from a shell that ricocheted, splitting the front of a limber chest without exploding it and cutting open a bundle of a battery member's clothing. By five in the evening the battle was over and the battery ceased fire. During the three hours, it had fired 459 rounds of ammunition.

That evening the battery crossed the river over one of the pontoon bridges laid by members of a New York volunteer engineer regiment and next day headed towards Brandy Station, remaining there until 26 November. With the rest of the army, it then crossed the Rapidan and headed towards Mine

Run. Getting into position by the morning of 30 November, the battery opened fire on Lee's works. Firing continued for about an hour, with apparently little damage being accomplished despite the 200-odd rounds expended. Meade could not winkle Lee out from his works, and Lee could not trap Meade away from a line of retreat. The campaign proved, for both sides, pretty much a failure, and Meade began to fall back. On 1 December the battery recrossed the Rapidan and on the 3rd went into camp at Brandy Station. After ensuring that the camp was fairly well set up, Henry was granted leave and, on 12 December, he went home. He would spend Christmas with his family, but all too soon, on 29 December 1863, he was back in camp.

At home Henry probably heard of the plan to merge the Commonwealth's batteries into a formal regiment, which would give at least three battery commanders field grade rank. It is possible that he wanted one of those slots for himself. Or perhaps Captain Randolph, not liking Henry and finding it impossible to bring the Massachusetts man to trial, tried another way to get rid of him. In any event, on 30 December he wrote to the Massachusetts governor asking him 'to consider favorably the claim to promotion of Captain J. Henry Sleeper, 10th Mass. Battery.

'I am sure from my knowledge of Captain Sleeper's merits that he will fill the office and perform the duties of any grade among the field officers of the proposed Regiment with honor to himself and credit to the state,' Randolph wrote.[11] Randolph's letter was favourably endorsed by two major generals: Brigadier General Henry Hunt, previously the army's chief of artillery, and the army's judge advocate.

On 10 January Henry left for another short leave, this time to go to Baltimore. He returned three days later. On 26 January he was granted another short leave in Baltimore, returning to camp three days later. But Henry was getting tired of life as a battery commander. He tried to get a discharge, writing on 25 February 1864 that he had 'served three years and six months continuously, that my entrance into service for three years dated from Sept. 1861. as 1st Lieut, that my muster into service as Captain was dated Oct. 1 '62. From the first date to the present I have never been voluntarily remustered or signified my intention of remaining in the service for a new term of three years. Had musters been allowed for a less term than three years, at date of last muster, I should not have accepted the muster for three years.' He signed himself Capt. and Br[vet] Maj 10th Mass By.'[12]

Henry was not the only battery commander who was thinking of leaving the service. Because the artillery did not have regimental organisations for its volunteer batteries, there were few promotional opportunities for a battery commander. Henry Hunt, the chief of artillery for the Army of the Potomac, complained to the army's chief of staff on 21 February 1864: 'Many of our best officers of field artillery have left that arm to accept the promotion in foot artillery and elsewhere that they could not obtain in their own branch of the service.'[13] Hunt wanted to be allowed light artillery regiments with a full complement of field grade officers to solve this problem. His sensible suggestion was not acted upon, and the flow of good captains out of the field artillery continued. But not, for the moment, Henry: the army refused to let him go and he chose not to take the other way out and resign. He would soldier on.

On 1 March 1864 Henry hired an enlisted man to act as a body servant. It was not that common for an officer to acquire an enlisted man as a servant. It was much more usual to hire one of the many black civilians, most of whom were escaped slaves, who hung around the fringes of the army. Considered legal 'contraband of war' and therefore not liable to be returned, these men were available for fairly low wages and proved quite capable. One such black servant, an escaped slave, who fell in with a lieutenant of the 4th Maine Infantry, recalled that his officer, a Lieutenant Carr, said to stick with him and he would see the young black through. 'Carr did stick to me, and I stuck to him, for he was my foster-father. I could look up to no one but him, and on toward Richmond the army marched and I with it, carrying my officer's grub and my own, his blanket and mine – onward and forward to the front of the Confederate capital.'[14] Officer and servant could, and often did, form quite close relationships.

During the winter the army was reorganised, smaller corps being merged into larger ones for greater efficiency. The men were dismayed at losing their old corps identities, and Henry was given the choice of a new unit, since the III Corps was essentially disbanded. Henry chose the II Corps, identified by the clubs they wore as corps badges. On 8 April the battery left its old quarters and moved to the II Corps cantonment area, near Stevensburg. Otherwise life went on as usual. In quiet times, the men had more time to get in trouble, with whiskey available and tempers rendered short by boredom and concern for folks back home. Henry had to reduce two sergeants to the ranks on 10 April, promoting two battery privates in their place.

Finally, snows melted and green buds appeared. A new general, Grant, had arrived from the west to drive the Army of the Potomac on its final thrust to destroy Lee's army. On 3 May the battery was ordered to pack up and it was on the road by nightfall. By the next morning they were on the other side of the Rapidan and into the Wilderness. There the dense woods and tangled brush meant that artillery was largely valueless. The men did have a short, fierce counter-battery fight, but for the most part they lay around and listened to the sounds of musketry.

Although the Army of the Potomac had been badly battered in the Wilderness, Grant directed it to push on southward to try to find a way around Lee's flanks. The summer settled down into a continuous fight from the Wilderness until the Federal forces finally swung around Richmond and ran into Confederate defences below Petersburg. At that point the fluid war became a siege war.

'The Tenth Massachusetts Battery,' wrote a correspondent for the *New York Evening Post* after Cold Harbor, one of the battles in this campaign, 'commanded by Captain J. Henry Sleeper, is one of the best in the service. It has been engaged seventeen times since our army has crossed the Rapidan, and was one of a very few batteries which managed to get into the fight of Thursday and Friday at the Wilderness. It has come to be called the saucy battery in Hancock's Corps, of which it is a part.'[15]

Another correspondent, this one for the *New York Times*, described Cold Harbor:

'About nightfall a desperate charge was made by the rebels on our extreme left, where a number of batteries of our Second Corps were in position. A perfectly devilish volley of musketry was delivered from their works, accompanied by the dismal howling which, in Dixie, has superseded honest cheering, and out they came piling over the breast-works, and for a short time having things just as they wanted them. Their success was very short-lived, for in a moment Sleeper's Tenth Massachusetts Battery, Adams's Rhode Island Battery, Sixth Maine Battery, and others were pouring canister into them in so effective a manner that they were forced to protect themselves in front of our breast-works, from which, later in the evening, they were expelled.'[16]

So far, the battery, and Henry in person, had been lucky. On the whole, there had been relatively few casualties in its ranks. That would change. At the end of June the battery was posted to Ream's Station, near Petersburg, on the Weldon Railroad, a vital link for Richmond and for Lee's army with the south. There the battery would be in support of the V Corps, which had earlier seized the vital station. This Federal move could not go unchallenged. On 25 August, just as battery members were preparing dinner, a cavalry regiment, Winsor Smith's 1st Maine, suddenly burst through the area as if pursued by the entire Confederate army. They were followed by Federal infantry as the battery stood to its gun-line. Finally Confederate small arms fire began hitting cannoneers and battery equipment.

'Early in the action,' Billings recalled, 'Captain Sleeper, who is riding slowly along in the rear of the guns, utterly regardless of the danger, is shot through the arm and soon after departs, leaving the Battery in charge of Lieut. Granger.'[17] Henry was fortunate; he was mounted, so he could ride back to a brigade hospital, where he learned that no bone was broken, although one was nicked, and that his arm would not have to be amputated. He was additionally lucky in that shortly after he rode off to the rear, the battery was overrun and most of its members captured.

Henry's wound was treated at the brigade hospital. Then, as the wound did not appear to be life-threatening, he was allowed to go on a disability leave for twenty days. He went to Boston where he could be easily visited by family and friends. His wound was slow to heal. In September a surgeon submitted documentation that he would not be fit for duty for at least twenty days and his leave was therefore extended thirty days. As late as 5 October 1864 a surgeon reported that the wound was 'still suppurating' and he was unfit for duty. However, it must finally have healed, for on 29 October he reported back for duty with the 10th. Then the battery went into winter quarters. In Henry's absence several of its senior officers, including the first lieutenant who had assumed command while Henry was recovering, were killed. New officers had been assigned to the battery. Henry would have to work hard to get his new team as efficiently drilled as his old one.

Shortly afterwards, Henry received a letter from the War Department, dated 2 December, notifying him that he was promoted to the rank of 'Major of Volunteers by brevet, in the service of the United States...'[18] He would, however, never serve as a field grade officer with the Union Army. He had already put in his request for a discharge as having served his three full years, and in late February 1865 he was notified that he would shortly be mustered out of service.

'On the 27th of February Maj. Sleeper severed his connection with the Company, and in a short speech, delivered with ill suppressed emotion, turned us over to Lieut. Adams,' a battery member recalled. 'He told us that if we ever came to Boston he should feel slighted if we did not give him a call; that anything he could do for us would be cheerfully done, and concluded by wishing us all a safe return home.'[19]

That day Henry signed his last pay voucher and was officially mustered out of the army. On his return home to Boston, he found a letter from Major General Alexander S. Webb, chief of staff of the Army of the Potomac:

'Sincerely regretting that you should have been induced to resign the command of your Battery I hope that you will always remember that you carry with you the very best wishes of all with whom you have been connected for four years. Intimately acquainted with you for the whole period of your services I congratulate you upon your military record with the hope of seeing you at no distant day giving a practical helping hand to those who are still striving to put down the Rebellion.'[20]

An editorial in *Harper's Weekly* added its own commendation:

'Captain Sleeper is but an example of what qualities the events of the war have developed in many of our young men of wealth. The only son of wealthy parents, before the war broke out he bade fair to lead a life of mere enjoyment. But when the sons of Massachusetts were called to arms, he at once devoted himself to the service of his country. He soon showed that he possessed the qualities needed in a commanding officer. His battery has been repeatedly mentioned in general orders, not only for its conduct under fire but also for its constant good order and efficiency.'[21]

NOTES

1 *ORs*, Series I, Vol. 2, p. 406
2 Headley, P. C., *Massachusetts in the Rebellion*, Boston, 1866, p. 178
3 Horrocks, James, *My Dear Parents*, New York, 1982, p. 23
4 *ORs*, Series III, Vol. 1, p. 551
5 *ORs*, Series I, Vol. 11, Part 1, p. 622
6 Billings, John D., *The History of the Tenth Massachusetts Battery of Light Artillery in the War of the Rebellion*, Boston, 1909, p. 27
7 ibid, p. 30
8 ibid, p. 44
9 Headley, P. C., op. cit., p. 524
10 Sleeper, Henry J. military records, National Archives
11 Billings, op. cit., p. 196
12 Sleeper, Jacob Henry, military personal records, National Archives
13 *ORs*, op. cit., Series I, Vol. 33, p. 582
14 Lear, Charles A. C., 'Recollections of the War,' *Bulletin of the Historical Society of Montgomery County Pennsylvania*, Spring 1963, p. 301
15 *Harper's Weekly*, New York, 9 July 1864, p. 1
16 ibid.
17 Billings, op. cit., p. 314
18 ibid, pp. 337–8
19 ibid, p. 395
20 ibid, p. 395
21 *Harper's Weekly*, op. cit.

15
Winsor Bruce Smith
Sergeant, 1st Maine Cavalry Regiment

On 23 August 1862, twenty-year-old Winsor Bruce Smith walked over to the Portland, Maine, recruiting office of the 1st Maine Cavalry Regiment to join up. The recruiting officer, Charles W. Ogilman, carefully noted that his latest recruit had brown hair, blue eyes, a light complexion and stood five feet nine inches high.

The 1st Maine was already a seasoned unit by the time Winsor decided to join its ranks. It had been formed in Augusta, Maine, the previous October, after the Union Army's dreadful defeat at the First Bull Run. John Goddard had then been authorised to raise the regiment and became its first commander. By 31 October, 1861, it had been fully organised in its first camp at Augusta, Maine, where it began training.

Winsor, son of one of the city's photographers, was quite likely not an experienced cavalryman; indeed, as a city boy, he was probably not even an experienced horseman. He was, however, in good company. Even the regiment's new colonel was by profession a lumberman; and the better part of one entire company was made up of seafaring men, fishermen and the like. So why pick such a specialised branch of the service, especially when so many Portland men were going into one or another of the various infantry regiments recruiting there? Because, wrote Edward Tobie, a member of the regiment who became its post-war historian, having won the Medal of Honor, 'there was something about the cavalry service, a dash and excitement which attracted those men who had read and remembered the glorious achievements of "Light Horse Harry" [Lee, a commander of cavalry in the southern campaigns of the War of American Independence]... and of "Morgan's Men" in the revolutionary war.' Indeed, Tobie thought that 'men who had read much in history or in fiction, preferred the cavalry service'.[1]

Not only were Winsor and his fellow recruits of the new 1st Maine regiment not horsemen, they were not much in terms of soldiers. 'The average Maine volunteer was less familiar with the use of fire-arms than with the uses of theodolites or telescopes,' recalled Charles H. Smith, who eventually became the regiment's colonel. 'With revolver in hand, the trooper was more likely to shoot off his horse's ears, or kill his next comrade, than hit an enemy, however near.'[2]

Fortunately, Thomas Hight, the regiment's lieutenant colonel, had some knowledge of cavalry service, and he quickly assumed the role of teacher to everyone, from colonel to private. His task was not easy, as the regiment had yet to be issued basic cavalry weapons. Indeed, the men began learning sabre drill with laths they had shaped into swords – which proved an utter failure. Sabre drill was abandoned until army authorities passed out sabres and heavy, 0.44 calibre Colt Army revolvers to the regiment in March 1862. Each trooper carried one of these weapons in a holster on the right side of his waist belt. Each man also received a tarred-black, cotton haversack in which to carry rations and a tin canteen that could be worn slung from the left shoulder or tied to a saddle. Unfortunately, the army did not have enough carbines for the entire regiment, so each company received six breech-loading Burnside carbines to be used by pickets.

The men learned to travel light. Recalled one cavalry captain:

'His inventory might run as follows: A shirt, a pair of socks (and often he has only those he wears), a housewife or needle-book, paper and envelopes, a tin cup, and bag which contains his coffee and sugar mixed together. Some men carry a towel and soap. The great effort is to learn to get along with the very least possible.'[3]

One unusual aspect to Winsor's new regiment, compared with other hard-riding, hard-soldiering horse outfits, was an early order issued by Colonel Goddard that prohibited the use of profanity. He later announced that he would not have any commissioned or non-commissioned officers in the regiment who had not signed a temperance pledge.[4] Indeed, Goddard insisted on strict discipline, ordering men who crept out of camp at night and had the misfortune to be caught to be placed briefly under guard with a heavy ball linked to their ankles by a long chain.

Winsor was assigned to Company K, which was largely composed of seafaring men from towns similar to his own. He reached the regiment's camp in September 1862. The men he found there were unhappy with conditions. Prior to August, the regiment had not served together as a single unit. Typically for Union cavalry, it had been ordered to send a company here and a company there, some serving as scouts and others as headquarters guards. 'Whose kite are we going to be tail to next?' was the catch-all phrase in the camp of the 1st Maine.[5] In the meantime, the Confederates united their cavalry and consistently rode over the Federal forces. Indeed, Smith arrived at a camp that was shy three entire companies, then serving on detached duty, as well as 210 individual officers and men on similar duties.

Winsor and his new colleagues were put into a 'fresh fish' squad, the term soldiers used to refer to raw recruits. Non-commissioned officers of the company took turns teaching them the rudiments. According to the period cavalry manual:

'The recruit commences his instruction on foot. The first week after his arrival at the regiment is employed exclusively in instructing him in all the details of discipline, police, and interior service, and in those relating to his dress and the grooming of his horse.

'He is taught to mount without saddle on both sides of the horse.

'He is taught the name and use of the principal parts of the arms and equipments, and the manner of keeping them clean; the manner of rolling the cloak, of folding the effects, and of placing them in the valise.

'These different instructions are given by the corporal of the squad, under superintendence of the sergeant and officer of the platoon.

'At the end of this week, the recruit commences the first lesson on foot; he continues to be instructed in the above-mentioned details.

'The recruits are drilled on foot twice a day, when possible, an hour each time. Their instruction on horseback is commenced at the same time with the sabre exercise.'[6]

Winsor and his fellow recruits had joined a regiment that had been on the march since early in September when word reached the Army of the Potomac that Lee's men were crossing into Maryland. The regiment, minus four companies that had been detached to serve as headquarters guards, reached the outskirts of Frederick where they had run into a brief scrap with Confederate cavalry on 12 September. While the rest of the army pressed on west, following the lead they had received when Lee's orders, wrapped around three cigars, fell into Union hands, the 1st remained in Frederick. Colonel Samuel Allen, commander of the 1st Maine Cavalry, had been appointed military governor of the city, and the regiment was ordered to serve as the city's provost guard. So there was time for Winsor to get more training than many recruits who had joined regiments already on the march and about to go into battle.

The men of the 1st were assigned living quarters in the town, the regiment taking over the jail and other public buildings. Soldiers became policemen, patrolling saloons and houses of prostitution as well as the railroad depot. Some officers and men were assigned to check papers on railroad passengers, making sure that their journeys were authorised. Those whose papers were not in order were sent on to the authorities in Baltimore.

One night, local southern sympathisers set fire to the jail to free their friends. Within half an hour, the Maine cavalrymen had sealed off the area and made sure none of their prisoners escaped. The other highlight of their tour, besides missing the bloodiest day of the war at the nearby battle of Antietam, was providing an escort to President Lincoln who stopped in the town on his way to visit the Army of the Potomac. Finally, however, on 2 November, the regiment was once again assigned to duty with a combat brigade in the army – apart from Colonel Allen and his staff who remained in Frederick. In January the colonel resigned, and Lieutenant Colonel Calvin S. Douty took over command of the regiment.

By now trained at least in the basics of a cavalry private's duties, Winsor served on picket and reconnaissance patrols in rain, snow, and sleet from the regimental post near Stafford Court House, Virginia. When the Army of the Potomac's new commander, Major General Ambrose Burnside, ordered a cross-country assault on Richmond, the 1st Maine was sent through icy streams and rain-soaked woods to reconnoitre his line of advance. The miserable weather took its toll; between 1 March and 1 November 1862 the regiment lost 700 horses, mostly through fatigue, and the number grew steadily. Although the regiment had put in several requests for new clothing, including greatcoats and boots, the requisitions had not been filled and the men were not only wet and cold but ragged as well.

Burnside had decided to try to storm over Lee's blockade of the northern route to Richmond at Fredericksburg. Under cover of artillery, his men would lay pontoon bridges across the Rappahannock River and then the infantry would move up the heights and through Lee's lines. Once the bridges had been built and infantry had cleared the town below the heights occupied by Lee's men, the 1st Maine was ordered to cross to the southern side of the river. Winsor's company, along with Company G, was detailed to support a section of artillery below the centre of the Confederate line, Marye's Heights. The Union guns drew counter-battery fire from enemy artillery. After several near misses, the Maine cavalrymen were replaced by Federal infantry. The two companies rejoined the rest of their regiment, drawn up in support of a regular US Army battery. Here, too, counter-battery fire brought down shells all around the Maine men. Most had to dismount and calm their horses, which were getting skittish at having to stand still under fire. By nightfall, when Burnside finally called off his abortive assaults, a number of horses and men had been wounded by shell fragments. Still, they argued, they were luckier than the infantry they had seen falling like flies before them that day.

On 15 December the 1st Maine was ordered to its winter quarters near Belle Plain Landing. The men went to work immediately building log cabins, using tents for roofs, and mud-lined barrels for chimneys. There they sampled the delights of Virginia mud, thick gooey stuff that stuck to everything and was said to be deep enough for a mule to sink in past its ears. 'Mud rules supreme, and as nasty and sticky a mud as Virginia ever produced,' one man wrote home. 'There are but few days that could have been called comfortable what with the frequent visits made by sleet, rain, snow, drizzle and even hail.'[7] Such bad weather would tend to limit drills, but work on building the camp, especially digging drainage ditches and corduroying stables so that the horses could be kept dry, seemed unending. Indeed, the men sang a special regimental song with the refrain, 'Six days shalt thou labor and do all that are able, and the seventh attend inspection and corduroy the stable.'[8] When off duty the men huddled in their huts, talking, writing letters, reading anything they could find, and playing cards and other gambling games.

In fact, the men who remained in 'Camp Mud', as they called their winter quarters, were the lucky ones. Regimental members spent about half of their time on picket duty several miles away, along the Rappahannock River. Both sides set up picket posts on their banks of the river but rarely exchanged pointless shots. They usually declared truces while they patrolled. Some even sent small boats back and forth, trading newspapers and southern tobacco for northern coffee, which was not available in southern camps.

Here Winsor received the first pay he had seen since joining. At $13 a month, this amounted to $52. Most men sent much of their money home, either to help with family expenses or to have deposited in the bank. Being unmarried, and since his father presumably made a decent enough living as a photographer, Winsor probably had a good part of his pay banked. The rest would have been spent at A. Collamore or Aurelius Parker's sutler store.

Winsor spent only a short time in 'Camp Mud,' for in February 1863 he was assigned as an orderly to the headquarters of Brigadier General Gabriel René Paul. Such duties may have sounded attractive, since they implied warm quarters, but as a rule they were not all that pleasant. Most commanders, especially old regular army men, required their orderlies to be in dress jackets with brightly polished brass every day, a far cry from the relaxed field standards to which Winsor must have been accustomed.

Since important messages that required explanation were mostly conveyed by officers, the orderly's main job was to take relatively unimportant messages to subordinate commanders. Generals found, however, that some

175

orderlies were intelligent enough to be entrusted with almost any type of message. Colonel Richard Coulter, commanding the 1st Brigade, 1st Division, I Corps, in his official report after Gettysburg, commended one 1st Brigade mounted orderly, Sergeant Johnson of the 1st Maine. 'The promptitude with which he conveyed orders and communicated information was highly creditable. He has proved himself on this as well as on other fields to be a brave soldier,' the colonel wrote.[9]

On the march, an orderly would carry the large flag that announced to all interested where the general's headquarters were situated. Others rode along behind, waiting to carry messages as required. When not so occupied, orderlies were kept busy with chores for the officers who were invariably to be found at headquarters, such as carrying their trunks and setting up their tents.

Paul, a regular army officer and West Point graduate in the class of 1834, was a hero of the Mexican War in which he had been breveted major. He had stayed in the army ever since, while many of his classmates dropped out to get better-paid civilian jobs. When the war began, he was an infantry major in New Mexico. Distinguishing himself in fighting out there in 1862, he had been commissioned a brigadier general of volunteers in September 1862. Presently he commanded the 3rd Brigade, 1st Division, I Corps, a brigade made up of New Yorkers.

Paul appears to have been pleased with Winsor's performance, since he promoted the Portland man to the grade of corporal on 1 July 1863, which gave him a dollar a month more pay. Corporal's stripes came with added responsibility. According to the standard US Army cavalry manual of the period:

'The Corporals should be capable of executing all the lessons mounted and dismounted, and should be qualified to teach the *school of the trooper dismounted*, and at least 4 lessons mounted.

'Their theoretical instruction should include, in addition to these lessons, all the details relative to the functions of their grade in the interior service, both in garrison and in campaign.'[10]

Smith now had the insignia of his new grade, two yellow chevrons, worn points down, sewn on the sleeves of all his uniforms. These were issued sewn to a dark blue backing so they could easily be set in place by the individual himself or, if he were totally inept with needle and thread, by a friend or tailor, of which there were usually several in any unit. As well, his new grade was marked by an inch-wide yellow stripe down each sky blue trousers leg.

As it happened, Winsor would have no chance of another promotion on Paul's staff. At the battle of Gettysburg, on the very day he promoted Winsor to the grade of corporal, Paul, probably accompanied by his orderlies as usual, tried to rally the men of the I Corps who had been pushed back through the town, up towards the cemetery. Suddenly a bullet smashed into his right temple, passing behind his nose, and tearing out his left eye. The general fell, apparently mortally wounded, blood streaming from his face and covering his uniform. His staff and orderlies ran to him, and carried him to the rear. Although Paul survived, he was blinded and retained only traces of the senses of smell and hearing. His active army days were over.

Paul's staff and band of orderlies was broken up and Smith was returned to duty with his own company. Changes had occurred in his absence. When he left the company for his detached service, the regiment had been armed only with sabres and revolvers, but in January 1863 it had become fully armed with the addition of new Sharps carbines. These were breech-loading, single-shot 0.52 calibre weapons that were greatly admired by their users. According to one Union ordnance officer, 'A cavalry carbine should be very simple in its mechanism, with all its ... parts well covered from the splashing of mud, or the accumulation of rust and dust. Sharps carbine combines all these estimable qualities.'[11] The regiment was no longer split into companies all over the army's organisational charts. Instead, the cavalry had been merged into one corps, as the Confederates had done earlier. Now it would fight on an equal footing with the enemy.

The spring brought a new campaign as the Army of the Potomac went to engage the enemy at Chancellorsville, while the Union cavalry swung right around the Confederates to cut off their communications and break up their supply trains. On this large raid, however, Winsor's company was detailed as rearguard for its brigade, and therefore saw little action. What they got instead was a long miserable ride in almost constantly rainy weather.

After the fiasco that was Chancellorsville, the 1st moved to Warrenton Junction where the men spent many days in the saddle on patrol, looking out for southern guerrillas. On 8 June, however, the regiment was ordered to join the main cavalry for an attack at Brandy Station, the first great cavalry battle of the war and a major disappointment to Confederate cavalry who prior to this had been master of every field. The battle marked the first time Winsor and his close friends or 'pards', made a full-blown, sabres-drawn charge. The Maine men smashed through a counter-charge and drove the Confederates back nearly a mile before breaking off to reform. The regiment lost forty men killed, wounded and missing, and took seventy-six prisoners together with the battle-flag of the 4th Virginia Cavalry.

Yet Brandy Station, no matter how depressing for the Confederates or exhilarating for the Federals, was only a footnote, the prelude to Lee's next invasion of the north. In early June the Confederates, screened by their cavalry, began heading up towards Maryland and Pennsylvania. The Federals, initially unaware of the Confederate move, returned to their old camps, the 1st back to Warrenton Junction. Soon, however, scouts reported Lee's army on the move, and the cavalry mounted up to try to find where the grey soldiers were heading.

They met them first near Aldie, a village in the gap in the Bull Run Mountains east of Ashby's Gap in the Blue Ridge. The first Federals on the ground were driven back by Confederates, and the 1st Maine, placed on the left of the Union line, came straight at the dismounted southern troopers in a sabre charge. The Confederates fell back, but the regiment's colonel was hit by two bullets and fell from his horse dead. Charles Smith, then serving as second in command, took over, leading the regiment the next day as fighting continued. Again Winsor avoided being hurt in the fierce fighting which resulted in a southern withdrawal.

The morning of 21 June brought another clash around the town of Upperville, where many of the 225 men in the regiment fought in the manner that had become standard for cavalry. The men rode up to the position they were to hold. Three out of every four men then dismounted and advanced to their line on foot. The fourth took the other three men's horses and fell back a safe distance. The three on the line would fight in a loose skirmish order, ducking behind whatever cover they could find as they fired their short-range carbines. The fourth would keep an eye on the front, ready to bring up the horses if needed for a rapid advance or retreat. Fighting this way at Upperville, the men of the 1st captured three field grade officers and seventy-five enlisted Confederates.

The regiment had lost a number of horses so far, and after Upperville returned to Aldie to refit and get new mounts. After this brief rest, they were back under way on the 26th, heading to a point where the armies were unintentionally gathering – the town of Gettysburg – arriving there on 2 July. The 23 officers and 396 men of the 1st were posted some three and a half miles east of the town. On 3 July they moved to support an artillery battery, and then to help defend a position on the right flank during the cavalry battle that was overshadowed by Pickett's Charge in another part of the field. Regimental losses were light.

On 6 July the cavalry, including the 1st, headed after the retreating Confederates. On 15 July the 1st ran into a strong enemy force near Charleston, West Virginia. Heading into the town as ordered, the Maine suddenly met heavy fire. Colonel Smith later reported:

'Having advanced nearly a mile, we surprised the pickets of the enemy, and drove them until we were met by a regular line of dismounted skirmishers; then the engagement became general. I deployed six companies, kept two companies on the pike to charge the centre of the enemy from time to time after his flanks were sufficiently forced back, and kept but three small companies in reserve and to guard our flanks and rear. Thus, by a bold front and two hours' severe skirmishing, we drove a very much larger number over a mile and from several good positions, when ordered to retire and join the column.'[12]

Winsor survived the battle unharmed. Overall, however, the efforts of the cavalry were not sufficient to prevent Lee's men from escaping back into Virginia.

That fall, the new commander of the Army of the Potomac took his army into Virginia for a series of manoeuvres designed to pin Lee's troops down and finish them off. Lee, however, was too clever for him and both armies danced around with minimal results. Each day was similar for the men of the 1st, as described by their colonel in a letter home:

'The countryside in front is green with gently rolling land, cut here and there by fences, a winding stream, and some clumps of trees. In the distance you would see a white puff of smoke, hear a report, and then the flashing explosion of the shell, bursting and scattering death. The thin line of blue skirmishers advance on foot under cover of the trees, hills, fences or whatever can give them some cover. Soon the carbines are heard, at first scattered here and there, but then faster and faster. Then is heard a fearful "yell" as the entire column starts the charge. The gun is limbered to be withdrawn only to be abandoned when some of the horses are shot. The enemy fall back towards a new position stopping now and then to fire back at our troops. The indifferent Surgeons in their green sashes go trotting up followed by a few ambulances. And, thus, the day goes...'[13]

Finally, Meade abandoned the campaign and retired to his winter camp. Once the men had built their stables and huts there, Winsor came in for a part of the corporal's duty he had avoided while serving as an orderly: the stable-guard. 'In each company,' a period military guidebook stated, 'a corporal has charge of the stable-guard. His tour begins at retreat and ends at morning stable-call. The stable-guard is large enough to relieve the men on post every two hours. They sleep in their tents, and are called by the corporal when wanted. At retreat he closes the streets of the camp with cords, or uses other precautions to prevent the escape of loose horses.'[14]

By winter Winsor had been in the field with his regiment for over a year. He was getting homesick. After the Mine Run campaign the regiment went into winter quarters, and many of the men received short furloughs. According to Army Regulations, furloughs were not a right due the men, but a privilege that could be granted by commanding officers at their whim. Rarely were they granted while the army was in the field actively campaigning. But winter quarters, with the slow, dull routine there, provided a chance to allow some of the men to get some home-cooked meals. Generally, only the better soldiers received furloughs, although this winter was to be different as enlistments for the original troopers were coming to an end. To any who would re-enlist for three years or who added two years to their enlistments, the army offered a bonus of $402 – quite a sum for someone making $14 a month – and a thirty-five-day furlough. Winsor was one of these. With no official transportation provided, his trip back to Portland was complicated and time-consuming: catching a ride to Washington, from there a train to Philadelphia, another to New York, and then more rides up to New England. Nonetheless, in December 1863 he went home on furlough, at which time his father, Portland photographer Benjamin F. Smith, took the picture of him seen here.

In January 1864 he was back with his regiment. A month later he found himself under the command of Colonel Eric Dahlgren who was leading a cavalry raid into Richmond itself to free prisoners of war there and – if papers found on the colonel's body are to be believed – quite possibly to do more, including burning the city and killing top Confederate executives. Again Winsor's luck held out during the raid. Ambushed after being misdirected by a local guide, the colonel was killed, and most of his men were killed, wounded or captured, only a few escaping to Federal lines. Winsor was one of the few.

On 1 May 1964 Winsor was promoted to the grade of sergeant, with monthly pay of $17. He had to replace his pair of chevrons with three chevrons on each sleeve and a yellow stripe an inch and a half wide on each leg. He also had to receive more education in the duties of the cavalry in his new job. According to the period manual:

'The sergeants should be capable of executing, dismounted and mounted, all that is prescribed by this book; and should be able to teach the lessons of the *school of the trooper*, and to command a platoon in the *school of the squadron mounted*.

'The theoretical instruction of the sergeants should include the *basis of instruction*, the *school of the trooper*, the *school of the platoon*, and the *school of the squadron* also the regulations for the interior service in garrison and in campaign, so far as their grade is concerned.'[15]

The 1st Maine, especially Winsor's Company K which served as a battalion skirmish company, saw a great deal of action over the spring and summer of 1864 as Grant attempted to wear down Lee's army, constantly driving south after being stopped in the Wilderness, past Spottsylvania and Cold Harbor, around Richmond and up from the south towards Petersburg, through which a number of railroad lines passed between the southern capital city and its sources of supply.

On 29 September at 4 a.m., the Federals began a push on their left. The 1st was part of a Federal cavalry force sent to capture the vital Petersburg & Weldon Rail Road line that ran between Petersburg and Weldon, North Carolina, bringing up supplies to the besieged Confederates, on the left of the final Confederate line before Petersburg. Quartermasters made sure each soldier had his full complement of sixty rounds of carbine ammunition, twenty rounds of pistol ammunition, rations for himself for three days and forage for his horse for two days. The men met the enemy early, pushing through several lines by nine in the morning until halted by a firm Confederate stand along Hatcher's Run. Shortly after noon, the 1st was sent to find a way around the enemy up the lower Church Road toward Popular Spring Church. It, too, ran into stiff opposition, and had to fall back. Then, in the late afternoon, the Confederates counter-attacked, driving the Federals back some distance before they could reform their ranks and stop the enemy drive. Further Confederate attacks almost cut off the 1st, which fell back quickly, leaving behind eleven dead, sixty-two wounded and eight missing, as well as other individuals who just had the misfortune not to hear the commands to fall back or get cut off by swarming greybacks.

This time Winsor's luck did run out. He had been captured near the Wyatt Farm and was quickly herded off to a temporary receiving camp set up for captured Federals by Confederate provost guards behind their lines. There he would lose his equipment and quite possibly personal items such as boots – always in demand by ill-shod Confederates – blanket, watch and money. From there Winsor and others captured on the site were marched off to railroad cars to take them to the first of a series of Confederate prison camps that would be his home until January 1865.

With paroles and exchanges no longer in general effect between the warring sides, the one way out of prison for Winsor, save being freed by advancing Federal troops, was to get sick, badly sick. The same day Winsor was captured, the commander of the prison camp at Elmira, New York, was told to ensure all prisoners got so ill that they could not be put back into the field within two months ready to be returned south. Winsor was one of those who made it back north under these conditions. After several months, his health failing rapidly, he was paroled north to Camp Parole, near Annapolis, and assigned to the 3rd Battalion, Paroled Prisoners.

The paroled men in this organisation had no official duties; and most, indeed, were able to do little more than eat and lie in bed.

In April 1865 Winsor was officially exchanged, but his cavalry days were over. He had never recovered from his prison ordeal and was sent home for recuperation; but his doctor wrote to officials on 10 April that Smith was 'laboring under gastro-enteritis with which he is now confined to his bed, and is wholly unable to rejoin his regiment and will be unfit for the duties of a soldier for at least nine weeks to come'. Checking to make sure this was an accurate statement, the army had Smith report to a military surgeon in Portland, who examined him on 2 May 1865. He found the sergeant 'suffering from the effects of confinement in Rebel prisons from want of food and clothing there'. He, too, did not believe that Smith would be ready for duty in the near future.[16]

On 24 July 1865 Sergeant Winsor Bruce Smith was therefore discharged from duty in Augusta, Maine, under War Department General Order No. 77, before his fellow 1st Maine veterans. The rest of his regiment who had survived returned to Augusta on 9 August 1865 and were likewise mustered out of the service of the United States.

NOTES

1 Tobie, Edward P., *History of the First Maine Cavalry*, Boston, 1887, pp. 3–4
2 Starr, Stephen Z., *The Union Cavalry in the Civil War*, Baton Rouge, Louisiana, 1979, p. 138
3 Glazier, Willard, *Three Years in the Federal Cavalry*, New York, 1874, p. 170
4 Tobie, op. cit., pp. 20–1
5 Starr, op. cit., p. 239
6 St. Geo. Cooke, Philip, *Cavalry Tactics, or the Regulations for the Instruction, Formations, and Movements of The Cavalry of the Army and Volunteers of the United States*, Philadelphia, 1862, pp. 22–3
7 Holmes, Torlief S., *Horse Soldiers In Blue*, Gaithersburg, Maryland, 1985, p. 68
8 ibid, p. 70
9 *ORs*, Series I, Vol. XXVIII, Part I, p. 293
10 St. Geo. Cooke, op cit., p. 23
11 Coates, Earl J., and Dean S. Thomas, *An Introduction To Civil War Small Arms*, Gettysburg, Pennsylvania, 1990, p. 45
12 *ORs*, Series I, Vol. XXVII, Part 1, p. 980.
13 Holmes, op. cit., p. 110
14 Le Grand, Louis, *The Military Hand-Book and Soldier's Manual of Information*, New York, 1861, p. 42
15 St. Geo. Cooke, op. cit., p. 23
16 Smith, Winsor B., service record, National Archives, Washington, DC

16
Lyman B. Sweeney
Private, 86th Indiana Infantry Regiment /
Second Class Private, Signal Corps

It was the young men, those at the beginning of their lives, who felt most strongly the desire to get into battle to save the Union. 'In September [1861] I was helping a neighbor stack grain and we heard there was going to be a war meeting at our little log school house. I went to the meeting, and when they called for volunteers, Harrison Maxon, Edgar Houghton, and myself put our names down,' wrote then fifteen-year-old Elisha Stockwell. 'My father was there and objected to my going, so they scratched my name out which humiliated me somewhat.'[1]

The regulations were clear: The only individuals who could be accepted into the army were those who were free, white, male, between the ages of eighteen and thirty-five, at least five feet three inches high, able-bodied, free from disease, sober, of good character and habits, and able to speak English at least fairly well. Anyone under the age of twenty-one required the written consent of a parent, guardian or master. Many parents, however, refused to let their children go off to what they knew was, at best, a highly unsafe place. Young Stockwell, shortly after being disgraced by his father at the public meeting, ran into one of his friends who had managed to enlist and decided to join him in the army. Telling his parents he was going off to deliver a load of coal, he joined his soldier friend on a trip to camp and once there, volunteered. 'Mr Houghton [the father of his soldier friend] told the captain the circumstances, and the captain got me in by my lying a little, as I told the recruiting officer I didn't know just how old I was but thought I was eighteen. He didn't measure my height, but called me five feet, five inches high. I wasn't that tall two years later when I re-enlisted, but they let it go, so the records show that as my height,' Stockwell wrote.[2]

Indeed, after the war Brigadier General Charles King wrote:

'So long as the recruit appeared to be eighteen years old and could pass a not very rigid physical examination, he was accepted without question; but it happened, in the early days of the war, that young lads came eagerly forward, begging to be taken – lads who looked less than eighteen and could be accepted on bringing proof, or swearing that they were eighteen. It has been since shown that over eight hundred thousand lads of seventeen or less were found in the ranks of the Union army, that over two hundred thousand were no more than sixteen, that there were even one hundred thousand on the Union rolls who were no more than fifteen.'[3]

So when Lyman B. Sweeney told the recruiting officer of Co. D, 86th Indiana Volunteer Infantry when the regiment was formed in September 1862 in Lafayette, Indiana, that he was eighteen years old, we cannot be sure that was perfectly accurate. Most likely he was accurate when he told officials that he was then a student in Indiana and had been born in rural Westmoreland County, Pennsylvania, which was his permanent residence. Indeed, the fact he enlisted in an out-of-state regiment, in an area where neither he nor his father would have been known, makes his age suspicious. We also know that he helped his father, a farmer and shoemaker. Indeed, many in his family opposed his joining the army, and Lyman, like Elisha Stockwell, had to enlist without his father's knowledge. The true facts about him listed in the form were that he stood five feet ten and a half inches tall, with blue eyes, light coloured hair and a fair complexion.

Lyman's regiment hardly had time to get equipped when it was ordered to Cincinnati, Ohio, on 5 September, then being rushed on through Covington, Kentucky, arriving in Louisville, Kentucky, on 30 September. They would not spend much time there, either, as the Confederates in that state were falling back, and the 86th began slogging in pursuit over muddy roads in a cold autumn. The Confederates were not beaten, however, and struck the Union pursuers at Perryville on 8 October. The 86th, held in reserve, fortunately missed the bloody fighting there. The Confederates were only partially successful, and continued their withdrawal into eastern Tennessee.

After a breather, the Union pursuit continued towards Nashville, Tennessee, 22 October. The troops reached that important city on 7 November, where they remained until 26 December. Then they headed after the Confederates again, the two armies colliding at Stone's River on 31 December. On the left of the Union line, in pouring rain, stood Lyman and his comrades of the 86th, in what one of them called an 'anxious suspense'. 'The orders were to be ready at a moment's notice. The lines were forming. Batteries were being placed into position. Dark columns stood noiseless in the rain. Hospitals were established in the rear, and the musicians and other non-combatants were detailed to bear the stretchers and attend the ambulances. Medical stores were unpacked and countless rolls of bandages placed at hand for use. Provision trains were brought up and rations issued.'[4]

The Confederates struck with a fury at daybreak on the 31st. The Federal line held, then slowly fell back in some places. Elsewhere entire units disintegrated. The 86th, on the right where many of the heaviest attacks fell, fell apart into, at best, small squads. The regiment left its colours and ninety-nine men taken as prisoners on the field. The next day, both sides, badly blooded, stayed in their lines, the Federals taking advantage of the lull to repair their positions. A day later, a fierce Confederate assault was broken up; the southern troops fell back, leaving the Federals in command of the field. Lyman had managed to escape when his regiment fell apart, and soon was back in the ranks of the reformed 86th.

A weary Federal army then went into winter camp at Murfreesboro, where they would remain until June. By the time the 86th would break camp, however, Lyman would no longer be with them. In April, 1863, Lyman was detailed for signal duty to headquarters, Department of the Cumberland. 'The Signal Corps of our Army is composed of officers and enlisted men, detailed from different regiments, with special reference to their fitness for the duties required of them,' wrote an officer of the Army of the Cumberland in 1863:

'The officers are instructed in the use of the signals used before they go into the field, and are forbidden to carry with them any thing that would give the enemy information leading to the discovery of the system in case of capture. The object of the organisation is to keep up constant communication between the different parts of the army and the different commanding generals, and to closely scan and discover the movements of the enemy. For this reason, the officers are furnished with powerful telescopes and marine glasses, and are usually located on the tops of high elevations, or other commanding positions.'[5]

The whole concept of signal duty was novel among armies of the world at that time. Signal detachments had their origins in the mind of an army surgeon, Albert James Myer, stationed in the west. A student in a system of communications designed for the deaf and dumb, Baine's telegraphic alphabet, which used simply dots and dashes, without pauses, he noticed that a flag wigwam system could send these dots and dashes easily over the long distances in the clear western air. Working with a West Point instructor, Edward Porter Alexander, he devised such a system and on 27 June 1860 was named the Signal Officer of the US Army. Myer's system was adopted in the Army of the Cumberland when Major General William Rosecrans assumed command in October 1862. One of the first things he did was to create a signal corps for that western force. Captain Jesse Merrill, an infantryman from the 7th Pennsylvania Reserve Regiment, was the appointed chief signal officer of the department and sent west from the Army of the Potomac, where he had been trained in Myer's system, to organise a signal service in that army. Merrill's newly assigned signalmen were broken down into small detachments and assigned to different corps headquarters.

Not every US Army officer was keen on the work of the Signal Corps. Major General William T. Sherman, for one, wrote that, 'I have little faith in the signal-service by flags and torches, though we always used them; because, almost invariably when they were most needed, the view was cut off by intervening trees, or by mists.' Instead, wrote Sherman, 'For the rapid transmission of orders in an army covering a large space of ground, the magnetic telegraph is by far the best, though habitually the paper and pencil, with good mounted orderlies, answer every purpose.'[6]

Since the signal service was forbidden by the War Department to use telegraphic equipment, it had to resort to flag communications. Lyman therefore learned to use signal flags and torches. An Army of the Cumberland officer wrote in 1863:

'In the first place, then elevated positions are chosen, between which communications are made by means of a flag in the daytime and of a torch at night. The alphabet of the code consists of certain definite figures, different combinations of which represent the letters of the ordinary English alphabet. Of these figures there are but few, a sufficient variety being obtained by different combinations of the same figures. Thus, 11, 14 may mean A, while 14, 11 may mean D; and so on. Each figure of the alphabet is represented by a definite number of dips or wavings of the flag or torch. For transmission of messages, different-colored flags are employed, as best suits the state of the atmosphere. There are now in use at Murfreesborough one black with a white center, one white with a red center, and one all red.'[7]

The second part of the corps mission was to learn about the movement of the enemy. 'In addition to the ordinary duty of transmitting messages, the officers and men of the corps act as scouts, keeping a constant watch upon the movements of the enemy, as they are able to do from their commanding location, and reporting the results of their observations to head-quarters without delay.'[8]

Lyman and his fellow Signal Corps members would have plenty to do, for in June the Army of the Cumberland broke the Confederate lines south of Murfreesboro. The Confederate Army of Tennessee had to fall back, but at every point it halted the Federals and turned the southern flanks in a series of brilliant manoeuvres, aided greatly by signal detachments that kept track of enemy forces and kept Rosecrans's subordinates in close communications. Finally, the Confederates found themselves in Chattanooga. Rosecrans, after a delay of several weeks, reached the Tennessee River, crossing it below Chattanooga. Again the Confederates had to retreat as Rosecrans took the city on 9 September.

Reinforced by an entire corps from the Army of Northern Virginia, the Confederates returned to the attack. They decided to hit Rosecrans's army near the Chickamauga Creek, cut him off from Chattanooga, where he could dig in, and destroy the Army of the Cumberland. On 17 September signal stations on Lookout Mountain, towering over Chattanooga, reported seeing columns of dust, indicating large bodies of men on the move, but were unable to say where these men were headed. Indeed, their reports were that a large body of infantry was headed through Dug and Catlett's gaps, when in fact it was merely cavalry feeling out the Union positions south of the line, the main Confederate objective.

On 19 September the Confederates struck, largely undetected by Lyman and his fellow signal operators. In a rugged two-day fight, the Federals were forced back, but largely escaped to hold Chattanooga. There they were besieged, Rosecrans, who no longer had the confidence of the government, being replaced by Major General George Thomas on 19 October.

The siege was an especially slow time for the Signal Corps. Even when the army was on the move, work was sporadic. 'The labor required of the corps is confining, but not severe,' wrote an Army of the Cumberland officer. 'For days there may be little to do, and, again, both officers and men may be constantly employed during both the day and night. They sleep when they can, and are expected to be ready at a moment's warning.'[9] The soldiers were paid while there, but there was little to buy in the besieged town. Gambling, although strictly forbidden in the Army of the Cumberland, became a major pastime. 'In all kinds of out of the way places, you can see groups of soldiers, and if you crowd in, you will find a rubber blanket spread on the ground with soldiers sitting on it, piles of money all about and dice boxes rattling, or maybe cards, and many of the poor fellows are soon fleeced of all they have,' an officer recalled.[10] Rations grew short, and the men were hungry. It would not have been an especially happy time in Lyman's life.

On 25 November, Grant having arrived on the scene, the Federals struck the Confederate line, first weakening their left, then storming over the top of Lookout Mountain. The Confederate army, totally broken, fled, not stopping until survivors reached Dalton, Georgia. Further campaigning, how-

187

ever, was out of the question as even high-level, aggressive Federal officials had to admit that bad roads and uncertain supplies meant that campaigning in the area could not be done after 6 December. Both armies went into winter camp to prepare for their 1864 campaigns.

Lyman would not be with them. Apparently enjoying signal work more than being an infantryman in the line and impressing his superiors, he applied, and was allowed, to take an examination to see if he would be considered fit to join the Signal Corps. It was an honour to be selected to take this examination for duty in the corps. One period manual writer indicated that:

'Recruiting officers for the signal corps are instructed to be very rigid in their examination of recruits. They should be active, athletic young men, of medium size; quick, intelligent, with superior eyesight; of good judgment and undoubted courage. They should have at least a good common-school education, and be able to write well.'[11]

On passing the exam, he was discharged from the 86th Indiana and, on 31 December 1863, he enlisted in the Signal Corps of the United States Army for a term of three years.

A genuine formal branch of the service solely devoted to communications was new in the army. It had been authorised, after proving the value of the detachments in the field, by Congress on 3 March 1863, to consist of a colonel, a lieutenant colonel, two majors, a captain for every corps or department, and at least eight lieutenants, with one sergeant and six privates for each officer. Eventually some 300 officers and 2,500 enlisted men would serve in the corps. Officers were to be paid as cavalry officers, while enlisted men received pay equal to those in the Corps of Engineers, giving Lyman, as a second class private, $13 a month, much of which he sent home to help support the family.

Lyman received a new uniform, consisting of a waist-length dark blue jacket fastened at the cuffs with three buttons and eleven buttons up the front. His trousers were the type worn by mounted troops, with extra lining sewn in the seat and down the legs. As of orders issued on 22 July 1864, he would wear a badge on his left sleeve consisting of 'crossed signal flags, on dark blue cloth, to be embroidered in silk; color of flags, one red with white center and one white with red center; size of flag three-fourth (¾) of an inch square, center one-fourth (¼) of an inch square, length of staff three (3) inches.'[12] Sergeants would wear the same badge over their yellow chevrons. Although there was no official cap badge for enlisted men, many wore the officer's badge which was similar, with metallic embroidery of thirteen gold stars above the crossed flags on a black velvet oval. For weapons, one signalman recalled, 'we had Colt's revolvers.'[13]

Although Lyman had been on active duty in the Signal Corps for eight months, now that he was formally mustered into the new corps he would be sent to the Signal Camp of Instruction in Georgetown, a small village just west of Washington in the District of Columbia. To make sure the right individual was sent and trained, the local signal officer sent a descriptive sheet to the camp headquarters bearing Lyman's description, place of birth, occupation and information on his enlistment – a single-sheet personnel record. This was recorded in the camp's Descriptive Book, a copy of which eventually went to the Adjutant General's office in Washington. Before an age of electronic data exchange, the paperwork done within the army was mountainous.

The Signal Camp of Instruction had been authorised in December 1862. Signal Corps members, originally only officers, were sent to the camp where they were trained in all aspects of the signal service, including military telegraphy, although civilian telegraph companies managed to get the War Department to turn over all field telegraph equipment to a newly organised US Military Telegraph Company on 10 November 1863. Signal Corps members had to take control of the telegraph trains in the field from time to time and therefore had to be familiar with the equipment involved. After passing an examination, the trainees were ordered to different commands in the field. If they failed, they were returned to their original line regiments.

Here Lyman received formal training in much beyond the simple flag signals he had used earlier. The corps used Coston signals at night, a system of coloured lights in which white flares meant one, red flares meant two, and green meant three. The mixture of different coloured flags was also simplified, white flags with a square red centre being the most common in use. However, red flags with a white centre were used for signalling at greater distances, having proved more visible, while plain black flags were used against snow.

He would also be taught the most guarded secrets of the army, the use of a cipher disk to send messages in code. A Signal Corps officer after the war explained the use of the cipher disk:

'Two concentric disks, of unequal size and revolving on a central pivot, were divided along their outer edges into thirty equal compartments. The inner and smaller disk contained in its compartments letters, terminations, and word-pauses, while the outer, larger disk contained groups of signal numbers to be sent. Sometimes this arrangement was changed and letters were on the outer disks and numbers on the inner. By the use of prearranged keys, and through their frequent interchange, the secrecy of messages thus enciphered was almost absolutely ensured.'[14]

Lyman spent January and February 1864 in his camp. Life was good there; training was extensive but not arduous, while the taverns in Georgetown and sightseeing in Washington provided much off-duty relief. In March he passed his final examinations and was assigned to the signal station in Cumberland, Maryland. That area was covered with signal stations, so that communications could be sent rapidly from any point of the front back to Washington. As well, the stations, built either on the tops of hills or featuring tall wooden towers, could observe the area, looking for enemy movement.

A Massachusetts infantryman stationed near Fort Lyon, Virginia, wrote in March 1863:

'A detachment of the Signal Corps has been sent to Forts Lyon and Worth, and it is really amusing to witness their interchanges of dumb signals by flags in the daytime and colored lanterns at night. Some 1 or 2 men are to be detailed from the 34th to join this corps. Any member of the Signal Corps is not allowed to converse or even speak to, any person aside from his own organisation and they are confined to a tent by themselves. The reason of this secrecy is to prevent any of the signals from being exposed.'[15]

As a further mark of their corps, lacking any regulation badge, many corps members wore silver shields some inch and a half square with an enamelled signal flag in the centre, lettered 'SIGNAL CORPS USA' above the flag. Some soldiers had their names engraved under the flag as well.

A month after arriving at Cumberland, Lyman was sent on to be a part of the detachment at Martinsburg, West Virginia, the headquarters for Signal Corps detachments in the region. According to Captain and Chief Signal Officer Franklin Town, the post there consisted of 13 officers and 161 enlisted men and controlled posts at Martinsburg and Mills' Gap, a post on North Mountain, near Gerrardstown about twelve miles from Martinsburg. Used primarily to observe enemy movements, the latter post was high enough so that those at it could see Charlestown, Maryland Heights near Harper's Ferry, and other vital posts. However, the main purpose in gathering so many members of the small corps was to train teams for duty in the Valley of Virginia in 1864.

'If we have no action for a few weeks, the party will be in good order for it, and I hope the party will be able to render all the service required of it by the time it has duty to perform in the face of the enemy,' Town reported on 30 April 1864. 'The officers and men are all disposed to use their best efforts, and no labor will be spared to meet the utmost expectations of the commanding officer of the corps and the major-general commanding department.'[16]

The Valley, scene of so much previous fighting, was fairly quiet in early 1864. The Federals were nominally in control of most of the land, although guerrilla bands struck often and largely at will. Lyman was sent on to a post at Round Hill near Strasburg, Virginia. The area was a hotbed of Confederate guerrilla action; Companies B and C, 43rd Battalion of Virginia Cavalry – Mosby's Rangers – were prowling in the area, hunting for supply wagons and attacking remote posts. On 10 May they attacked a cavalry outpost near Front Royal where they captured a captain and fifteen men, along with seventeen horses. They were a constant danger.

The signalmen were given the job of watching out for them, from their elevated posts, and then following them, leaving signs for other troops to come behind and capture them. Such missions were part of their regular jobs. According to the manual produced by Albert Myer in 1864, 'A Signal Party should be sent to follow an enemy cavalry force.'[17]

So it was that on the evening of 12 May 1864 a group of Signal Corps troops left the station at Round Hill on a routine scouting mission. When they failed to return the next morning, the officer in charge gathered a rescue party that included Lyman. Riding off, the men separated and Lyman was not seen again. According to his commander he was 'probably captured by guerrillas'.[18] If so, and there was little reason to doubt it, his fate would be, at best, uncertain. Federal soldiers hated and feared the guerrillas, calling Mosby's men 'the most detestable characters that the war produced', adding that the guerrillas were 'human hyenas'.[19] Indeed, the chances of surviving a capture by southern guerrillas were poor; Mosby's men captured one Federal soldier that spring trying to burn a house and, according to a civilian witness, the rebels 'hung him instanter'. Moreover, the civilian was given to understand that Mosby warned the Federals that if they continued to burn houses the guerrillas would kill every prisoner they took.[20]

Lyman was not caught burning houses, however, and managed to survive his capture. Indeed, the guerrillas sent him back to Richmond where he became a regular prisoner of war, the Federal government being so notified. Sometime after his capture his family was informed that Lyman had survived and been sent to Camp Sumter, better known under the name of its nearby village, Andersonville. He arrived at a post already terribly overcrowded and short of supplies.

The prison itself consisted of little more than a block of 26 acres surrounded by a 15-foot-tall wood stockade. A walkway connected guard towers along the fence where guards were stationed, muskets in hand, ready to shoot anyone who passed the 'dead line', a waist-high fence inside the walls, some distance from the walls. No barracks had been built inside the stockade nor were there trees to provide shade; the only water was a sluggish stream that fed foetid water slowly through the camp. The camp sanitary facilities were located at the end of this stream, near where it finally worked its way out of the stockade. By the end of July 1864, 26,367 soldiers and sailors were crowded inside the stockade fence, living in makeshift tents pieced together from scrounged pieces of canvas, or ponchos and poles, or in burrowed holes in the ground.

Some Union prisoners preyed on newcomers, beating them up and stealing their money, clothes and any equipment they had brought into the camp with them. While some of these bullies worked alone, others formed into gangs. The worst band was led by an Englishman named Willie Collins but better known to those who feared him as 'Mosby', his band being known as 'Mosby's Rangers.' His group were terrorising the camp even before Lyman arrived and continued thereafter without any interference from Confederate guards. One prisoner noted in his diary of 27 June:

'Raiders going on worse than ever before. A perfect pandemonium. Something must be done, and quickly. There is danger enough from disease, without being killed by raiders. Any moment fifty or a hundred of them are liable to pounce upon our mess, knock right and left and take the very clothing off our backs. No one is safe from them.'[21]

Eventually a number of law-abiding prisoners organised themselves, and on 3 July, after a fierce brawl, captured Collins and his band. The camp administration allowed the Federal prisoners to try the raiders themselves. The trial, predictably enough, ended with unanimous guilty sentences. On 11 July – Lyman probably in the crowd around the gallows watching – the six bullies were hanged; the rope used for Collins, a large man, broke, forcing him to be hanged a second time before he died.

It was not a good time to be a prisoner. Supplies of all sorts were hard to come by, and exchange did not exist. One prisoner complained in April that his rations consisted of 'pig feed (corn meal) about three ounces of salt pork, and half a pint of beans.'[22] Indeed, one Union prisoner noted in his dairy on 17 May, around the time Lyman must have arrived, 'The sandy soil fairly alive with vermin. If this place is so bad at this time of the year, what must it be in July, August and September? Every man will die, in my estimation, but perhaps we may be relieved before then. We'll try and think so anyway. New prisoners die off the fastest.'[23]

The prisoner was right; things would get worse. Two days later he noted, 'Nearly twenty thousand men confined here now. New ones coming every day. Rations very small and *very* poor. The meal that the bread is made out of is ground, seemingly, cob and all, and scourges the men fearfully. Things getting continually worse. Hundreds of cases of dropsy. Men puff out of human shape and are perfectly horrible to look at.'[24]

Even nature conspired against the prisoners, with heat in July rotting many of the local crops in the fields. By late August there was such a famine, that many of the men developed severe symptoms of scurvy as well as the general pangs of hunger. By the war's end, there were some 12,912 graves dug outside the stockade fence. Their only hope now was a rapid approach from Sherman's troops, then in Atlanta. The Confederates reacted against this threat by building new camps to house their prisoners. Many of Andersonville's prisoners, including Lyman, were sent on to Camp Lawton in Millen, Georgia, in September.

However, conditions were not better at Camp Lawton, described by one of the first prisoners to arrive there as nothing more than 'pine woods by the side of a considerable stream.'[25] A later arrival described the post:

'The stockade is similar to that at Andersonville, but in a more settled country, the ground high and grassy, and through the prison runs a stream of good pure water, with no swamp at all. It is apparently a pleasant and healthy location. A portion of the prison is timber land, and the timber has been cut down and lays where it fell, and the men who arrived before us have been busily at work making shanties and places to sleep in. There are about six thousand prisoners here, and I should judge there was room for twelve or fifteen thousand. Men say they are given food twice each day, which consists of meal and fresh beef in rather small quantities, but good and wholesome. The rebel officer in command is a sociable and kindly disposed man, and the guards are not strict, that is, not cruelly so.'[26]

Such optimism was to be short-lived. Living standards actually fell below Camp Sumter standards. Guards, angry at the defeat of southern armies across all fronts, killed prisoners on the spot for crimes such as coming too close or asking questions. It was already too late for Lyman; he was one of those who would die at Millen. According to what his family was told, he died from starvation there on 1 November 1864. He may indeed have died that way; many did. Yet many more died of poor diets rather than lack of anything to eat; and many simply gave up the desire to live, becoming victims of what Confederate doctors called 'nostalgia' or 'mental depression'. This deep depression robbed the men of their resistance to the many diseases, and they simply laid down and died.

This is demonstrated by the statement of a Signal Corps officer after the war:

'Did a non-combatant corps ever before suffer such disproportionate casualties –killed, wounded, and captured? Sense of duty, necessity of exposure to fire, and importance of mission were conditions incompatible with personal safety – and the Signal Corps paid the price. While many found their fate in Confederate prisons, the extreme danger of signal work, when conjoined with stubborn adherence to outposts of duty, is forcefully evidenced by the fact that the killed of the Signal Corps were one hundred and fifty per cent of the wounded, as against the usual ratio of twenty per cent.'[27]

NOTES

1 Abernethy, Byron R., ed, *Private Elisha Stockwell, Jr. Sees the Civil War*, Norman, Oklahoma, 1958, pp. 3-4
2 ibid., p. 6
3 Miller, Francis, ed., *The Photographic History of the Civil War,* New York, 1909, Vol. 8, p. 190
4 Cozzens, Peter, *No Better Place To Die,* Urbana, Illinois, 1991, pp. 71–2
5 'An Officer,' *Annals of the Army of the Cumberland*, Philadelphia, 1863, p. 303
6 Sherman, William T., *Memoirs*, New York, 1990, pp. 888–9
7 'An Officer,' op cit., pp. 305–6
8 ibid, p. 307
9 ibid, p. 307
10 Cozzens, Peter, *The Shipwreck of their Hopes*, Urbana, Illinois, 1994, p. 49
11 Kautz, August, *Customs of Service for Non-Commissioned Officers and Soldiers,* Philadelphia, 1864 , pp. 67–8
12 Emerson, William K., *Chevrons*, Washington, DC, 1983, p. 48
13 Todd, Frederick P., *American Military Equipage 1851-1872*, Providence, R.I., 1977, Vol. II, p. 401
14 Miller, Francis, op cit., pp. 316–18
15 Drickamer, Lee C. and Karen D., eds., *Fort Lyon to Harpers Ferry,* Shippensburg, Pennsylvania, 1987, p. 88
16 *ORs*, Series I, Vol. 33, p. 1027
17 Gibbs, Pam, '1864 Manual of Signals,' *The Signal Cipher*, Louisville, Kentucky, March 1991, p. 1
18 Sweeny, Lyman B., military record, Signal Corps, National Archives
19 Wert, Jeffrey D., *Mosby's Rangers*, New York, 1990, p. 162
20 ibid., p. 164
21 Ransom, John, *John Ransom's Diary*, New York, 1963, pp. 86–8
22 Dougherty, Michael, *Diary of a Civil War Hero,* New York, 1960, p. 84
23 Ransom, John, op cit., p. 72
24 Ransom, John, ibid., p. 73
25 Meredith, Roy, ed, *This Was Andersonville*, New York, 1956, p. 226
26 ibid., p. 132
27 Miller, Francis, op cit., p. 318

17

John D. Thomas
Acting Ensign, US Navy

John D. Thomas stood in front of Father Alligote and the altar of St
Anne's Episcopal Church in Montreal, Canada, and slipped the gold ring
on to the fourth finger of the left hand of Bridget Mary Ellen O'Shea, a
nineteen-year-old Irish girl, while repeating the words from the Book of
Common Prayer: 'With this ring I thee wed, and with my body I thee wor-
ship, and with all my worldly goods, I thee endow: in the Name of the
Father, and of the Son, and of the Holy Ghost. Amen.' Outside the church
it was a typical Canadian summer day, this 14 August 1861. Across the border, war was raging, and after the wedding the two journeyed south, to the
United States.

John was born in Charleston, Maine, a descendant of the Thomas clan
who first arrived from England on Maine's rocky shores in the mid-seventeenth
century. They had come to America largely because they were Puritans, driven
by a strong sense of religious duty dedicated to creating the Kingdom of God
on earth. Traditionally, Maine folk are as hard as their rocky soil and as clan-
nish as the foxes who hide in their woods. So it was to suit her husband's family, who still lived in East Corinth, Maine, that Bridget Mary took to calling
herself Ellen Thomas.

John himself had been born on 27 February 1846. He was thus little
more than fifteen, four years younger than his bride. He stood five feet, eight
and a half inches tall, with brown hair, black eyes and a generally dark complexion. His hometown, East Corinth, is almost in the centre of the state,
slightly north of Bangor, and far from the sea. Yet John had sometime previously made his way to the shore and shipped aboard one of the many craft that
anchored in Maine's harbours. By 1861 he was a professional sailor.

The Civil War, however, threatened John's profession. True, the Ameri-
can South, the new Confederate States of America, was not a maritime power.
No US Navy ships were taken south or even captured in seaworthy condition.
The south lacked major shipyards, facilities to make much-needed naval equip-
ment, or sufficient trained seamen to man the few ships ready to take on the
Federal navy blockading southern ports.

Yet, the Confederate naval effort was directed by an intelligent and able individual, Secretary of the Navy Stephen Mallory, and he immediately decided that a two-pronged attack on the US Navy was not only possible, but that he was the man to do it. First, he would defend his entire 3,000 miles of coastline, including seaports such as Charleston, South Carolina and Galveston, Texas. Second, he would send out ships to destroy northern merchant ships.

To achieve his first objective, he commissioned the construction of powerful, though not very seaworthy, iron-clad ships designed to stop any US Navy ship afloat.

Mallory planned several ways of taking aggressive steps to destroy northern commerce. As a first step, the Confederate government, quite against the policy of most civilised nations of the time, issued letters of marque to private armed ships, authorising them to attack enemy merchant shipping, as early as May 1861. Patriotic citizens soon began to mount any sort of ordnance they could find on any vessel that could float, and set out in pursuit of the foe. In all, some fifty letters were issued, though not all of these represented seagoing vessels. At first these lightly armed craft drew blood, capturing a number of merchant ships bound from ports in South and Latin America to northern ports. Eventually, however, civilian companies realised that there was better money to be earned by running the blockade, which became increasingly effective, with goods than by privateering.

Moreover, Mallory's attempts to build his own commerce raiders in European shipyards and man them with southern officers and largely European crews paid much better dividends. The most famous raider, the *Alabama*, spent only twenty-three months at sea, but took sixty northern ships that, along with their cargoes, were worth millions of dollars. This resulted in skyrocketing maritime insurance rates. Shipowners switched their ships' flags, largely to European ones, so that the vessels would appear to be neutral if captured by Confederate cruisers. The US merchant fleet swiftly declined in numbers as Mallory's raiders took to the high seas.

Northern merchants cried out for help. 'The undersigned, who are largely engaged in commerce in this city, respectfully suggest that it is advisable for the Government immediately to charter or purchase twenty of the best clipper ships that can be obtained, and arm and place them in commission at once for the protection of our commerce against privateers,' wrote the managers of W. F. Weed & Co. in New York to Gideon Welles, the Secretary of the Navy, on 18 April 1861. A group of presidents of maritime insurance companies wrote the President the same day: 'We entreat you to take immediate measures to protect American commerce in the Southern waters, and we respectfully suggest the purchase or charter of steamers, of which a number can befitted from here without delay.'[1]

The US Navy had to seek out and destroy these commerce-raiding vessels, no easy task. For one thing, there were not that many ships available. Indeed, the navy could only draw on a fleet of some seventy-six vessels, of which just a handful were steam-powered, to participate in the blockade of all southern ports declared by April 1861. Of these, a mere twelve ships were stationed along the American coast, while the rest were in waters from Brazil to Africa. It would take time to assemble a fleet, from purchases and newly built ships, large enough to accomplish such a task; and it would take time to man such a fleet. Almost a quarter of the 1,554 US Navy officers either left the service or were dismissed, their loyalties being suspect, at the outbreak of war. All the ships already in service were somewhat undermanned, and when hostilities began only 7,600 enlisted seamen were in the navy, with a further 200 men either in training or ready for assignment to a ship in service.

The navy immediately sent agents to look at merchant ships, now idle, with a view to purchasing the fast sailers among them, arming them and sending them against Confederate cruisers. It even bought ferries, which would see good service in rivers too narrow for larger vessels to turn about when brought under fire. The navy very rapidly purchased an additional 136 vessels for the fleet, putting another 52 on the stocks immediately to be built.

There was still the problem of manning these new vessels. The navy authorised commandants of navy yards, as at Brooklyn and Philadelphia, to enlist seamen. At the same time, other officers were sent to open naval rendezvous, which were actually recruiting stations, in all principal seaports. They found a ready source of manpower. As the number of ships decreased, merchant seamen were now often unable to find work. True, many joined the Union army, which offered fairly generous bounties whereas the navy could offer none. Not until 1 July 1864 would Federal bounties equal to those given for joining the army be allowed for naval enlistees. Of course, there was always a chance of getting a part of the value of every enemy ship captured – the traditional prize money – but this was not money in hand as were bounties. Still, many old salts, more comfortable at sea than in a land-based organisation, were happy to hear Lincoln's call for 18,000 men to serve in the US Navy for terms ranging from one to three years. A steady steam of men entered naval service.

Recruiting, however, was not all that was wanted. In June 1862 Welles had to admit to one of his squadron commanders that 'more than 3,000 men are now wanting for the ships of war'.[2] Qualification standards were lowered. Men without any experience, rated as 'landsmen', were admitted to the navy's service. On 16 September 1862, John left his wife, now pregnant with their first child, and reported to a naval rendezvous at Boston, Massachusetts, to join up. His seaman's pay would be $18 a month and, with a new child, that would be important. Besides his regular pay, he would also receive an extra $1.50 a month, paid in lieu of a daily ration of grog, which had been banned as of 1 September that year. From that point on, ratings would find themselves joining a dry navy.

John was immediately sent to the USS *Ohio*, an antique ship of the line, now used as a receiving ship off the Boston Naval Yard. The *Ohio* would not have looked out of place with Nelson's fleet at Trafalgar. She had been laid down in 1817, a 2,757-ton, wood-walled sailing ship that carried, in her prime, 74 guns spread over three decks, and a crew of 840 officers and men. By this point in her history, however, she was little more than a floating barracks used to house and train naval recruits. A recruit sent aboard the *Ohio* wrote later:

'For almost three weeks the old *Ohio* was my home, and I was so well content with having at last found a way into the navy I was quite satisfied to remain on board. The *Ohio* was an old Line-of-battle-Ship, with what seemed to me countless portholes for guns on three decks, and her vast bulk was a great attraction to my unaccustomed eyes. I passed hours roaming about her great decks, studying the fittings of a war ship, and watching the boys at their different games and diversions. There were some three or four hundred people on board, and probably two-thirds of them were boys of sixteen to eighteen years. The food was abundant and good, and there was little for us to do but turn out at six o'clock in the morning, sweep the decks, eat our three meals, and turn in after hammocks were piped down at eight bells (eight o'clock) in the evening.'[3]

There John received his uniform, a dark blue visorless cap, a dark blue pullover shirt worn over a lightweight blue, white or red shirt, dark blue wool trousers cut wide at the ends of the trouser legs, a black kerchief to be tied around the neck, black tied shoes, and a heavy dark blue wool pea jacket or pea coat. For summer, he would have white cotton uniforms, but the cold winds in Boston harbour made the dark blue wool cosy even in September.

John also got his first taste of navy life on the *Ohio*. Being an old sailor, his first meal probably did not come as much of a shock as it did to another naval recruit who recalled, 'Our first meal on board the *Dolsen* was served to us standing on the main deck and consisted of a tin pan of rice and what the boys called "salt horse". I ate the rice but when I tasted the salt horse [actually beef] I thought it was the saltiest morsel I ever had in my mouth so I gave it a flip into the river, but we got used to it after awhile because salt horse, salt pork, rice, and bean soup with hardtack was the "chief of our diet".'[4] As well, sailors received coffee, tea, butter, dried apples, desiccated potatoes, vinegar and molasses, plus seafood caught from the ship.

Receiving ships were intended to teach new sailors their crafts. There they would perform tasks that ranged from holy-stoning the decks to gun drill, all under the eye of experienced navy petty officers and commissioned officers. Holy-stoning the decks was done once a week on the *Ohio*. 'Then on all three decks the operations of holy-stoning begins, so called from the queer name bestowed upon the principal instruments employed. These are ponderous flat stones with long ropes at each end, by which the stones are slidden about, to and fro, over the wet and sanded decks; a most wearisome, dog-like, galley-slave employment,' wrote novelist Herman Melville, who shipped out on a US Navy frigate some years earlier. 'For the byways and corners about the masts and guns, smaller stones are used, called *prayer-books;* inasmuch as the devout operator has to down with them on his knees.'[5]

Other skills to be learned included handling sails and small boats, as well as drills in handling cutlasses, 0.36 calibre Navy revolvers and rifles. The recruits also learned how to take care of themselves against old hands all too eager to victimise them by stealing their possessions or bullying them. Yet not all was safe and pleasant on board the receiving ships. One officer described his ship as 'a floating hell'; and one group of men arrived on the USS *Fernandia*, according to her captain, from a receiving ship, 'all in debt, their entire pay being swallowed up by their clothing bills. The reason is because they have had all their clothes stolen.'[6]

John would not stay long on the *Ohio*. On 24 October 1862 he was ordered to report to the USS *Sabine*, a frigate which until only a short time earlier had been home to William McCann (see Chapter 9). Gathering all his clothes, John happily left the old ship of the line, and headed for his new command.

The *Sabine* was another classic sailing ship, laid down in 1823 and finally commissioned in 1858. The 1,726-ton frigate was 202 feet long, and carried two 8-inch smoothbores and thirty-six 32-pounder guns. Over 450 officers and men shipped out with her as crew. In appearance, without steam power, she looked much like the frigates that had fought the naval war in 1812 against the British Royal Navy.

On 28 October, a few days before John's arrival, the Navy Department had issued orders to Commodore Cadwalader Ringgold, commander of the *Sabine*:

'Proceed with the US Frigate *Sabine*, under your command, on a cruise in search of piratical vessels, particularly the *Alabama*, or *290*, and for the protection of our commerce. Your cruise will be by the Azores and Cape Verde, touching at those islands; thence to the coast of Brazil and back to New York, capturing any vessels you may find engaged in depredating on our commerce or in conveying supplies to the rebels.'[7]

On 2 November, All Souls Day, the *Sabine* slipped out of New Haven harbour and set out on her long voyage. Days quickly fell into a regular pattern. John spent his nights in a hammock slung up on the berth deck, with only 18 inches separating him from his neighbours on either side. A marine bugler would sound reveille at 5.45 in the morning. Boatswains and bo'suns mates would then patrol the berth deck, calling for all hands to rise and lash up the hammocks that hung among the ship's guns. This was done in short order, and the seamen began cleaning the berth deck with saltwater and holy-stoning the spar deck, not a favourite activity. 'Another job we didn't like was holystoneing and washing down the decks,' a Union sailor recalled. 'One day it would be the duty of the Starboard watch and the next day we of the Port watch had to do this work.'[8]

Other sailors would polish all the ship's brass fittings, from bell to gun carriage parts. Some men climbed aloft to check and adjust the rigging and sails. Only after all this was done, and the men had cleaned themselves up, were hands piped to breakfast, usually around eight in the morning, at the start of the forenoon watch.

After breakfast, save on Sundays and holidays, 'beat to quarters' was played and every officer and man had to report to his battle station. The officer of the division would inspect them there, and this was followed by various drills, ranging from boarding and small arms drill to full gun drill. 'As the specific object for which a man-of-war is built and put into commission is to fight and fire off cannon, it is, of course, deemed indispensable that the crew should be duly instructed in the art and mystery involved,' wrote novelist and seaman Melville. 'Hence these "general quarters", which is a mustering of all hands to their stations at the guns on the several decks, and a sort of sham-fight with an imaginary foe.'[9]

Training, however, was not identical every day. It would be varied by drills for abandoning ship, repelling boarders, fire and collision drills, and drills in the use of the giant guns.

At noon, the seamen would be allowed to go below decks for dinner. Then there was more work on the ship or drill in the afternoon, apart from Saturdays and Sundays. 'The galley (kitchen) fire of ships of war used to be started at seven bells of the mid-watch (3.30 a.m.); and the officers, and most of the men, who next came on duty, managed to have coffee, the latter husbanding their rations to this end,' wrote one officer.[10] Supper was served at four.

'The common seamen in a large frigate are divided into some thirty or forty messes, put down on the purser's books as *Mess No.* 1, *Mess No.* 2, *Mess No.* 3, etc. the members of each mess club, the rations of provisions, and breakfast, dine, and sup together in allotted intervals between the guns on the maindeck,' Melville wrote. 'In undeviating rotation, the members of each mess (excepting the petty-officers) take their turn in performing the functions of cook and steward.'[11] In fact, the mess cook was not a true cook, but simply received issued food from the purser or outside sources, took it to the ship's cook to prepare, and carried the meal from the galley to his mess-mates.

Such was the regular weekday routine. Saturday afternoons were left free for men to patch, mend and clean their gear for the following day. At ten (four bells) on Sunday morning, after a muster for church service, the captain would inspect all hands who would be drawn up, hammocks and ditty bags in hand. The first Sunday of every month was also given over to a general muster, with the reading of the *Articles of War*. The rest of the day was free for all except those required for the smooth running of the ship.

John was rapidly promoted to the grade of Captain of the Hold, the condition of which was his responsibility. Most importantly for his family, which grew with the birth of his son Walter on 19 November 1862, was his raise to $20 a month. As well, he was authorised to wear a petty officer's badge on his left sleeve above the elbow, 'an eagle and anchor, of not more than three inches in length, with a star of one inch in diameter, one inch above. The same device, embroidered in blue, to be worn on the sleeves of their white frocks in summer.'[12] These devices were not issued, but were generally embroidered by the petty officer himself on a cloth backing and then sewn to the uniform.

In the event, there was little excitement on the voyage, as the *Sabine* never intercepted any Confederate cruisers. In December 1862 the ship put in at the Cape Verde Islands, its first port of call. Such a call provided a break from routine but little activity, except for those allowed shore leave. 'Unless you happen to belong to one of the numerous boats, which, in a man-of-war in harbour, are continually plying to and from the land, you are mostly thrown upon your own resources to while away the time. Whole days frequently pass without your being individually called upon to lift a finger,' Melville recalled.[13] Some men spent their time gambling, while others tried to buy and bring aboard proscribed items, especially liquor, from the many boats that roamed around the ships. Music was a welcome diversion for men who had their own instruments, such as banjos, and some ships even formed their own bands. Many of the men passed time tattooing one another; during one such session John's left forearm was tattooed with the figure of a woman wrapped in a flag.

Many used the time to sew new clothes or decorate old garments. 'Encouraged by the good weather, the men got out their diddy-bags and boxes, bought blue cloth or flannel, sewing silk, etc. of the purser, and employed their spare hours in cutting and making shirts and trousers,' wrote an enlisted man on blockade duty. 'Inspired by the good example, I bought some blue flannel, black sewing silk, etc., got out my "housewife", and cut and made for myself a flannel shirt, working fancy stars on the collar and a crowsfoot at the bottom of the neck opening.'[14]

All in all, though, the voyage was a disappointment to all hands. On its return, the Sabine was posted to the North Atlantic Blockading Squadron, to watch for blockade runners as well as Confederate cruisers. Now there would not even be the odd ports of call to break up the deadly dull routine of cruising back and forth in search of an all too rare sail. 'Blockading was desperately tedious work, make the best one could of it,' wrote young naval officer A. T. Mahan.[15]

Eventually, even this duty came to an end and the Sabine turned for home. There was little prize money to share as the frigate put into Providencetown, Massachusetts, in September 1863, where John, who had enlisted only for a year's tour of duty, was discharged on the 15th of the month. He returned home for his first meeting with his young son. While there his daughter Gertrude was born in July 1864.

The US Navy back home had continued to grow during the time John and his mess-mates were at sea. Whereas on 1 December 1861 she had 264 vessels with 2,557 guns, by the Christmas of 1863 that John spent with his family in Maine, the navy boasted 427 vessels with 3,268 guns. It was still difficult to get enough experienced seamen as crews for these vessels, let alone those presently under construction. But it was even harder to get trained naval officers.

At the beginning of the Civil War the profession of US Navy officer was limited to a relatively small number of men in a closed society. Many were related by family ties, with young sons shipping at tender ages as midshipmen on board ships of their fathers' friends. For example, Commodore David Porter, who had begun as a midshipman and was a highly successful captain in the War of 1812, left behind a legacy to the navy that included two sons, David and William, both of whom attained flag rank, and an adopted son, David Farragut who became the US Navy's first full admiral.

Whereas the army had already built a military academy at West Point, it was not until 1845 that the navy authorised a naval academy at Annapolis to train its young officers professionally. The number of midshipmen at the academy was limited by law to 515, but the actual number was always considerably lower than that. Worse, at the outbreak of the war, some 322 officers resigned their US Navy commissions to enter the Confederate Navy.

Something had to be done and therefore on 24 July 1861 Congress voted:

'That the temporary appoints made, or which may be made, by the Secretary of the Navy, of acting lieutenants, acting paymasters, acting assistant surgeons, acting masters and masters' mates, are hereby ratified and confirmed as temporary acting appointments until the return of the vessels in which they are respectively employed, or until the suppression of the present insurrection, as may be deemed necessary; and the rate of compensation allowed for the several grades specified is hereby legalised and approved.'[16]

Eventually some 7,500 such officers were commissioned into the wartime US Navy. Initially these volunteer, acting officers were to be drawn largely from the officers of merchant ships now out of work. However, as there were not enough candidates to be drawn from this source, essentially anybody with maritime service under their belts was invited to apply for such a commission.

Moreover, with the large variety of vessels placed into navy service, and their organisation into squadrons, the ancient rank system of the pre-war navy had to be changed. At the war's outbreak, there were only midshipmen, masters, lieutenants, commanders and captains. If several ships were banded together, one captain was given the temporary rank of commodore; the rank of admiral, thought to be somewhat royalist and élite, was forbidden. On 16 July 1862 several more ranks were added to this list. A rear admiral was named as the highest possible rank, while that of commodore was made a permanent rank. A lieutenant commander was inserted between the lieutenant and the commander, while the ensign became the lowest regularly commissioned officer, a midshipman being essentially an officer cadet.

John spent the end of 1863 and most of 1864 on shore. Making a living was not easy, however, and his heart was still with the navy. In late 1864 he applied for a commission and was interviewed by a board of regular US Navy officers. Here years of experience both as a deep-water sailor and as a naval petty officer paid off. He passed his examination, and was awarded a commission as a volunteer acting ensign on 23 December 1864. He was now, by Act of Congress, an officer and a gentleman.

John was assigned to a new ship, the USS *Muscoota*, an unarmoured steam vessel laid down in 1862 and due shortly to be commissioned. John joined her for the final touches of her building and launching on 5 January 1865. She was a 1,370-ton ship with side wheels and her single inclined direct-acting engine directly amidships between the wheels. She carried a 9-inch smooth bore, two 100-pound rifled guns, two 20-pound rifled guns and two 24-pounders. Although she had two masts, they were not designed as her primary propulsion method.

John's world was vastly different now. Instead of sleeping in a hammock slung up amidst the cannons of the berth deck and only inches from other sailors, surrounded by coughing and snoring and the movement of men going on and coming off duty all night, he now had his own stateroom. It had a door that could be closed for privacy, although the top of the door was made with slats for ventilation below decks. He had his own bunk, built against the bulkhead over four drawers to hold all his belongings. As well, he had a chair, a dresser or desk and a washstand. Shelves over the bunk held additional books and photographs of his family. He hung his new uniforms on pegs on one bulkhead.

Although he now had many more uniforms, they cost him. Whereas previously he had been issued uniforms and equipment, he now had to buy them. His dark blue hat had a patent leather visor and a cap badge of a gold wreath around a silver anchor. His dark blue double-breasted coat had a single narrow stripe of gold, topped with a gold star, on each cuff. His trousers were plain dark blue in the winter and white during the summer. Moreover, certain items such as a business-suit dark blue blouse for fatigue wear, a straw hat for summer, and vests for all seasons, were usually part of a naval officer's attire. When at sea, he now received $1,200 annually, which was a good living wage, but much of his first wages was spent on uniforms.

In addition, he had to supply himself with mess gear and a belt and sword. One newly commissioned paymaster remarked on his new sword with disgust that 'I had to go to the expense of $16 for one of those useless toys, for it is nothing else – for service we use a ship's cutlass, this is for mere dress. My expenses have been enormous. I dare not figure it up myself.'[17]

Moreover, whereas the navy had provided food and drink for Chief of the Hold Thomas, Volunteer Acting Ensign Thomas was expected to pay for his own provisions, and sometimes for a servant as well. He would eat this food in the wardroom, the large room on to which his stateroom door opened. It had a large table in the middle, with chairs around it, lanterns hanging overhead, and a serving board at one end of the wardroom. 'All the Commissioned officers, numbering eleven, are in our mess & eat in the ward room,' wrote a paymaster of a typical navy warship's wardroom. 'We provide all our own dishes & table furniture as well as provisions. One of our number is chosen as caterer, who makes all the purchases & sees that the food is properly prepared. The cost to each of us for our dishes &c & provisions for two months is $70.00 – not very cheap board.'[18] Part of this money went towards liquor, for, unlike the berth deck, the wardroom was then not dry.

As an ensign, John was a line officer, rather than one of the civil officers such as the paymaster or surgeon. In some of the navy's smaller vessels he could have served as the boat's captain. The *Muscoota*, however, shipped a full complement of 190 officers and men. Therefore, his duties in action were to serve as captain of a section of guns or, if the captain desired, to lead boarding parties. From day to day he would serve as officer of the deck, taking control of the ship in the captain's absence. Otherwise, his time would usually be spent in the wardroom, reading, writing home or chatting with his peers around the wardroom table.

By early 1865, when the *Muscoota* had finished her sea trials, there was little need for as large a fleet as before. All southern ports except one were occupied by Union soldiers, and that one was under close siege. European governments finally stopped their shipyards from supplying the Confederate Navy, and essentially only one cruiser was still at large, and that one in the Pacific Ocean. The Mississippi River had long been under firm Union control. Thus John's new ship did not see any action before the war came to an end. Even so, he suffered the only health setback of his naval career while aboard the *Muscoota;* he developed yellow fever or malaria – the diagnosis was unclear.

The navy could not get rid of all its ships immediately; and since John evidently enjoyed naval life, he stayed on after the war ended while many other volunteer acting officers resigned their commissions as quickly as possible. Indeed, he even transferred to the USS *Saco*, an 836-ton gunboat whose steam engines drove a screw propeller, making her one of the most modern wooden ships in the navy. She had been built especially for fast inshore cruising, and had been commissioned on 11 July 1864.

Despite suffering insomnia and vertigo, apparently as a result of his tropical disease, John showed little sign of wishing to return to civilian life. But

he was not a naval gentleman with a well-connected family or Annapolis training. As the navy sold off its ships, it beached many of the jumped-up officers
created during the war. John's time was limited, and on 21 December 1867 he
was honourably discharged. He went back to the merchant marine after the
war, finally retiring to Leadville, Colorado, where a man seeing an oar would
ask what that was, in 1899. There he died of a strangulated hernia on 23 July
1914, just as America was heading into yet another war.

NOTES

1 Rush, Richard and Robert H. Woods, eds., *Official Records of the Union and Confederate
   Navies in the War of the Rebellion*, (hereafter *ORN*), Washington, 1894, Series I, Vol. I, pp.
   9–10
2 Still, Dr. William, 'The Common Sailor', *Civil War Times Illustrated*, February 1985, p.
   26
3 Hunter, Alvah F., *A Year on a Monitor and the Destruction of Fort Sumter*, Annapolis,
   Maryland, 1991, p. 8
4 Mulligan, John D., 'Navy Life On The Mississippi River,' *Civil War Times Illustrated*,
   May/June 1994, p. 66.
5 Melville, Herman, *White-Jacket, or The World in a Man-of-War*, New York, 1892, p. 84
6 Still, op. cit., p. 30
7 *ORN*, op. cit,. p. 522
8 Mulligan, op. cit., p. 69
9 Melville op. cit., p. 64
10 Mahan, A. T., *From Sail to Steam*, New York, 1907, p. 144
11 Melville, op. cit., p. 57
12 Schuyler, Hartley and Graham, *Illustrated Catalog of Civil War Military Goods*, New York,
   1985, p. 86
13 Melville, op. cit., p. 152
14 Hunter, op. cit., p. 31
15 Mahan, op. cit., p. 174
16 Official, *Laws relating to the Navy and Marine Corps and the Navy Department. July 1,
   1865*, Washington, 1865, p. 95
17 Daly, Robert W., ed., *Aboard the USS Monitor: 1862*, Annapolis, Maryland, p. 17
18 ibid, p. 20

18

Charles J. Trotter

Sergeant, 23rd Indiana Infantry Regiment /
Acting First Assistant Engineer, US Navy

On 1 July 1861, in New Albany, Indiana, Charles J. Trotter, a twenty-five-year-old native of Jeffersonville, Indiana, raised his right hand and was sworn into the service of the United States Army, as part of a brand new unit, Company B, 23rd Indiana Volunteer Infantry Regiment. Charles was six feet tall, taller than the average soldier of the period, weighed a stocky 190 pounds, and had grey eyes, dark hair and a light complexion. Apparently considered by his officers and peers a good soldier, he was named a sergeant upon his enlistment.

The regiment was officially mustered into the service twenty-eight days later, and on 15 August it was moved to Paducah, Kentucky, to do garrison duty and to begin training for the forthcoming campaign. Once the training day was over, many soldiers were allowed to visit the town and neighbourhood. Out of camp there was plenty to do. Fun-loving Charles even had his arms tattooed. Inevitably, too, there were prostitutes. One Federal soldier wrote to a friend from Pulaski, Tennessee: 'There are four whorehouses here where a man can get a single jump for 3 dollars, five dollars for all night in Tennessee money. You may think I am a hard case, but I am as pious as you can find in the Army.'[1]

Charles, too, appears to have been a bit of a 'hard case'. After only a couple of months in Paducah he reported to his regimental surgeon, complaining of sores that were bothering him. The doctor took one look at them and reached for his file of blank discharge papers. According to Charles's army record, he 'was discharged the service at Paducah, Kentucky, December 22, 1861, by reason of syphilitic ulcers on the tibia'.[2]

Syphilis, a sexually transmitted disease, is first detected as small, painless ulcers, such as Charles reported to the regimental surgeon. A secondary stage, indicated by transient fever and rash, arrives several weeks later, soon to clear up spontaneously. Thereafter the disease may become dormant for years until the signs of a third stage. At that point the infection eats away at vital organs, including blood vessels and the brain.

During the war there were 73,381 reported cases of syphilis in the four years of the Union Army's existence. It was not an uncommon cause for dismissal. All told, nevertheless, the army discharged only 1,779 white and 86 black volunteers during the war for this reason. By comparison, however, 9,002 white and 358 black volunteers were discharged for hernia and 1,555 white and 43 black volunteers for piles. However, by 31 December 1864 2,330 men had been admitted to the Soldiers' Syphilitic Hospital in Nashville, Tennessee, from the western army. Early in the war, when a need to retain men was not as obvious at it would by 1864, men with symptoms of the dreaded disease were sooner discharged than treated. Had Charles developed the disease towards the end of his three-year enlistment, he probably would have been retained in the army after a hospital stay.

In truth, though, there was no known cure for syphilis – nor would there be one for another fifty years. A surgeon stationed in California during the war wrote that he used smallpox vaccination for the disease:

'I inoculate every case of chancre. If the virus take, I treat locally and hygienically alone; if it fails to produce chancre after the third inoculation, I use protiodide. The cures in both series of cases is generally reasonably prompt, occupying from fifteen to rarely sixty days.'[3]

Another western Army doctor cauterised primary ulcers with nitrate of silver, using 'black wash' until the ulcer healed. The most common treatment, however, used since the eighteenth century, involved mercury: hence the saying, 'A night with Venus, a lifetime with Mercury'. Surgeon Ezra Reid, 21st Indiana, used a steam bath with mercury vapour for 'mercurial fumigation, which deposits the mercury on the surface on the body', especially following cauterisation on primary chancres. The fact is, however, nothing cured, and only time hid the disease until its final deadly outbreak.

Charles was not ready to get out of the war that soon. After discharge, he might possibly have received civilian medical attention, but eventually his symptoms would have vanished regardless of medical aid, leaving him apparently quite healthy. But because the army would obviously not be happy to find him as a new recruit, he decided to draw on his engineering background and apply for a commission as an engineer in the sea-going services. His application was approved, and on 1 October 1862 he was commissioned as an acting third assistant engineer in the US Navy. It was the lowest grade of naval officer, but still a cut above being an infantry sergeant. His pay as such a serving officer would now be $750 a year.

The rank of an engineering officer was not considered very prestigious. The US Navy is a branch of the service exceptionally mindful of tradition. It was born in an age of sail, of iron hearts and wooden ships. The addition of steam engines to propel its ships was not a change that sat at all well with its corps of officers. Nonetheless, on 31 August 1842, Congress authorised the Engineer Corps of the Navy, with a Chief Engineer, two 1st Assistant Engineers, two 2nd Assistant Engineers, and three 3rd Assistant Engineers for each steamship in the navy. As technical personnel, much like sailmakers or carpenters, these engineers were warrant officers, caught in that limbo land between the officers' wardroom and the ratings' berth deck. There was considerable grumbling on the part of trained engineers about this, and on 30 June 1846 Congress authorised the President to appoint 'chief engineers of the navy', with 'the advice and consent of the Senate'.[4] This made chief engineers commissioned officers equal, in theory, with executive officers on deck.

Recruiting the talented and trained individuals to manage the cranky steam engines of the period was difficult since only a warrant grade was offered. Not only was the pay poorer than for a merchant marine engineer, but the social status was on a level with a craftsman. Such individuals would certainly not be welcome in better houses, as were men wearing the gold epaulettes and cuff lace of navy officers. At the same time, the opening of the US Navy Academy in Annapolis, Maryland, exposed its future leaders not just to wardroom talk, but to qualified scientific expertise as well. Younger, better educated naval officers were, by the end of the 1850s, increasingly important in the service, and they appreciated the value of engineers, unlike the veterans of the War of 1812 who still ran the navy. Moreover, the engineers were all placed in a separate Bureau of Steam Engineering, whose head reported directly to the Secretary of the Navy. As such, he had influence that was not mitigated by having to be passed through a chain of command that included line officers. He could take the case of the Engineer Corps directly to the civilian Secretary.

Therefore, on 13 January 1859, on the eve of the Civil War, the Secretary of the Navy ordered that all engineers would thenceforth be commissioned officers. Chief engineers of more than twelve years' service were to rank with captains. Chief engineers of less than twelve years' service rated with lieutenants. First assistant engineers rated next after lieutenants, and therefore just above masters. Second assistant engineers rated next after masters, and hence above midshipmen. Third assistant engineers rated with midshipmen. These ranks were considered 'relative' or 'assimilated', meaning that while they were considered true commissioned officers and authorised all the perks of service, they were not allowed to exercise military command. Indeed, their command authority was limited to those within their own corps, i.e. lower-ranking engineers and ratings in the engine room. Line naval officers still regarded the commissioned engineers as little more than glorified mechanics.

As a result, it was less difficult to be directly commissioned from civilian life as a naval engineer than as a naval officer in any other speciality. Moreover, there were no naval engineering schools to teach these new recruits about marine engineering or naval traditions: they had to learn as they went along. While the problem was one that cut across the entire fleet, both blue water as well as brown water, it seemed to be especially pressing in the river squadrons. Writing about engineer officers on the Mississippi, Rear Admiral Farragut informed the Secretary of the Navy in July 1863: 'The majority of them know very little of their duties and their engines are cut up and ruined by neglect and want of proper care.' The Secretary turned to the Chief of the Bureau of Steam Engineering with a note that the problem came from 'employment of incompetent and neglectful persons in the engineer department.'[5] He asked the chief to try to improve the quality of commissioned engineers, especially among those who had temporary assignments during the war. It was a problem never fully solved, given distances and lack of a formal naval engineering school, even though the chief did try, as far as possible, to screen and train applicants. It was another reason why line officers thought little of the engineers in their wardrooms.

The navy badly needed men of all types for its operations on the western rivers. Originally the army had manned a fleet of armoured rams designed for river warfare, but by mid-1862 the navy began building its own river men-of-war. One of these was the *Chillicothe*, designed to be a large, side-wheel paddle ship. Some 160 feet long, she had two inches of armour around her gun deck, with three inches of armour around the forward-mounted pilot-house. The deck was covered with armour an inch thick. Her original armament included two 11-inch smooth-bore cannon on pivots so they could fire through ports over the bows, abeam or at an angle aft. She was driven by two engines and three boilers powering the side wheels and two screws. At maximum power, she had a speed of seven knots. Ships' engines were designed to be extremely strong, able to withstand neglect, given the difficulty in finding skilled maritime engineers to run them. Fuel economy and power were sacrificed to the principle of having a fool-proof engine.

Such was the situation for Charles when he accepted his navy commission. He was only one of five engineer officers – the fourth in line of succession – assigned to duty on board the newly built USS *Chillicothe*.

On 22 October 1863 Lieutenant Commander John G. Walker replaced the ship's previous captain, whose services, it was felt, were needed more in St Louis. His report indicated that the new gunboat was less than a perfect warship:

'I found the contractor at work on board putting a light hurricane deck over her and filling in her gun ports, 9 inches on each side and 9 inches at the bottom.

'Her ports had already been cut out on the upper side 5 inches, so that about the ports both wood and iron is patched a good deal and therefore deficient in strength. This will, however, be protected in a measure by the port shutters when in place. When underway she worked enough to open a seam a half inch or more all the way across the deck over the engines. The contractor is now trying to strengthen her by iron straps fore and aft under the deck and bolted through it. She is a scow, without knees or anything to strengthen her and, I think, very weak. She leaks forward when underway about the plating bolts, and her deck leaks very badly.

'The quarters for officers and men are small, badly ventilated, and extremely uncomfortable. Houses could be built on deck at very small expense, which would do much for the health and comfort of the officers of the vessel.

'The wheel is in the gun tower, between the two forward ports, and very much in the way of the guns in action, while pilots can only see ahead, which, in the river, I take it, is a grave objection to its present position. A pilot house should be built abaft and joining the gun tower high enough to look over the top of the tower, with look-out holes in all directions.'[6]

Walker was not to stay long. On 14 November 1862 Lieutenant Commander James P. Foster replaced him as the ship's captain. Foster reported her almost ready for duty, and rented a nearby room for a naval rendezvous with her new crew. Luckily he was able to start with at least a skeleton crew that had been sent to defend the ship only two months previously; and by December he had assembled enough men for a complete crew, one of only two such gunboats to do so. However, the water was still too low for the ship to pass over the bar and descend down the river. Winter snows finally raised the water, and by Christmas Day, 1862, she had arrived for duty with the rest of the US Mississippi Squadron, commanded by Acting Rear Admiral David D. Porter. Porter assigned her to the first division of larger vessels, under command of Captain Henry Walke. The squadron was to help the army in its attempt to take the fortress on the Mississippi, Vicksburg, which blocked free passage north and south.

On 10-11 January 1863 the *Chillicothe* was part of the force sent to capture Fort Hindman, Arkansas. The ships steamed up to just below where the fort, on a high bluff, overlooked the White River. One sailor on another ship in the squadron later recalled the fight: 'We steamed close up to the battery and bullets as well as shells fell about us like hail. We fought until it was so dark we could tell where the battery was only by the flash from their guns.' The ships withdrew from the indecisive battle that evening, only to return the next afternoon. 'The Guerrillas kept up a continual fight trying to pick off our men. The Tinclads in our rear kept pouring in shells and doing their best to help and look after the Guerrillas,' the sailor recalled.[7] The fort fell on 11 January to the combined army/navy force.

The emphasis in early 1863 was on clearing the Mississippi River of Confederates who had built fortifications at many places along the river, especially near the important town of Vicksburg. The question was how the navy might best be used in such a campaign.

Porter agreed to a combined arms operation which would see him send his ships through the Yazoo Pass, which had earlier been used by small vessels, to take Yazoo City by surprise. Each ship was to carry a company of infantry who would land and take the town, which then could become a base of operations for the army. Porter later wrote about this expedition:

'To describe the difficulties which attended this expedition would be impossible and they could only be realised by those who saw them. The pass had been closed up for many years and trees had grown up in the middle of the channel which had become dry after the levee was built across its mouth. Great rafts were left in this dry channel as the water ran off and bushes and vines now grew thickly around them and tied them together as with withes. Overhanging trees joined together over the channel – and their branches were so low that steamers could not pass without having their smoke-pipes knocked down and all their boats and upper-works swept away.'[8]

The bottom of the *Chillicothe* was stove-in by a stump and sailors worked desperately to keep it in place by shoring it from above. Despite such damages and being able to proceed only at a snail's pace, the expedition pressed on. Finally, on 11 March 1863, the *Chillicothe* came around a bend in the Tallahatchie within range of the guns of Fort Pemberton.

Immediately the Confederate gunners got her range, striking her within minutes of her being seen. A lucky southern shot jammed a port shutter closed. Orders came down to the engine room to reverse engines, then hold her so that just her bow could be seen. This would allow her guns to exchange fire with the Confederates, while hiding most of her bulk. Charles and his engine room crew responded, and held her there for about an hour. Finally, after seeing that little damage was being done to the Confederate fort, the ship's captain had her withdrawn. She returned again in the afternoon, only to be even worse manhandled.

'She proved herself to be a poor vessel for resisting shot,' Porter recalled. 'During the afternoon fight she lost four men killed and fifteen wounded.'[9]

The ship and others returned to exchange fire again two days later, with slightly better luck. Once more, however, they had to withdraw without having destroyed their target. They returned on the 13th and had hardly begun firing when a Confederate heavy artillery shot penetrated the *Chillicothe*. Even so, wrote Porter, 'The "Chillicothe" remained in action one hour and thirty-eight minutes, and then had to withdraw for want of ammunition, besides being much cut up by the enemy.'[10] Having repaired the damage, the ship continued in service on the Tallahatchie through to the end of the campaign on 23 March. She then returned to patrol duty on the Mississippi, supporting the army effort against Vicksburg.

Charles went on leave in June 1863, marrying Minnie E. Green back home in Clark County, Indiana, on 9 June. Hardly had he returned to his ship when the Confederate garrison at Vicksburg surrendered, on 4 July.

The Mississippi was now a Union waterway, but it would be the duty of the ships along the river to patrol it and prevent the Confederates from crossing it. This duty would largely be deadly dull, with brief moments of pure terror when guerrillas struck. The only problem was that nobody knew when those moments would arise. 'My sailors having had quite a dull time lately, and no fighting,' one ship commander, Commander John Hart, wrote home in December 1862. Stopping alongside the river bank from time to time to send a ship's boat ashore so that the cooks could buy fresh food, the officers and men often got to know local residents. Some of them invited the sailors to dinner, and Hart noted 'how odd it is to dine in this way, for at least eight or ten armed men pickett off about the premises so that the Guerrillas cannot catch us.'[11]

There was constant concern about being sniped on by guerrillas. A sailor on the *Cincinnati* recalled:

'We had to go to quarters regularly three times a day. At night we had to get our guns ready for action so that if we were attacked by Guerrillas we would be ready for them. Instead of being on watch part of the time, our whole Starboard or our whole Port watch would have to be on duty. We didn't like this as it gave us so little time to sleep, besides we had our day duties to care for, i.e. scrubbing decks, cleaning bright work, coaling ship and being called away in one of the small boats now and then. This of course kept us out of mischief even if we did not get much rest.'[12]

Otherwise, life turned into a routine. Hart described a typical day for a senior officer on a patrolling gunboat:

'It may be a pretty day, and I call "Sassage" – fill my pipe – and go on deck, and I find the crew looking fresh and clean and at exercising under their officers – perhaps I find some faults, give some trivial order, and this is done to let the people know that I am moving about the decks[.] If any gross negligence has taken place I raise a row that startles the people, and then I seem to get pacified slowly, – it is strange how one must do these things, as it were, on principle, with all the appearance of anger, when none is felt, – but it makes things wholesome – Then I hail the "Winona" and ask how Capt Weaver is, which he answers by asking how I am, – and perhaps he says –"Shall I take you up in my gig, I'm going ashore to call on the Colonel?" – and I say "I don't mind if you do" – so along comes Weaver with his dog Standy up in the bows of his boat, and we go on shore with our pipes, and go to "Head Quarters" to read papers and bother Colonel Holcomb for an hour or two, – and then for a walk and talk with Weaver[,] the confounded dog bothering us for he is always straying away so far that much breath has to be expended in whistling to him, – Then perhaps a visit to some gentleman's house, then to the Provost Martial's [sic] office, then a stroll along the levee, perhaps on board of some river boat, – then seeing my gig coming for me, – I bid Weaver good day, promising to see him in the evening then I go on board and write reports and official letters till dinner, which is ½ past 4 – then a quiet sound snooze for an hour, – then I read 'till it is time to meet Weaver, who gets out his cigars, lemons, hot water and I believe Whiskey and then we sit and discuss and argue and wrangle 'till we both get weary[.] When I return to my state room and torment "Sassage" till he snaps and barks at me, and then I get out Elly's picture, pick out a book and read and read 'till 11, 12, or 1 o'clock in the morning, – There now is a fine day's work.'[13]

When on the ship, the officers, including Charles, found most of their social life in the wardroom. Judging from material found on the USS *Cairo*, which sunk suddenly after hitting a mine, wardrooms on the *Chillicothe* were well equipped. China was ironstone supplied by J. J. Brown in New Albany, while silver was plate, made by Rogers and Brothers and Hartford Manufacturing Co. A handsome wooden ice chest was found on the remains of the *Cairo*, as well as whiskey, rum, champagne and wine bottles. The *Cairo* was also equipped with a complete officers' bathroom, including a toilet and shower, and the similar *Chillicothe* must have had much the same. A shower would have been especially welcome after spending several hours in an engine room in the hot Mississippi summer.

Fleeing slaves often made their way to the gunboats. A sailor from the *Cincinnati* later recalled:

'We took on board a lot of contrabands, and they were a jolly lot of darkies right from the plantation. They would get together at night and give us a gay old time, a regular plantation jig. The names of the leaders were Aleck, Charley and Black Hawk. Alex would do the patting and Charley and Black Hawk would do the dancing and the usual shouting and yah yahing. Our powder monkey was George Washington, black as midnight with the thickest lips I ever saw on a darky. We were constantly picking up contrabands as we went down the river but we didn't always keep them because oftentimes their masters would claim them and our Captain would give them up.'[14]

On 9 October 1863 Charles received a promotion, jumping him over the next rank of second assistant engineer. He was now officially an Acting First Assistant Engineer, making a respectable $1,250 a year. He would also be the second engineer of his ship, under command of Chief Engineer A. W. Hardy. The rest of the engineering staff on board included Acting Second Assistant Engineer J. W. Hymen and Acting Third Assistant Engineers J. W. Terrell and Anthony Lane.

The dull days of river patrolling were soon to end. The *Chillicothe* was part of the largest inland waters fleet ever put together, one gathered to serve on a raid organised under Major General Nathaniel P. Banks to go up the Red River into Texas in early 1864. Its purpose was both to acquire cotton and to garrison Texas across the border against a French army in Mexico. An army force of 30,000 was to move to Alexandria, Louisiana, to meet the fleet at the mouth of the Red River. Despite a river that was lower than expected, making it difficult for deeper draught ships such as the *Chillicothe* to negotiate the narrows, the expedition pressed forward. Indeed, it was not until the end of March that all the ships crossed 'the falls' at Alexandria and were heading upriver.

On 8–9 April the Federal soldiers and Confederate defenders clashed at Sabine Crossroads and Pleasant Hill. The Federals were held, and Banks decided to abandon any attempt to take Shreveport. In the meantime, however, the navy pressed on toward Loggy Bayou, almost halfway between Grand Encore and Shreveport. Reaching there, they learned of the army's retreat, and turned back. On 12 April *Chillicothe* ran aground, to be hauled off the next day. 'We got under way this morning at sunrise and steamed down – ahead of the *Chillicothe* steamed in advance,' a Marine officer on the *Cricket* noted in his diary of 13 April.[15] Confederates fired on the passing ships as they tried to get back towards Alexandria.

Once at Grand Encore, army and navy top brass met to discuss renewing the advance on Shreveport. They learned there that part of the army was to be sent immediately to Sherman, thus greatly reducing the overall force.

Navy officers expressed their concern about sailing on the Red River, which had fallen even lower than before. They decided on 21 April to return to Alexandria, the army arriving there three days later. The navy, slowed by the loss of the *Eastport* to a Confederate mine, was there shortly afterwards. However, they then found that the river had fallen so low that many of the ships, including *Chillicothe*, were unable to pass over the falls. They were trapped.

It was an army engineer, Lieutenant Colonel Joseph Bailey, who suggested building a dam on the falls to raise the water level to a suitable depth. Porter accepted the idea, later writing:

'Every man in the fleet was engaged in the operations connected with the construction of the dam, conveying stone in boats to weight the big cob-frames forming the dam, moving the frames into position – a tedious and dangerous duty – and floating down the logs which were cut and hauled by the soldiers to the river banks. Many boats had to be kept lying on their oars day and night ready with hawsers, and at least three thousand soldiers were constantly working up to their necks in water.

'While this was going on, all the forges in the fleet were employed in making long iron bolts to bind the dam together. Getting the iron off the sides of the vessels to lighten them – a most harassing and difficult job – employed many men. In addition, all the heaviest guns had to be taken on shore.'[16]

On 8 May the job was done and the pressure of the backed-up water flushed two barges out of position on 9 May, setting a stream of water through the opening. Although four ships got out safely on the back of this tide, *Chillicothe* was not among them. The men went back to work, rebuilding the dam and waiting for the waters to build up again. Finally, on 12 May it was ready. 'The balance of the boats came over the falls today with the exception of *Chillicothe* and *Ozark*,' a marine noted in his diary of 12 May.[17] The next day Charles's ship flowed up and over the falls. It was free.

Essentially, after the abortive Red River Campaign, *Chillicothe*'s major campaigning days were over. The rest of the war would be spent on routine patrolling. On June 8, near Simmesport, on the Atchalfaya River, she was part of an expedition sent to reconnoitre reports of Confederate batteries. There were, in fact, two Confederate 30-pound rifled cannon, which opened fire on the warships. Their shots could not penetrate the armour, however, and the navy sent a landing party ashore, under cover of cannon fire, which quickly drove off the Confederates and captured the guns.

It would be the last action of Charles's war. He would manage to visit his wife again in March 1865. Charles was honourably discharged on 20 October of that year, and their first child, Harry, was born on 4 December. The *Chillicothe* did not stay in the navy's service much longer; she was sold to a civilian company on 29 November 1865.

Despite the disease that ended his army service, Charles lived a good number of years, dying on 10 April 1914 of – according to the death certificate issued by the City of Chicago – bronchial pneumonia, with erysipelas as a secondary contributing factor. Erysipelas is an acute disease of the skin and surrounding tissue marked by spreading inflammation which is caused by a virus. Such could be a description, phrased so as not to embarrass his widow, for the final stage of syphilis. Minnie Trotter lived on until 14 June 1931.

NOTES

1 Lowry, Thomas P., MD, *The Story the Soldiers Wouldn't Tell*, Mechanicsburg, Pennsylvania, 1994, p. 35
2 Trotter, Charles, Army personnel records, National Archives, Washington, DC
3 Lowry, op. cit., p. 105
4 *Official Laws Relating to the Navy and Marine Corps and Navy Department July 1, 1865*, Washington, 1865, p. 63
5 Sloan, Edward William III, *Benjamin Franklin Isherwood Naval Engineer*, Annapolis, Maryland, 1965, p. 34
6 *ORN*, op. cit., pp. 448-9
7 Mulligan, John D., 'Navy Life On The Mississippi River,' *Civil War Times Illustrated*, May/June 1884, p. 71
8 Porter, David D., *Naval History of the Civil War*, Secaucus, New Jersey, 1984, p. 300
9 ibid, p. 301
10 ibid, p. 301
11 Hart, John E., 'Commanding The USS Albatross,' *Civil War Times Illustrated*, March, 1975, p. 30
12 Mulligan, op. cit., p. 70
13 Hart, op. cit., p. 31.
14 Mulligan, op. cit., p. 70
15 Jones, James P., and Edward F. Keuchel, eds., *Civil War Marine*, Washington, DC, 1975, p. 48
16 Porter, op. cit., p. 526
17 Jones and Keuchel, op. cit., p. 56

No. 2.

RECORD OF DEATH AND INTERMENT.

Name and number of person interred.	*David A. Barnett*
Number and locality of the grave . .	
Hospital number of the deceased . .	*4193*
Regiment, rank, and company	*99ᵗʰ Pa. Vols. Sergt. of Comp. B.*
Residence before enlistment	*Peach Bottom*
Conjugal condition, (and if married, the residence of the widow) . . }	*Single*
Cause of death . . . . }	*Gunshot Wound of Knee, Amp. of Thigh Death from Pyaemia.*
Age of the deceased	*22 Years*
Nativity	*Penn*
References and remarks . . . . . }	*Mother is C Barnett, Peach Bottom York bt Co Pa.*
Date of death and burial	*November 26ᵗʰ 63, November 28ᵗʰ 1863.*

[A duplicate of this Record has been forwarded to the Sexton, and another remains at this Hospital.]

To

Brig Genl L Thomas
Adjt Genl U S Army

SIR:

It becomes my duty to inform you that the person above described died at this Hospital as herein stated; and that it is desired his remains should be interred with the usual military honors.

Respectfully,

W Thomson
Asst. Surgeon U. S. Army.
in charge.

MILITARY HOSPITAL, *Douglas*

This copy of Record is to be transmitted to the Adjutant General at Washington immediately after the place of burial and the number of the grave have been ascertained and registered. The above notification is to remain attached.

On David Barnett's death, this form was filled out in triplicate, one going to the Adjutant General's headquarters, one to the sexton of the graveyard in which he was buried, and one remaining in the hospital. Paperwork was a vital part of Civil War soldiering. (National Archives)

Index